Rediscover Catholicism

A SPIRITUAL GUIDE TO LIVING

WITH PASSION & PURPOSE

MATTHEW KELLY

Beacon
PUBLISHING

REDISCOVER CATHOLICISM

Table of Contents

Prologue: Imagine This...   5

Introduction: Where to From Here?   11

PART ONE: We Become What We Celebrate

1: OUR UNIVERSAL HUNGER   20

2: THE PREVAILING PHILOSOPHY   25

3: IS JESUS STILL RELEVANT?   31

4: SEARCHING FOR IDENTITY   39

5: WHAT ARE WE CELEBRATING?   49

PART TWO: The Authentic Life

6: WHAT IS THE AUTHENTIC LIFE?   59

7: THE PATH IS WELL TRODDEN   73

8: EVEN A BLIND MAN KNOWS. . .   83

9: WHAT SETS THEM APART?   108

10: THEIR ATTRACTION AND INFLUENCE   118

11: WHO WILL BE NEXT?   123

PART THREE:
The Seven Pillars of Catholic Spirituality

12: CONFESSION   137

13: DAILY PRAYER   163

14: THE MASS   193

15: THE BIBLE   217

16: FASTING   235

17: SPIRITUAL READING   253

18: THE ROSARY   269

PART FOUR: Now Is Our Time

19: TIME FOR A CHANGE   275

20: LEADERSHIP   296

21: RETURN TO VIRTUE   304

Prologue

Imagine this.

You're driving home from work next Monday after a long day. You turn on your radio and you hear a brief report about a small village in India where some people have suddenly died, strangely, of a flu that has never been seen before. It's not influenza, but four people are dead, so the Centers for Disease Control is sending some doctors to India to investigate.

You don't think too much about it—people die every day—but coming home from church the following Sunday you hear another report on the radio, only now they say it's not four people who have died, but thirty thousand, in the back hills of India. Whole villages have been wiped out and experts confirm this flu is a strain that has never been seen before.

By the time you get up Monday morning, it's the lead story. The disease is spreading. It's not just India that is affected. Now it has spread to Pakistan, Afghanistan, Iran, Iraq, and northern Africa, but it still seems far away. Before you know it, you're hearing this story everywhere. The media have now coined it "the mystery flu." The President has announced that he and his family are praying for the victims and their families, and are hoping for the situation to be resolved quickly. But everyone is wondering how we are ever going to contain it.

That's when the President of France makes an announcement that shocks Europe: He is closing the French borders. No one can enter the country, and that's why that night you're watching a little bit of CNN before going to bed. Your jaw hits your chest when a weeping woman's words are translated into English from a French news program: There's a man lying in a hospital in Paris dying of the mystery flu. It has come to Europe.

Panic strikes. As best they can tell, after contracting the disease, you have it for a week before you even know it, then you have four days of unbelievable symptoms, and then you die.

The British close their borders, but it's too late. The disease breaks out in Southampton, Liverpool, and London, and on Tuesday morning the

President of the United States makes the following announcement: "Due to a national-security risk, all flights to and from the United States have been canceled. If your loved ones are overseas, I'm sorry. They cannot come home until we find a cure for this horrific disease."

Within four days, America is plunged into an unbelievable fear. People are wondering, *What if it comes to this country?* Preachers on television are saying it's the scourge of God. Then on Tuesday night you are at church for Bible study, when somebody runs in from the parking lot and yells, "Turn on a radio!" And while everyone listens to a small radio, the announcement is made: Two women are lying in a hospital in New York City dying of the mystery flu. It has come to America.

Within hours the disease envelops the country. People are working around the clock, trying to find an antidote, but nothing is working. The disease breaks out in California, Oregon, Arizona, Florida, Massachusetts. It's as though it's just sweeping in from the borders.

Then suddenly the news comes out: The code has been broken. A cure has been found. A vaccine can be made. But it's going to take the blood of somebody who hasn't been infected. So you and I are asked to do just one thing: Go to the nearest hospital and have our blood tested. When we hear the sirens go off in our neighborhood, we are to make our way quickly, quietly, and safely to the hospital.

Sure enough, by the time you and your family get to the hospital it's late Friday night. There are long lines of people and a constant rush of doctors and nurses taking blood and putting labels on it. Finally, it is your turn. You go first, then your spouse and children follow, and once the doctors have taken your blood they say to you, "Wait here in the parking lot for your name to be called." You stand around with your family and neighbors, scared, waiting, wondering. Wondering quietly to yourself, *What on earth is going on here? Is this the end of the world? How did it ever come to this?*

Nobody seems to have had their name called; the doctors just keep taking people's blood. But then suddenly a young man comes running out

6

of the hospital, screaming. He's yelling a name and waving a clipboard. You don't hear him at first. "What's he saying?" someone asks. The young man screams the name again as he and a team of medical staff run in your direction, but again you cannot hear him. But then your son tugs on your jacket and says, "Daddy, that's me. That's my name they're calling." Before you know it, they have grabbed your boy. "Wait a minute. Hold on!" you say, running after them. "That's my son."

"It's okay," they reply. "We think he has the right blood type. We just need to check one more time to make sure he doesn't have the disease."

Five tense minutes later, out come the doctors and nurses, crying and hugging each another; some of them are even laughing. It's the first time you have seen anybody laugh in a week. An old doctor walks up to you and your spouse and says, "Thank you. Your son's blood is perfect. It's clean, it's pure, he doesn't have the disease, and we can use it to make the vaccine."

As the news begins to spread across the parking lot, people scream and pray and laugh and cry. You can hear the crowd erupting in the background as the gray-haired doctor pulls you and your spouse aside to say, "I need to talk to you. We didn't realize that the donor would be a minor and we . . . we need you to sign a consent form."

The doctor presents the form and you quickly begin to sign it, but then your eye catches something. The box for the number of pints of blood to be taken is empty.

"How many pints?" you ask. That is when the old doctor's smile fades, and he says, "We had no idea it would be a child. We weren't prepared for that."

You ask him again, "How many pints?" The old doctor looks away and says regretfully, "We are going to need it all!"

"But I don't understand. What do you mean you need it all? He's my only son!"

The doctor grabs you by the shoulders, pulls you close, looks you straight in the eyes, and says, "We are talking about the whole world here. Do you understand? The whole world. Please, sign the form. We need to hurry!"

"But can't you give him a transfusion?" you plead.

"If we had clean blood we would, but we don't. Please, will you sign the form?"

What would you do?

In numb silence you sign the form because you know it's the only thing to do. Then the doctor says to you, "Would you like to have a moment with your son before we get started?"

Could you walk into that hospital room where your son sits on a table saying, "Daddy? Mommy? What's going on?" Could you tell your son you love him? And when the doctors and nurses come back in and say, "I'm sorry, we've got to get started now; people all over the world are dying," could you leave? Could you walk out while your son is crying out to you, "Mom? Dad? What's going on? Where are you going? Why are you leaving? Why have you abandoned me?"

The following week, they hold a ceremony to honor your son for his phenomenal contribution to humanity . . . but some people sleep through it, others don't even bother to come because they have better things to do, and some people come with a pretentious smile and pretend to care, while others sit around and say, "This is boring!" Wouldn't you want to stand up and say, "Excuse me! I'm not sure if you are aware of it or not, but the amazing life you have, my son died so that you could have that life. My son died so that you could live. He died for you. Does it mean nothing to you?"

Perhaps that is what God wants to say.

Father, seeing it from your eyes should break our hearts. Maybe now we can begin to comprehend the great love you have for us.

Where to from Here?

The past several years have been a tough time to be Catholic in America. In many ways this is a time of tragedy for the Church. The abuse of our children is a tragedy. The scandal of the cover-up is a tragedy. The fact that the entire priesthood has been tarnished by a small group of troubled priests is a tragedy. The absence of bold and authentic leadership is a tragedy. Morale is low and the number of Catholics leaving the Church is higher than ever before. The effects of all these tragedies are far reaching. They have left society at large with a very low opinion of Catholicism and caused many Catholics to be ashamed of the Church.

I have spent hundreds of hours reflecting on where we are in our journey as a Church, and one thing that has become startlingly clear is that we have forgotten our story.

Catholicism is more than a handful of priests who don't know what it means to be a priest. There are 1.2 billion Catholics in the world. There are sixty-seven million Catholics in America—that's at least fifteen million more people than it takes to elect an American president. And every single day the Catholic Church feeds, houses, and clothes more people, takes care of more sick people, visits more prisoners, and educates more people than any other institution on the face of the earth could ever hope to.

Consider this question: When Jesus was alive, where were the sick people? Were they in hospitals? Of course not; there were no hospitals at the time of Christ. The sick were huddled at the side of the road and on the outskirts of town, and that is where Jesus cured them. They had been abandoned by family and friends who were afraid that they would also become sick.

The very essence of health care and caring for the sick emerged through the Church, through the religious orders, in direct response to the value and dignity that the Gospel assigns to each and every human life.

Allow me another question: How many people do you know who were born to nobility? Men and woman whose parents are kings, queens, dukes, earls, duchesses, knights, and so on? Not many, I suspect, and probably none. Well, that is the number of educated people you would know if the Catholic Church had not championed the cause to make education available to everyone. Prior to the Church's introduction of education for the common man, education was reserved only for the nobility. Almost the entire Western world is educated today because of the Church's pioneering role in universal education.

The global reach and contribution of the Church is enormous, but the national impact of the Church on every aspect of society is also impressive, though largely unknown. In the United States alone the Catholic Church educates 2.6 million students every day, at a cost of ten billion dollars a year to parents and parishes. If there were no Catholic schools these same students would have to be educated in public schools, which would cost eighteen billion dollars. The Catholic education system alone saves American taxpayers eighteen billion dollars a year.

In the field of secondary education the Church has more than 230 colleges and universities in the U.S., with an enrollment of seven hundred thousand students. And the Catholic and non-Catholic students educated in our schools and colleges go on to occupy many of the highest positions in any field. In terms of health care, the Catholic Church has a nonprofit hospital system comprising 637 hospitals, which treat one in five patients in the United States every day.

Beyond our national and global impact, the local contribution Catholics make in every community, on a daily basis, is nothing short of remarkable. Every city and town has its own stories, but allow me just one example to make my point. In Chicago there are hundreds of Catholic organizations that serve the needs of the people of that city. One of those organizations is Catholic Charities. This year the local chapter of Catholic Charities in Chicago will provide 2.2 million free meals to the hungry and the needy in that area. That's 6,027 meals a day—just one small example of our enormous contribution. Every city has a hundred stories like this one.

Our contribution on a local, national, and global scale remains phenomenal even in spite of our faults, inefficiencies, and recent scandals, and yet the Church is despised by millions of ordinary Americans, while most Catholics want to crawl under the table when people start talking about the Church in a social setting. We have forgotten our story and as a result we allow the anti-Catholic segments of the media to distort our story on a daily basis.

The tragedy continues on another level as well. It is disturbing that at a time when millions of Catholics are angry and disillusioned with the Church there has been no significant effort to remind Catholics of who we really are, no strategic effort to raise our morale among Catholics, no organized effort to remind the world that, for the past two thousand years, wherever you find Catholics, you find a group of people making enormous contributions to the local, national, and international community.

We have spent more than two billion dollars settling lawsuits, but we have not spent a single dime on any special initiative to encourage Catholics in America to continue to explore the beauty of their faith. We have not spent a dime reminding the culture at large of the enormous contributions we make to society as a Church. We have not spent a dime inspiring Catholics at a time when more are disillusioned about their faith and the Church than perhaps ever before. And that is a tragedy.

The book you are holding (and the campaign to provide free or low-cost copies to every Catholic in America) is the beginning of our attempt to raise morale among Catholics, remind ourselves that there is genius in Catholicism, and engage disengaged Catholics. In the future we hope to launch a series of billboards and television and radio commercials that remind people of the incredible impact the Church has had and that inspire Catholics to stay engaged.

Imagine a large billboard on any of Chicago's busy, backed-up freeways. No photos would be required, just this simple text: THIS YEAR CATHOLIC CHARITIES WILL PROVIDE 2.2 MILLION FREE MEALS TO THE HUNGRY AND THE NEEDY OF CHICAGO. WE DON'T ASK THEM IF THEY ARE CATHOLIC—WE JUST ASK THEM IF THEY ARE HUNGRY. REDISCOVER CATHOLICISM.

The point is we have forgotten our story, and in doing so, we have allowed the world to forget it as well. We have allowed the anti-Catholic segments of the media to distort it on a daily basis. Our history is not without blemish; our future will not be without blemish. But our contribution is unmatched, and it's needed today more than ever before.

I admit that I have been as angry and frustrated as most people about what has happened, what is happening, and what is not happening in the Church. I suppose the question we should consider together is: What will we do with our frustration and our anger?

It seems many people have just stopped thinking about it. They have disengaged from the Church to one extent or another and are getting on with their lives. Some refuse to come to church anymore. A great many have stopped contributing financially. Others have left the Catholic Church for their local nondenominational church. And some have tried to ignore the fact that they are angry about what has happened.

None of these are suitable solutions for me. The past fifteen years on the road have convinced me of these things:

1. There is genius in Catholicism, if we will just take the time and make the effort to humbly explore it.
2. There is nothing wrong with Catholicism that can't be fixed by what is right with Catholicism.
3. If you and I are not part of the solution, we are part of the problem.
4. If sixty-seven million Catholics in the United States stepped it up a notch, something incredible would happen.

So let's decide, here and now, today, to begin to explore the genius of our faith, to be part of the solution, and to step it up a notch.

It seems clear to even the most casual observer that something is missing. So where do we go from here?

Two thousand years ago, a small group of people captured the attention and intrigued the imagination of the entire Western world. At first, these people were thought to be of no consequence, the followers of a man most considered to be nothing more than an itinerant preacher. But when this man was put to death, a dozen of his followers rose up and began telling people about his life and teachings. They began telling the story of Jesus Christ. They were not the educated elite of their time, they had no political or social status, they were not wealthy, and they had no worldly authority, yet from the very beginning people were joining this quiet revolutionary group one hundred at a time.

As their popularity soared, the prevailing authorities grew fearful of their power, just as they had been afraid of their leader. In some places, the authorities tried to put an end to this new group by randomly killing some of its members. But those chosen considered it the highest honor to die for what they believed. This only intrigued the hearts and perplexed the minds of the people of their time even more.

This small group of people were the first Christians. They were the original followers of Jesus of Nazareth and the first members of what we know today as the Catholic Church.

As the centuries have passed, much has changed. Today, Catholicism is the largest faith community on earth. With more than a billion members across the globe, we are no longer the small minority group the first Christians were. Responsible for the birth of both the education and health care systems that stand as pillars in our modern society, we continue to lead with excellence in these areas. Throughout the centuries, the Church has also been the largest benefactor of the arts, nurturing the elements of cultural life that have the ability to elevate the human heart, mind, and spirit so effortlessly to the things of God. In these United States, where Catholics were once not permitted to apply for certain jobs, there are now more publicly elected officials who are Catholic than any other religious affiliation. The Church is one of the largest landowners in the world, holding property in almost every community, from the most remote rural locations to the most sophisticated cities. In this modern day and age, when the life and dignity of the human person is being threatened at almost every turn, the Catholic Church remains the world's premier institutional defender of human rights. The Church today is a global entity of considerable proportions.

We have come a long way from our humble beginnings. And yet, as great as our achievements may be, as great as our numbers are today, we seem unable to capture the attention and intrigue the imaginations of the people of our own time the way our spiritual ancestors did.

The story of Jesus Christ is the most powerful in history and has directly or indirectly influenced every noble aspect of modern civilization. But amid the hustle and bustle of our daily lives, it is easy to become distracted and distance ourselves from this story. From time to time, someone comes along who reminds us of the spellbinding power the Gospel has when it is actually lived. Some of these men and women are the saints who have become household names; others are just ordinary people: parents and grandparents, nurses and schoolteachers, financial advisers and entrepreneurs.

We have become too comfortably a part of the modern secular culture, and this comfort has resulted in a dangerous complacency toward the life-giving words of the Gospel. Too often, we listen to these words but do not allow them to penetrate our hearts and transform our lives. There is something ultimately attractive about men and women *striving* to become all that God created them to be. It is this striving that we need to rediscover as a Church.

This striving that is so important to the life of the Church is not the human striving that says, "Let's come up with a plan and make things happen." Rather, it's the striving that relies upon the Spirit of God to illumine, instruct, and guide us at every turn. God doesn't want to control us, nor does he want us to ignore him. God yearns for a dynamic collaboration with each and every single one of us.

The first Christians were not perfect; nor were the saints. They lived in communities that were torn by strife in ways remarkably similar to what we are experiencing today, and they struggled with the brokenness of their own humanity in the same way you and I do. But they were dedicated to the basics.

Catholicism is not a football game, but Paul once compared the Christian life to athletics, and I would like to continue the analogy. Championship winning teams are not necessarily those with the most talented players or the most ingenious new plays, nor are they necessarily the teams with the most resources or superior knowledge of the game. The very best coaches will tell you that teams that win championships are those that focus on the basics and master them together.

We need to get back to the basics.

I know this may sound cliché or trite, but when Catholics dedicate themselves to the basics of our rich and dynamic spirituality extraordinary things begin to happen.

The first Christians intrigued the people of their time. So did the saints, and so do ordinary people who embrace the Christian life today. In the great majority of cases they don't do anything spectacular. For the most part they commit themselves to doing simple things spectacularly well and with great love, and that intrigues people. We need to intrigue the people of our time in the same ways.

Whom does your life intrigue? Not with spectacular accomplishments, but simply by the way you live, love, and work.

If we live and love the way the Gospel invites us to, we will intrigue people. Respect and cherish your spouse and children, and people will be intrigued. Work hard and pay attention to the details of your work, and you will intrigue people. Go out of your way to help those in need, people will be intrigued. When we do what is right even if it comes at a great cost to ourselves, people are intrigued. Patience, kindness, humility, gratitude, thoughtfulness, generosity, courage and forgiveness are all intriguing.

God always wants our future to be bigger than our past. Not equal to our past, but bigger, better, brighter, and more significant. God wants your future and my future, and the future of the Church, to be bigger than the past. It is this bigger future that we need to envision.

One of the most incredible abilities God has given the human person is the ability to dream. We are able to look into the future and imagine something better than today, and then return to the present and work to make that richly imagined future a reality. Who is doing this for the Church?

For many years I have been reflecting on a single verse from Proverbs. It never ceases to ignite my passion for the Church. "Where there is no vision, the people will perish." (Proverbs 29:18) I have found this to be true in every area of life. In a country where there is no vision, the people will perish. In a marriage where there is no vision, people will perish. In a business, a school, or a family where there is no vision, the people will perish.

And it is with a heavy heart that I acknowledge that it seems as a Church we are without a vision, and as a result people are perishing. We need a Catholic vision for this place and this time, something simple and yet profound. A vision to inspire and mobilize Catholics young and old. A vision that can be understood by a seven-year-old as easily as it can by someone with degrees in theology and philosophy.

Some people may take offense at my suggestion that we are without a vision. Others, I am certain, would consider this preposterous. But if you asked one hundred Catholics what the Church's vision is for our times, I suspect you would get one hundred different answers. Or possibly many would have no answer at all. So either we don't have a vision or Catholics don't know what it is, but regardless, the result is the same: People are perishing.

This Catholic vision we are in search of is not the sole responsibility of the Pope, or of the cardinals and bishops. Your priest is not solely responsible for your parish's vision. We each have a role to play in imagining and working toward a future for the Church that will confound the skeptics and inspire the masses.

Many are calling for a return to the past. These people are reactionaries, not visionaries. Too often their cries are driven by a fear of uncertainty and a grappling for stability. Rather than placing their trust in God and cooperating with his future, they allow their humanity to get the better of them as they try to control things beyond their control.

God never goes back; he always moves forward. Adam and Eve were banished from the garden. God could have redeemed them and sent them back to the garden, but he didn't, for two reasons: God always wants our future to be bigger than our past, and God always moves forward.

So let us press on toward the future God has envisioned for us and for the Church. It is time for us to become a people of possibility again. Too much of what we do is governed by a very limited way of thinking. We gravitate toward what is manageable, rather than imagining what is possible. We have lost touch with best practices and settle for the way things have always been done. Now is the time for us to reimagine what incredible things are possible if we walk with God. Now is the time for Catholics to become a people of possibility. Imagine what sixty-seven million American Catholics are capable of. Imagine what more than a billion Catholics worldwide are capable of.

One thing is certain: Whatever we do or do not do will determine the future of humanity and the world.

All of this leads me to conclude that now is a time when we all need to rediscover Catholicism. I try to rediscover it every day, and when I seek in earnest to do so I am never disappointed. When I am able to set my ego and personal agenda aside, more often than not I am left in awe.

There are many, Catholics and non-Catholics alike, who do not want to rediscover Catholicism. Others think religion, and Catholicism in particular, has no place in the modern context. I will admit that Catholicism is old. But let me ask you a question. If you had an ancient treasure map, would you throw it away just because it was old? No. The age of the map doesn't matter. What matters is whether or not it leads to treasure. Catholicism is a treasure map: It may be old, but it still leads to treasure. Let's rediscover it together, and help others to do the same.

Matthew Kelly

Part One

WE BECOME
WHAT WE CELEBRATE

The Church (like so many other things in life) is not so much something we inherit from generations past or take over from our predecessors as it is something on loan to us from future generations.

Chapter One

OUR UNIVERSAL HUNGER

Throughout human history, there has never been a shortage of men and women willing to point humanity along the right path. Nor have the needs of the human family ever been a secret: food, shelter, meaningful work, companionship, freedom, forgiveness, acceptance, and love.

In every age, there is an abundance of people who try to speak to these very real human needs and announce the social implications particular to that time. These people stand at the crossroads and point humanity down a path they have never traveled themselves. In our own age, there is certainly no shortage of books, CDs, DVDs, podcasts, Web sites, radio shows, seminars, and television programs attempting to speak to our very real human needs in ways that are relevant and engaging.

But amid this apparent abundance there is a great poverty. I am not speaking of a material poverty. Rather, it seems in every place and in every time the shortage is always of men and women willing to *lead* humanity along the right path with the example of their own lives. In each moment of history authentic lives are ever so rare.

• Appearance vs. the Authentic •

Our own age seems to be governed by illusion and deception. We have built a whole culture based on appearance. Everything looks good, but scratch just below the surface, and you will discover little substance. Appearance has become a standard. We have grown so numb to the realities of good and evil that lying and cheating have become almost universally accepted as necessary evils. So we tolerate them, as long as they are performed in the dim light of *respectability*. Occasionally, in the midst of this cultural darkness, the great light of the human spirit shines forth with honesty and integrity. At those times we seem surprised, even taken off guard. Honesty, loyalty, and integrity seem almost out of place in the modern schema.

But beneath the surface, under the guise of appearances, this age, like any other, is made up of people like you and me. And if you listen carefully, if you look closely, you will discover that people are hungry. We were created to love and be loved, and there is a restlessness, a longing for more, a profound discontent with our lives and with our culture. We sense that something is missing, and deep within we know that nothing we can buy and no worldly pleasure will satisfy our restlessness.

This yearning preoccupies the human heart, and it is neither random nor accidental; everyone has it and we have it for a reason. The Holy Spirit (the "soul of our soul," as Pope Benedict XVI calls him) is at the source of these longings. It is the presence of God in the most interior part of ourselves that calls us to move beyond the surface concerns of our lives, to explore and experience something deeper.

Our hunger is not for appearances, nor is it for the fleeting and superficial; it is for something of substance. We are hungry for truth. The people of today are starving for the authentic, thirsting for the tiniest droplet of sincerity, aching to experience the genuine.

• Why Has Christianity Been Rejected? •

The hunger for truth and goodness is enormous, and yet at the same time Christianity (and particularly Catholicism) has been largely rejected. There are, of course, many people who faithfully attend church each Sunday, but increasing numbers are choosing not to come to church. This is particularly true among younger generations.

Most of us know good, intelligent people, contributing members of our communities, who won't have anything to do with Christianity. Many of whom were raised as Christians in one form or another. Sooner or later, we must begin to explore this ever-increasing phenomenon and ask some probing and uncomfortable questions: Is it possible that we failed to engage them? Did the hypocrisy of individual church members or leaders obscure their experience of God? Did we fail to feed them? Did we ever really welcome them?

Those of us who call ourselves Christian do so because we believe that the life and teachings of Jesus Christ are the personification of truth, sincerity, and authenticity, and, in a practical sense, simply the best way to live. If we are correct in this belief, and if the people of the twenty-first century really are hungering for authenticity and the best way to live, then as Christians we must ask ourselves questions such as: Why are more people not enthusiastically embracing Christianity? Why, in fact, are so many people so hostile toward Christ and his Church?

I sense it is because the people of today believe that Christians, Christianity, and perhaps Catholics in particular are as much a part of this culture of appearance and deception as anyone else. This is a harsh truth that needs to be faced. People's desire for truth has not diminished, but they have become wary, doubtful, skeptical, and, sadly, even cynical in their search for truth. And to be honest, I cannot blame them for their attitude. I do not agree with their position, but I understand it. And perhaps more important, I can see how they arrived at that place of philosophical confusion and theological desolation.

The cause of much of this confusion is the unprecedented proliferation of words, symbols, images, and every manner of communication in the latter part of the twentieth century. People are tired; they are worn out, overloaded with information, and overwhelmed with the social, political, and economic climate. They are not *striving* to thrive; they are merely trying to survive. This is a tired culture.

• The Cry for Help •

This cultural fatigue is creating a hopelessness in the lives of more and more people every day, and from the midst of that fatigue and hopelessness they are crying out for help.

More than ever, our non-Christian and non-practicing brothers and sisters are sending you, me, and all of Christianity a message. Though they are probably not aware of it, they are indirectly giving witness to the Gospel. For within the message the people of our times are sending us, there is a profound challenge for you and me to embrace a life rooted more fully in the example and teachings of Jesus Christ. Their message is clear, unmistakable, and disarmingly simple. Our siblings, parents, and children are sending us this message, as are our friends, neighbors, and colleagues. They are saying, whispering, crying out, "Don't tell me—*show* me!"

Their plea comes from a longing deep within them and represents their great hunger. They don't want to see another television evangelist, they don't want to read another book or hear another CD about Christianity, and they don't want to hear your amazing story of conversion. They want the real thing. They want to witness someone, anyone—just one will do—living an authentic life, someone whose words are supported by the authority of his or her actions. Someone striving humbly but heroically to live by what is good, true, and noble in the midst of—and in spite of—the modern climate.

They are not sending us this message merely to sound the childish cry of "Hypocrite!" Rather, theirs is a natural cry, a cry for help. They are saying to us, "Don't tell me—*show* me!" because they are so hungry for a courageous example of the authentic life, a life lived to the fullest, in this day and age. Seeing the conflicts and contradictions of your life and mine, they often cry "Hypocrite!" out of their hurt and anger. They are angry because the disappointment of discovering that we are not living the life we espouse robs them of their own hope to live an authentic life. They are disillusioned and searching, but they never cease calling out to us like sheep without a shepherd, wanting to be fed, wanting to be led to the pastures of kindness, compassion, generosity, forgiveness, acceptance, freedom, and love.

I have heard this cry a thousand times, but the words of one man echo in my mind like a bad dream that keeps returning to haunt a terrified child. They are the words of Mahatma Gandhi, a man for whom I have great admiration, who I believe strove with all his might to live an authentic life. I have studied his life and writings, but one passage stands out. It speaks to me with a clarity that pierces my heart.

In reference to the well-known fact that Gandhi read from the New Testament every day and often quoted the Christian Scriptures, a reporter once asked him why he had never become a Christian. He answered, "If I had ever met one, I would have become one." In his own way, Gandhi was saying, "Don't tell me—*show* me!" revealing his yearning for an example of an authentic life.

All this being said, I also believe there is a desire within each of us to live an authentic life. We desire not only to witness authentic lives but also to live an authentic life ourselves. We genuinely want to be true to ourselves. At times, we have perhaps resolved to live such a life with all the fervor we could muster. But distracted by the sweet seduction of pleasure and possessions, we have wandered from the narrow path. We know the truth, but we lack the discipline and strength of character to align the actions of our lives with that truth (cf. Matthew 26:41). We have given ourselves over to a thousand different whims, cravings, and fantasies. Our lives have become merely a distortion of the truth we know and profess. We know the human family's need for kindness, compassion, generosity, forgiveness, acceptance, freedom, and love, but we have divided our hearts with a thousand contradictions and compromises.

At every moment, the entire modern world kneels before us, begging, pleading, beckoning for some brave man or woman to come forward and lead them with the example of an authentic life.

In many respects our age is one of abundance, but amid this abundance (which at times may seem all prevailing) there remains a great hunger in the people of today. We have a universal hunger for the authentic, a longing to be and become and experience all we are capable of and created for. Everything good in the future (for ourselves, our marriages, our families, our communities, our Church, our nation, and humanity) depends on whether or not we will follow this longing.

Chapter Two

THE PREVAILING
PHILOSOPHY

When you think of philosophy, what comes to mind? Perhaps you recall a class in college that you had to take but never really understood, or maybe you think of the great philosophers such as Socrates and Aristotle. The truth is we are all philosophers, and we all have a philosophy.

In ages past philosophies have been well-thought-out approaches to life. The great minds of every era have grappled with universal and enduring questions: Who am I? Where did I come from? What am I here for? How do I do it? Where am I going? All of these questions lead from (and back to) the question that has preoccupied humanity from the very beginning: What is the best way to live? The more people who ask this question and rigorously pursue an answer to it, the more dynamic and vibrant a society will be.

Every culture is the fruit of the ideas and attitudes of its people. These ideas and attitudes come together in both people and cultures to form philosophies. Our own age is one of great philosophical poverty, and as a result we live in an age of tremendous moral and ethical confusion.

Today, there is little philosophical rigor in our culture. The way we consume information leads us to think less and less about more and more. We spend much of our time fixated on secondary questions (usually related to controversial and sensational issues) and very little time exploring the primary questions about our brief stay here on earth. This is why many of the philosophies we live our lives in allegiance to are absorbed through the culture rather than the result of any well-thought-out approach to life.

We each have our own philosophy, our own personal rule of life. This philosophy comprises a set of beliefs by which we choose to live. These beliefs are probably many and varied. A person might believe that there is one God, that the earth is round, and that you should never go anywhere without an umbrella. These beliefs are very different, but could coexist within one's personal philosophy.

What is your philosophy?

While you may not be able to articulate your personal philosophy, you call upon this "rule of life" many times each day. Every day you make hundreds of decisions. Some of these decisions affect what you eat and what you wear, while others affect the very direction of your life. In every case, these decisions are determined by your personal philosophy.

Communities also have philosophies. The philosophy of a community is made up of the collective philosophies of its members. A community could be as small as a family or as large as a nation. Your parish is a community, and a college campus is a community. In the present age, there are certain philosophical trends that are governing the decision process. I find these trends disturbing on many levels: They disturb me as a human being, as a brother, son, father, and member of a family. They disturb me as a citizen of a modern nation. They disturb me as a person of faith and as a Christian. And they disturb me as a Catholic, as an active, believing member of the one holy, catholic, and apostolic Church.

Although there are many philosophies influencing the modern schema, I would like to propose that there are three major practical philosophies upon which we have constructed our modern culture. I will leave it to the reader to decide whether we have built our culture on rock, like the wise man, or on sand, like the fool (cf. Matthew 7:24–27).

• Individualism •

The first of these practical philosophies is individualism. When most people today are faced with a decision, the question that seems to dominate their inner dialogue is, "What's in it for me?" This question is the creed of individualism, which is based on an all-consuming concern for self. In the present climate, the most dominant trend governing the decision-making process—and therefore the formation of our cultural belief system—is individualism.

No community, whether as small as a family or as large as a nation, can grow strong with this attitude. Individualism always weakens the community and causes the whole to suffer. In every instance it is a cancerous growth.

The social and political reforms of our age have exalted the individual in a way that is unhealthy for society as a whole. Under the pressure and guidance of a number of special-interest groups that represent only a fraction of society at large, the rights of the individual have been gradually elevated and ultimately placed above the rights of society as a whole. A perfect example is the recent situation in California, where a court banned public schools from using "under God" when saying the Pledge of Allegiance because one student found it offensive. The rights of the individual have been strengthened at all costs, with no regard for right and wrong, and often to the detriment of the whole. At the same time, everything has been done to weaken the rights of the Church, the State, and authority of any type.

All this has been done under the banner of false freedom. The false and adolescent notion is that freedom is the opportunity to do whatever you want, wherever you want, whenever you want, without the interference of any other person or party. This is not freedom.

Our culture places a very high premium on self-expression, but is relatively disinterested in producing "selves" that are worth expressing.

The fruits of individualism are no secret to any of us: greed, selfishness, and exploitation. What would become of a family or a nation in which each member adopted individualism as his or her own personal philosophy?

• Hedonism •

This naked individualism is only furthered by the present generation's assertion that pleasure is the supreme good. This assertion unmasks hedonism as the second philosophical mark of our age. Hedonism is the philosophy that emphasizes pleasure as the ultimate goal of life. The motto, the creed, the catch cry of the hedonist is, "If it feels good, do it!"

Under the guise of a supposedly *newfound freedom,* this ancient impostor has seduced and deceived present generations. This is the great paradox regarding the philosophical marks of our age. The people who promote and propagate them represent them as new and different, but if we undress these philosophies we quickly discover that the present cultural environment is based on failed ideologies of the past. We mistakenly believe that these philosophies are new and different. But, if we scratch just beneath the surface and look a little deeper, we will discover that the cultures that first employed these philosophies, or have since adopted them, can all trace their decline to them.

Whenever hedonism has emerged as a dominant practical philosophy in other cultures and subcultures, it produced men and women who were lazy, lustful, and gluttonous. Furthermore, hedonism has been a contributing factor to the demise of every culture and subculture in which it has featured significantly. The Roman Empire is a perfect example.

Hedonism is not an expression of freedom; it is a passport to enslavement by a thousand cravings and addictions. And in the end it produces not pleasure, but despair.

• Minimalism •

The third philosophical mark of our age perfectly complements the greed of individualism and the lust of hedonism in the demise of human character. Accompanying these other modern creeds, whose central tenets are "What's in it for me?" and "If it feels good, do it!" is the creed of minimalism. The minimalist is always asking, "What is the least I can do?"

A minimalist is always seeking to exert the minimum effort and receive the maximum reward. Consciously or subconsciously, people everywhere seem to be asking, "What is the least I can do and still keep my job? What is the least I can do and still get reasonable grades in school? What is the least

I can do and still keep my marriage alive? What is the least I can do and still stay physically fit? What is the least I can do and still get to Heaven? What is the least I can do . . . ?"

Minimalism is the enemy of excellence and the father of mediocrity. It is one of the greatest philosophical diseases of our age. Minimalism has infected every aspect of our lives and society, and tragically, it is also one of the philosophical diseases that is eating away at the Church.

It is within the philosophical realms of individualism, hedonism, and minimalism that most people make the majority of their decisions every day. These philosophies are being communicated powerfully yet subtly via every social, cultural, and political medium. Through movies and music, literature and fashion, government policy and education, these philosophies have nudged their way into every aspect of our lives. It didn't happen overnight; it has taken decades. We would have reacted if it had happened overnight, just as a frog will jump straight out if you drop it into a pot of boiling water. But if you put a frog in a pot of cold water and then slowly raise the temperature, it will stay in the pot even to its death.

With all this in mind, we shouldn't be surprised by the radical increase in sexual promiscuity and sex crimes today, or the cultural manipulation and destruction of the family unit, or the gradual but persistent political and cultural undermining of family values in our modern societies. It shouldn't surprise us that corporate and political fraud have escalated at alarming rates. Truth be known, we shouldn't be surprised that during my short lifetime more than nine times the number of people murdered in the atrocity we call the Holocaust have fallen victim to abortion in the United States alone. Teenagers walking into classrooms and shooting students and teachers, children killing their parents, adolescents killing themselves, and the dramatic and unprecedented increase in non-warfare violence shouldn't shock us. These are the signs of the times, and they are merely the fruits of the philosophies that mark this moment in history.

Any community that adopts these philosophies, whether that community is as small as a family or as large as a nation, does so at its own peril. A philosophy is a way of life. Individualism, hedonism, and minimalism will destroy every individual and community that practices them. They are ultimately self-destructive philosophies that destroy body, heart, mind, and soul.

The crisis of the modern world is a crisis of ideas. Ideas shape our lives and the world. Thought determines action. It would not be too soon for us to learn that ideas have very real consequences.

Chapter Three

IS JESUS STILL RELEVANT?

It should also come as no surprise to us that in this modern environment the relevance of Jesus is being undermined and questioned. The reason is simple: The philosophy of Christ is very different from the prevailing philosophies of our modern culture. In fact, they are completely opposed to each other. And yet, the teachings of Christ and these modern philosophies both claim to be the key to the fulfillment of a yearning that is common to us all.

• Our Quest for Happiness •

The human heart is on a quest for happiness. Every person yearns for happiness like the desert yearns for rain. You have a desire for happiness; I have a desire for happiness. This desire is universal, common to every member of the human family. We simply desire to be happy, and we act from this desire.

We often do things that we think will make us happy, only to discover that they end up making us miserable. This is often because we confuse pleasure with happiness. And sometimes long-term misery comes disguised as short-term pleasure. Under the influence of philosophies such as individualism, hedonism, and minimalism, we often seek the happiness we desire through pleasure, possessions, power, and the path of least resistance. Each of these may offer moments of happiness, but they end too soon, having lasted ever so briefly, and our quest for a lasting happiness continues. These moments of happiness are of course real, but only as real as a shadow: A person's shadow is real, but it is nothing compared to the actual person. So many of us spend a large portion of our lives chasing shadows.

The modern search for happiness is governed by individualism, hedonism, minimalism, and their fruits: greed, lust, laziness, gluttony, selfishness, exploitation, and deception. And yet, as these philosophies become more and more the focus of modern lifestyles, people seem to be filled with a greater discontent and unhappiness with every passing day.

Are we prepared to consider that these philosophies cannot deliver what they promise? Is it possible that there is something lacking in these philosophies that makes it impossible for the human person to find happiness through them?

• God and Happiness •

I believe God wants us to be happy. I believe God gave us this yearning for happiness that constantly preoccupies our hearts. It seems he has placed this yearning within each human heart as a spiritual navigational instrument designed to lead us to our destiny. God himself is the author of our desire for happiness.

As a father who takes a sincere and active interest in the lives of his children, God sent his only Son to respond to humanity's yearning for happiness, and to teach us how to satisfy that yearning. God sent his Son into the world to reconcile us with himself, certainly, but he also sent Jesus to show us how to live.

The philosophy of Christ is the ultimate philosophy of human happiness. It isn't just a way of life; it is *the* way of life. At the same time, the philosophy of Christ is one of self-donation. This is the great paradox of God's teaching. In our misguided adventures, we may catch glimpses of happiness as we live outside of the philosophy of Christ. You may even taste happiness for a moment living a life contrary to the philosophy of Christ, but these are stolen moments. They may seem real, but they are just shadows of something infinitely greater.

• The Attitude of Christ •

Jesus never asked, "What's in it for me?" He was not motivated by the individualist creed; he was motivated by a spirit of service. Far from advocating a hedonistic deification of pleasure, Jesus gently proclaimed a life of self-denial, saying, "Whoever wishes to follow me, let him deny himself and take up his cross." (Matthew 16:24) He certainly didn't ask himself, "What is the least I can do and still bring salvation to humanity?" No, he asked, "What is the *most* I can do?" For this is the question of the lover. The attitude of Christ forms a stark contrast to the philosophies of individualism, hedonism, and minimalism.

The life that Jesus invites us to live is very different from the lifestyle our modern culture invites us to live. Individualism, hedonism, and minimalism—and their various sibling philosophies, such as relativism and materialism—encourage us to do whatever we want, wherever we want, whenever we want. Jesus, on the other hand, invites us to a life of discipline and discipleship.

Having appeared to Mary Magdalene after his Resurrection, Jesus summoned the disciples to Galilee. When the eleven were gathered together on the mountain, Jesus said, "Go therefore and make disciples of every nation." (Matthew 28:19) He did not say, "Go and make followers of every nation."

It is easy to be a follower, but to be a disciple means to be a student—to be humble, docile, and teachable, and to listen. All this requires discipline. Christ invites us to a life of discipline not for his sake, but for our sake; not to help him, but to help us; not to make him happy, but to allow us to share in his happiness.

• The Role of Discipline •

Jesus said, "I have come that you may have life and have it to the fullest." (John 10:10) Discipline is the path that leads to "fullness of life." There are four major aspects of the human person: physical, emotional, intellectual, and spiritual. When we eat well, exercise often, and sleep regularly, we feel more fully alive physically. When we love, when we give priority to the significant relationships in our lives, when we give of ourselves to help others in their journey, we feel more fully alive emotionally. When we study our vision of ourselves and God, the world expands, and we feel more fully alive intellectually. When we take a few moments each day in the classroom of silence to come before God in prayer, openly and honestly, we experience life more fully spiritually. All of these life-giving endeavors require discipline. When are we most fully alive? When we embrace a life of discipline. The human person thrives on discipline.

Are you thriving? Or are you just surviving?

Discipline awakens us from our philosophical stupor and refines every aspect of the human person. Discipline doesn't enslave or stifle us; rather, it sets us free to soar to unimagined heights. It sharpens the human senses, allowing us to savor the subtler tastes of life's experiences. Whether those experiences are physical, emotional, intellectual, or spiritual, discipline elevates them to their ultimate reality. It heightens every human experience and increases every human ability. The life and teachings of Jesus Christ invite us to embrace this life-giving discipline.

Many people consider Jesus irrelevant today because he proposes a life of discipline. Is discipline, then, to be considered the core of Jesus' philosophy? No. Christ proposes a life of discipline not for its own sake, and certainly not to stifle or control us; rather, he proposes discipline as the key to freedom.

In the midst of the complexities of this modern era, we find ourselves enslaved and imprisoned by a thousand different whims, cravings, addictions, and attachments. As previously stated, we have subscribed to the adolescent notion that freedom is the ability to do whatever you want, wherever you want, whenever you want, without interference from any authority. Could the insanity of our modern approach to life be any more apparent? Freedom is not the ability to do whatever you want. Freedom is the strength of character and the self-possession to do what is good, true, noble, and right. Therefore, freedom without discipline is impossible. Strength of character is not stumbled upon in life's moments of need and temptation. Character is built little by little, over days, weeks, months, and years, with thousands of small and seemingly insignificant acts of discipline. Self-possession is not an unearned right;

it is the privilege of the few who build it, defend it, and celebrate it by disciplining themselves.

Is *freedom*, then, to be considered the core of Jesus' philosophy? No.

So what is the core of his philosophy? Well, as it turns out, the people of his own time were curious for an answer to this very question.

One day, while Jesus was teaching a large group of people in the synagogue, a man in the crowd asked our Lord a question. He was a learned man, one of those doctors of the law who were no longer able to understand the teaching God had revealed to Moses because it had become so twisted and entangled in the ways of men. He questioned Jesus, asking, "Teacher, which is the greatest of the Commandments?"

Jesus opened his divine lips slowly, with the calm assurance of somebody who knows what he is talking about, and replied, "You shall love the Lord your God with your whole heart, your whole mind, and your whole soul. This is the first and the greatest of the Commandments. And the second is like it, you shall love your neighbor as yourself. Upon these two rest the whole law and all the prophets." (Matthew 22:34–40)

Love is the core of Jesus' philosophy. But in order to love you must be free. For to love is to give your *self* freely and without reservation. Yet, to give your self—to another person, to an endeavor, or to God—you must first possess your self. This possession of self is freedom. It is a prerequisite for love, and is attained only through discipline.

• Jesus in History •

Before Christmas last year, I saw a Jewish scholar interviewed on television. The topic of discussion was the influence Jesus has exerted on human history. In summary, the scholar concluded, "The impact this man has had on human history is undeniable. Because of this man we call Jesus, the world will never again be the same. Because of Jesus, men and women will never think the same. Regardless of whether or not we believe he was the Son of God, because of this man who walked the earth two thousand years ago, men and women will never live the same, will never be the same."

Sometimes, in this turbulent cultural environment, which can be particularly anti-Christian, we can lose sight of the impact Christ has had on history. Caught up in the day-to-day challenges of our busy lives, we sometimes forget or overlook the unfathomable influence this one man has had and continues to have.

There are a great many people today who think that Jesus is irrelevant in the modern context. I suspect these people are suffering from a modern madness caused by an ignorance of self and history. As we get to know ourselves, our deepest needs, and the history of humanity, the relevance of Jesus Christ to modern man becomes startlingly clear.

Is Jesus still relevant?

Gather all the books that have been written about the life and teachings of Jesus. Add to them all the artwork Christian life has inspired. Now consider all the music inspired by Christ. Not to be forgotten is the fact that the Church nurtured and nourished the development of the arts for centuries. Christianity is the moral foundation upon which America and many other nations built themselves.

Now consider the fact that prior to Christ walking the earth, there was never any such thing as a hospital. Where were the sick when Jesus walked the earth? They were on the side of the road, left there to rot and die by relatives who feared for their own health.

How is it that we have also collectively forgotten that until the Church introduced education for the masses, there was never any such thing as an education for the common man? Education was only for the nobility until the Church recognized and proclaimed the dignity of every human person and introduced the idea that every person deserved an education. And how many cities, such as San Francisco, take their names from Christian roots?

All of these represent aspects of the measurable impact Christ has had on human history. And yet, these are all just dim reflections of the person who was and is Jesus Christ. Adding all of these together is still nothing compared to the impact Christ can have on your life, on my life. All the worldly success of Christ and the Church are insignificant compared to the change Christ wants to have in you and your life.

The life of Jesus Christ is indelibly engraved upon history; neither the erosion of time nor the devastating and compounding effects of evil have been able to erase his influence. Some people thought he was crazy; others considered him a misfit, a troublemaker, a rebel. He was condemned as a criminal, yet his life and teachings reverberate throughout history. He saw things differently, and he had no respect for the status quo. You can praise him, disagree with him, quote him, disbelieve him, glorify him, or vilify him. About the only thing you cannot do is ignore him, and that is a lesson that every age learns in its own way.

You can't ignore Jesus, because he changed things. He is the single greatest agent of change in human history. He made the lame walk, taught the simple, set captives free, gave sight to the blind, fed the hungry, healed the sick, comforted the afflicted, afflicted the comfortable, and in all of these, captured the imagination of every generation.

His teachings are not complex or exclusive, but simple and applicable to everyone, everywhere, in every time in history, regardless of age, color, or state in life. Beyond life's complexities, there is simplicity. Beneath the chaos and confusion of life, there is understanding. It is the Gospel, the good news. Within it and through it we find salvation. Part of that salvation is happiness—not the foolish, empty happiness that this modern age associates with getting what you want. But rather, a happiness deeper and higher than any we could imagine or design for ourselves.

Christ came to reconcile us with the Father, and in doing so, offered the satisfaction of this craving for happiness that preoccupies our human hearts. Love is our origin and our destiny. Our yearning for happiness is a yearning for love. Created to love and be loved, we seek out the fulfillment of our purpose. "God is love," (1 John 4:8) and our yearning for happiness is ultimately a yearning for God. The *Catechism of the Catholic Church* wastes no time in addressing this truth. The opening point of Chapter One, Section One, reads, "The desire for God is written in the human heart, because man is created by God and for God; and God never ceases to draw man to himself. Only in God will man find the truth and happiness he never stops yearning for."

Our desire for happiness is not going to go away. It is part of the human condition. Our quest for happiness is a quest for God. This is the genius of God. This yearning for happiness is the ultimate homing device, designed to draw us gently toward our eternal home. God creates us, places this desire within us, and sends us out into the universe. He does this knowing that sooner or later, if we can muster even the tiniest droplet of humility, the desire for happiness will lead us back to him—for no one else and nothing else can satisfy it.

Our yearning for happiness is a yearning for union with our Creator. Augustine's words echo anew in every place, in every time, and in every heart: "Our hearts are restless until they rest in you, Lord." Wherever men and women yearn for happiness, Christ will be relevant. He alone is the fulfillment and satisfaction of this yearning, and so for every person in every place and time he remains "the Way, the Truth, and the Life." (John 14:6)

Chapter Four

SEARCHING FOR IDENTITY

Today, perhaps more than ever before, we are struggling as Catholics to establish a positive identity in society. What has caused this identity crisis? How do we establish a vibrant identity for Catholicism in the modern world? These are questions that challenge us as individual Catholics, as parish communities, and as an international family of faith.

• The Mission •

The cultural settings of different ages may change dramatically, but two things remain the same in every place and in every time: the human heart's yearning for happiness and the mission of the Church. In fact, the mission of the Church is God's direct and intimate response to the human heart's unceasing desire for happiness.

At the dawn of this new millennium, it is essential that we remind ourselves that Christ did not entrust the Church with a social, political, or economic mission, but with a mission that is primarily spiritual. The mission of the Church is to proclaim the Gospel to the people of every nation in every age (see Mark 16:15). At the same time, as we live out this mission, it can and should impact the social, political, and economic order of the societies in which Christians live—indeed, every aspect of our lives. When we allow the Gospel to transform the way we live and love and work, it elevates every honest human endeavor and every aspect of society. The Gospel is alive and active. It has the power to transform our lives, our communities, our nations, and even the whole world. There is no word, thought, or action in our lives that is beyond the reach of the Gospel.

• The Adventure of Salvation •

Once we are aware of our yearning for happiness and the world's inability to satisfy it, the adventure of salvation begins. Our yearning for happiness is one way God invites us to join this adventure. God has a dream for you and a plan for your life. He wants to deliver you from everything that stands in the way of becoming the-best-version-of-yourself.

Throughout this book we are going to speak a lot about becoming the-best-version-of-yourself. With this term I am not suggesting a narcissistic, self-seeking approach to life. Rather, I am inviting you to a dynamic collaboration with God. It is in and through this collaboration that we become the-best-version-of-ourselves, in which the loving nature of God is most present.

God has a plan of salvation for each of us. Your adventure of salvation is unique and different from mine. In *The Rhythm of Life,* I write extensively about the relationship between our legitimate needs, our deepest desires, and our talents. It is through this relationship that God reveals to us our unique path of salvation. Francis of Assisi walked a different path than Teresa of Avila. They each became the-best-version-of-themselves, but they did it in different ways, according to their unique needs, talents, and desires. John Paul II lived a very different life than Maximilian Kolbe. Their paths were different, but the result was the same. Consider also for a moment the twelve Apostles. Each of them had very different talents and personalities, but Jesus called them each for a specific reason, to a specific role, and he calls you and me in the same way today.

God created us with legitimate needs. We all have legitimate physical, emotional, intellectual, and spiritual needs. The most basic understanding of these legitimate needs comes from considering our relationship to food, water, and oxygen. To eat and drink are legitimate needs. If you don't eat and drink, you will die. If you don't breathe, you will die even faster. God gave us these needs for a reason. When we hear them calling to us, we hear the voice of God.

Similarly, our hearts are filled with dreams and desires. The good dreams and desires that fill our hearts are placed there by God and stirred by the Holy Spirit, to call us along the path of salvation. One of the most ancient practices of Christian spirituality is the unveiling of the deepest desires of our hearts through contemplation and reflection. When we hear these deepest desires calling us forth, we hear the voice of God.

Finally, in creating us, God endowed us each with certain talents and abilities. He gave us these particular gifts as tools for life. He knew what talents and abilities we would need in our own unique journey. When we hear our talents calling us forth, we hear the voice of God inviting us to fully participate in the adventure of salvation.

It is through prayer, reflection, the Scriptures, the grace of the sacraments, the wisdom of the Church, and the guidance of the Holy Spirit that we discover and walk the path that God is calling us to walk. In our own way, we all seek out our individual destiny. Drawn by our yearning for happiness, we may seek to experience pleasure, possessions, and even power, but the world and all it has to offer can never content the human heart. God alone can satisfy the deepest cravings of our hearts.

It is the task of the Church to introduce us to our destiny by unveiling for us the mystery of God, who is our ultimate end and our destiny. It is the task of the Church to assist us in any way possible to fulfill this destiny. By "the task of the Church," I do not mean the job of your priest and your bishop and the parish staff. You and I have as much a role to play in the Church as any other member. Your role may be different from mine or a priest's, but it's no less important. What is critical is that each part of the one body fulfills its role to the best of his or her ability.

Allow me to re-articulate my last point in this way: It is your task and mine to introduce others to their destiny by unveiling the mystery of God for them. It is your task and mine to assist all those who cross our paths to fulfill their destiny. Serving others in this way will also allow us to fulfill our own destiny. This is one of the brilliant and beautiful ways that God has tied us all together.

By embracing the adventure of salvation we become with each effort more perfectly the person God created us to be. Christ has commissioned the

Church to guide and direct each of us along this path. Our dialogue and inter-action with the Church is designed to help us hear the voice of God in our lives, live the life God invites us to live, and become the-best-version-of-ourselves. Let us never forget that people do not exist for the Church—the Church exists for people.

It is for this reason that in every age the Church proclaims the unchanging truths of the life and teachings of Jesus Christ—the Gospel. In doing so, she invites us to a life of discipline.

There are certain disciplines that are associated with the lifestyle of an athlete that could also be compared with the lifestyle of a Christian. Athletes abide by certain diets and adhere to certain training regimens. They don't stay out all night partying, because they know they have to wake early the next morning for training. All these are part of an athlete's lifestyle. So it is with the life of a Christian. There are disciplines and practices that must be embraced and respected if we are to walk faithfully along the path of salva-tion, fulfill our destiny, become better-versions-of-ourselves each day, and enjoy the happiness God wants to fill us with. Your journey with God will require more discipline than any other quest you will pursue in this life.

• Catholics Today •

For years now I have spent endless hours wondering what God's vision for the Church was in the beginning and what it is today. I have explored Cath-olic history and studied the roots of Christianity. I have also wondered what the essential differences are between Catholics today and the first Christians. It's a difficult question.

For the first Christians, Christianity was a lifestyle. They shared a common life. Living in a community, they often worked together, prayed together, and studied the Scriptures together. Their faith was the center of their lives; it affected everything they did. They shared meals together, played together, and cared for each other in sickness. They allowed the principles of the Gospel to guide them in the activities of their daily lives. They comforted each other in their afflictions and challenged each other to live the Gospel more fully. There was unity and continuity between their professional lives and their family lives, between their social lives and their lives as members of the Church. They allowed the Holy Spirit to guide them in all they did. Then, at the pinnacle of their common life, they celebrated Eucharist together.

This is what many writers would have you believe. But was it really like that? If you read Acts 2:43–47, and just these verses, you could be lead to believe it. But the rest of Acts demonstrates that everything was not so idyllic among the first Christians.

The first deacons were chosen because the gentile widows were not being cared for by the Jewish members of the Church (Acts 6:1). There was conflict over how to treat the gentiles (Acts 15:1–21). Paul had to take Peter to task because he refused to eat with the gentile converts (Galatians 2:11–14). In his first letter to the Corinthians Paul severely criticizes the community for selfishness, with the rich eating with their friends and the poor in their midst going hungry.

The first Christians were not perfect, but there was a real rigor among them for truth. It may not have been true of every member, but as a community they were rigorously seeking the best way to live the Christian life. Are you and I rigorously seeking the best way to live the Christian life?

Today, amid the busyness and complexities of modern life, the great majority of Catholics are challenged merely to make it to Mass each Sunday. In modern society, a great separation has taken place between the various aspects of our lives. Many people feel that they need to leave the values and principles of their faith outside certain activities in the same way you leave a coat in a waiting room. The modern world tries to separate faith from reason, the professional from the personal, the means from the ends. This separationist approach destroys unity of life and creates the modern madness of feeling torn in two, which we experience because our very nature tells us that we cannot divorce faith from reason, or the personal from the professional, or the means from the end. Living the Gospel is difficult; it always has been and it always will be. This is what today's Catholics have in common with the first Christians, and with Christians of every place and time.

There has never been a time when the Church is the perfect society Jesus calls for us to be. There have been moments when certain individuals and communities have celebrated Christ's vision in awe-inspiring ways. But sustaining these moments is the real challenge. Think of how easy it is for you to turn your back on the-best-version-of-yourself. Consider how difficult it is for you to choose the-best-version-of-yourself in different situations each day. Now multiply that by 1.2 billion and you will have some sense of how difficult it is for the Church to be the-best-version-of-herself for even a single moment. Every time you engage in a self-destructive behavior, the Church becomes a- lesser- version- of- herself. And every time you bravely choose to become a- better-version-of-yourself, the Church becomes a-better-version-of-herself.

I don't know what the essential differences are between the first Christians and Catholics today. I do know that the ways of man will not get us from where we are today to where we are called to be. I also know that in every place and in every time since Pentecost the Holy Spirit has been present to guide you, me, and the whole Church. I am certain that the Church needs less and less of your ideas and mine, and more and more guidance from the Holy Spirit.

So pray with me for a moment.

Come Holy Spirit, fill the hearts of your faithful. Enkindle in us the fire of your love. Send forth your spirit and we shall be created, and you shall renew the face of the earth.

It is the Holy Spirit that will renew the face of the earth. Will it happen with a blinding flash of light? I suspect not. The renewal that the Church and the world so desperately need at this moment in history will happen in this way: You and I will abandon the illusion of control and surrender our hearts to the Spirit of God. We will allow the Holy Spirit to guide our words, thoughts, and actions one moment at a time. In this way, the Spirit will slowly bring renewal to our lives, our marriages, our families, our businesses and schools, our parishes, our nations, our Church, and to all humanity.

Whatever the successes of the early Church, they were the fruit of their faithfulness to Jesus Christ under the inspiration of the Holy Spirit. Whatever the failures of the early Church, they were the result of rejecting the Holy Spirit's guidance. The same is true of the Church today.

• Catholicism Is a Lifestyle •

It is equally important at this time in history that we ask, "What is Catholicism?" and "What does it mean to be Catholic?"

Catholicism is not merely a religion, or a sect, or a set of rules. When small minds and smaller spirits try to capture the essence of Catholicism, this is often what they tend to conclude. But Catholicism is more than a religion. It is more than just another movement. The essence of Catholicism is not sin, punishment, duty, or obligation, and it is more than a set of lifeless rules and regulations. Catholicism is *more*. It is more than most people think and more than most Catholics ever experience.

The essence of Catholicism is dynamic transformation. You cannot become more like Jesus Christ and at the same time stay as you are. To be Catholic means to be striving to live the Gospel, to be striving to become more like Jesus Christ. It is this dynamic approach to transformation that animates the human person—physically, emotionally, intellectually, and spiritually—and allows us to experience life "to the fullest." (John 10:10) When are you most fully alive? When you are changing and growing and exploring all you are capable of becoming.

God constantly calls us to new life. He continually invites us to higher and deeper places. Christ is constantly saying to us, as he did to Peter, "Put out into the deep water and lower your nets for a catch." (Luke 5:4) The world, on the other hand, is constantly calling us to the shallow water.

Catholicism is a dynamic way of life that encourages and empowers each individual to become the-best-version-of-himself or herself. Quite different from the pop psychology and secular philosophies of our time, this is not something we do to and for ourselves (self-help), but rather something that takes place in and through Jesus Christ. We may be able to help ourselves to a certain extent, but it is precisely because we cannot help ourselves to the extent that we need and desire that we need a savior.

The Catholic lifestyle, when it is authentically presented and embraced, promotes the integration of every aspect of our daily lives and every aspect of the human person. And as you journey toward your destiny, God intertwines your talents with the needs of others to allow you the privilege of touching them, serving them, and inspiring them as they make their own journey.

Catholicism is a way of life in which the giving and receiving happen in equal measure. It nurtures the individual, the local community, and the whole human family. Catholicism affects every area of our lives and is a guiding light in all of our decisions. It is both the philosophical and theological basis and the practical inspiration. Catholicism is a call to live an authentic life. When embraced as a lifestyle, it causes the elevation of every human activity. Catholicism provides the map and the tools for bringing each person into harmony with self, God, and others.

G. K. Chesterton wrote, "Christianity has not been tried and found wanting; it has been found difficult and not tried." This is particularly true of Catholicism. Of all the many people I know who have rejected Catholicism, or who are critical of it, I do not know a single person who has truly explored and embraced the Catholic lifestyle. If you *humbly* open your heart, mind, and soul to the genius of Catholicism, you will not find it wanting.

• Identity Crisis •

If you took a poll on the streets of any city in America this week and asked people to describe Catholics, what do you think they would say? To be honest, I am not sure. But I suspect the answers would be many and varied, and probably not overwhelmingly positive. At this moment in history as Catholics we have identity and image problems.

We have an identity problem because enough of us have not clearly defined and embraced an authentic Catholic lifestyle. If we had, when people heard that you were marrying a Catholic, they would just assume that he is an honest, prayerful, generous man. If we had, when you were looking for a job people would just assume that you are a hardworking, ethical, self-motivated contributor who pays attention to the details of your work just because you are Catholic. If we had, people would be actively seeking us out in all of life's situations, to be their spouses, neighbors, employees, employers, priests, teachers, and friends!

Instead, in the midst of a tumultuous and rapidly changing cultural environment, we have struggled as Catholics today to establish a vibrant identity. Plagued and persecuted by false stereotypes, burdened by scandals and the abuse of power, and lacking clear direction and bold initiative, we have failed to establish an authentic Catholic identity in the modern world. As Catholics at the dawn of the twenty-first century, we are in the midst of a serious identity crisis.

From where will we draw the guidance and inspiration to reestablish a vibrant Catholic identity in the world? At supper with his disciples for the last time, Jesus himself offered an answer to this question. His words are as fresh and relevant today as they were twenty centuries ago: "I give you a new commandment: Love one another. As I have loved you, so you should also love one another. This is how all will know that you are my disciples, if you have love for one another." (John 13:34–35)

The love that the life and teachings of Jesus Christ invite us to experience is real and relevant in every place and time, and the world is waiting for us to embody it. It is not a love of words and theories, but a love of action. It can be expressed in something as simple as helping someone in need, communicating our gratitude, feeding the hungry, or comforting the lonely. A few days ago I heard of a couple who had rented their home to a family because they were moving to another state for two years for a job opportunity. After some time the family renting their home started to struggle with their rent payments. When the couple inquired about the late or missing payments, they discovered that the father was out of work and one of the children was seriously ill. When the couple's two-year assignment was complete they moved back to town, but rather than displace this family at a time of crisis in their life the couple rented another home not even two blocks from the home they owned. They did this even though the family renting their home had not paid rent in almost a year. They did this even though they had to make personal sacrifices and considerable adjustments to their spending habits. This is the love of God, alive and active. This is a new and vibrant Catholic identity in the making.

How I wish that when people discovered you or I are Catholic, they could immediately conclude that we are honest, hardworking, generous, loving, joyful, compassionate, temperate, humble, disciplined, prayerful, and generally in love with life. You wouldn't need too many people like this to develop a positive reputation for Catholicism in a local community. I pray that God raises them up. I pray that God will transform you and me into Catholics of that caliber.

All it will take to radically alter the way Catholics are perceived in society today is for you and me to become . . . honest, hardworking, generous, loving, joyful, compassionate, temperate, humble, disciplined, prayerful, and generally in love with life.

Chapter Five

WHAT ARE WE CELEBRATING?

Traveling the world I have learned that every faith community has problems and issues. Every Catholic diocese and parish in the world has difficulties. In some places, I have seen these problems drain communities of energy and enthusiasm, causing division and resentment. In other places, the same problems have given birth to renewed energy and enthusiasm, and indeed have become the source of increased unity.

What causes such varied outcomes in such similar situations? I have observed two differences. The first is on a very human level: Some people are willing to admit their mistakes and others are not. As a Church, and as local faith communities, we should always be willing to face our shortcomings with humility, courage, and hope. When we admit we have big problems, people start looking for big solutions. The second difference is on a supernatural level: We should consider why problems occur in our lives and in the life of the Church. Do problems occur so that we can solve them? I don't think so. We are not here to solve the problems; the problems are here to solve us. This is one of the supernatural mysteries of our journeys here on earth.

When we approach any problem in the right way we become better-versions-of-ourselves. This is true for individuals, but it is also true for marriages, families, businesses, nations, and the Church.

Let's face it, you and I both know if we solved all the Church's problems today, there would be a whole new set of problems tomorrow. Does that mean we should not set about solving the problems? No, we absolutely should, but as with any activity in life we need to connect it to our essential purpose.

We do not do things and solve problems merely to get them out of the way so that we can get on with life. Doing things and solving problems are very much a part of life, and every moment of life is an opportunity to become a-better-version-of-yourself. But we need to be conscious of this truth in order to reap the harvest of each moment.

As Christians, as Catholics, as a Church, and as citizens, we should always take time to check and adjust the compass that guides us. To do this, we must ask ourselves soul-searching questions and courageously seek answers.

"What are we celebrating?" is one of those questions, because you can be certain that we are becoming whatever it is we are celebrating. We must ask this question of ourselves, of our Church, of our nation, and of our culture. And we would be wise to listen attentively to the answers, because these answers will utter prophetic truths about our future. We become what we celebrate.

If you walk into most teenagers' rooms and look around, what occupies the places of prominence? Posters of rock idols and movie stars who, for the most part, live lives unworthy of emulation; magazines filled with articles that subtly, and not so subtly, undermine the dignity of the human person and the values of our faith; iPods and CDs filled with music that redefines love as something selfish and sensual; and video games that too often celebrate violence, depersonalize the human person, and stifle the individuality and creativity that define a person's unique path toward God. We become what we celebrate, and this teenager will become a cloned conglomerate of the people and things he or she is celebrating.

When our children know more about teen pop idols than they do about Jesus Christ, isn't it time for us to reassess the place and priority our faith has in our lives? It is also time for us to develop innovative strategies and dynamic methods for communicating the faith to people of all ages, but particularly the young. Too often we adopt nineteenth-century solutions for twenty-first-century problems. Now is the time to explore new ways to communicate the Gospel, ways that demonstrate the genius and relevance of Catholicism to the modern lifestyle. Now is the time to celebrate our faith by living it in such a way that we capture the imagination and intrigue the hearts and minds of the people of our time.

We become what we celebrate. What are you celebrating?

• The Future of Catholicism •

As we look to the future, there are a great many challenges that face the Church. In my meetings with Catholic leaders in the United States, Europe, and Australia, the same issues seem to emerge consistently: Our parishes are emptying; we lack real contact with the youth; divorce is destroying families, dividing communities, and alienating whole families from Catholicism for generations to come; vocations to the priesthood and religious life are scarce; and the Church is facing a growing marginalization in the wake of an ever-intensifying secularity.

When these issues wander into the light, I have noticed that people tend to become very defensive. Perhaps we don't like to think of the Church as having problems, but we must, because problems bring with them the hope of solutions. If we continue to turn our backs on the real issues, they will continue to spread and grow like cancer in the body. And if no one is willing to admit that there are some big problems, no one will begin looking for big solutions to those problems.

There are a great many people who think the problem with the world today is that people don't come to church. They think the challenge is to bring people to church, but the real challenge is to bring the Church to the people. Fundamentally, that is what we are failing to do. We are failing to do as Christ did—namely, to reach out and meet people where they are in their need, in their brokenness. We are failing to carry out the mission Christ entrusted to us through our apostolic lineage (cf. Matthew 28:16–20). We are failing to carry out the mission of the Church, which is to proclaim the good news of the Gospel to the people of every age. It is reasonable that people would expect the Church to be able to articulate the relevance of the Gospel to their lives and relationships here and now. Together, we have a responsibility to demonstrate that walking with God and following the life and teachings of Jesus Christ is the best way to live.

If people do not come to church it is not their failure alone; it is ours as well. We should ask ourselves, "Why are they not coming to church?" People don't come to church because they don't see the value in it. If we convinced them of the value, if they really understood the richness and beauty of Catholicism, they would make church an indispensable part of their lives.

We are failing to feed them and engage them. I don't mean entertain them; I mean genuinely engage them. We are failing to meet them where they are and actively demonstrate that God invites them to live differently, and that if they live in the way God calls them to, every aspect of their lives will be better. They are hungry for us to reach out to them where they are in their own unique journey, to speak to them about their hopes and fears, their marriages, their careers, their cravings and addictions, the emptiness they sometimes feel when they are quiet and alone, their personal finances, their children, and every aspect of their lives. Engaging people means showing them how the Gospel can transform their lives. It means showing people that embracing the life God calls us to will liberate them from feeling torn in a dozen different directions. Engaging people means showing them how God intends to make their lives better. People know they are in pain, they know their brokenness, they know their emptiness, they know they have a spiritual hunger, but they think that going to church is irrelevant to modern living. Why do they think that? Because you and I have failed to show them the relevance of the life and teachings of Jesus Christ in the twenty-first century. As a Church, we have failed to show them how Jesus, the sacraments, the Gospel, the Eucharist, and Catholic spirituality in general can ease their pain, make them whole again, and bring meaning and purpose to their lives.

Certainly, we can become proud and obstinate and put our heads in the sand and say, "That's their problem." Or we can seek shallow consolation in the knowledge that "the gates of hell will not prevail." (Matthew 16:18) It saddens me when people take this attitude, because I don't think God wants you, me, or the Church just to survive. I think God wants us to thrive. Are you thriving? Or are you just surviving? Is the Church thriving? Or is it just surviving? An honest look at ourselves and our Church is in order.

And if we have the courage to take an honest look at the Church, the role we play in it, and the challenges facing it today, I suspect we will discover that Christ is renewing his Church at this very moment, even if we do not have eyes to see that. In every place and in every time, Jesus invites us to live the faith in more personal and intimate ways through vibrant and active community.

Your future, my future, and the future of the Church are all intimately related to one another. It is people like you and me who make up the Church. If the Church is not thriving, it is because you and I are not thriving.

The mission of the Church in this age is to share the life-giving gift of the Gospel with the people of our time. This is your mission. This is my mission. This is our mission together, and now is our time. We are the Church. The best way for us to fulfill this mission is to allow the values, principles, and spirit of the Gospel to transform our own lives. The only way to authentically achieve this is to become docile to the promptings of the Holy Spirit and thus allow God to transform our hearts. The most effective messenger is the one who lives the message. Francis of Assisi said, "Preach the Gospel at all times, and only when necessary use words." Our culture is hungry for authentic lives. Let your life speak.

• The Solution •

In every age, the Church experiences problems and difficulties. Our time is no different. The solution to the problems that plague our lives and the Church is unchanging and singular. The problems are many; the solution is solitary. Personal holiness is the answer to every problem. In every situation in my life, in every problem, in every difficulty, I know that if I allow the values and principles of the Gospel to guide me, it will turn out for the best. It will not always turn out as I wish, but I will be a better person for having lived the Gospel in that situation, and because of that, my future will be richer. I suppose that leads us to one of the fundamental questions that confront us all sooner or later: Do we actually believe that living the Gospel is life giving, that it will lead us to a better life, that it is the best way to live? If we don't, it is unlikely that we will celebrate the teachings of Christ in each moment of our lives.

Holiness is simply the application of the values, principles, and spirit of the Gospel to the circumstances of our everyday lives, one moment at a time. It is not complicated; it is disarmingly simple. But simple is not the same as easy.

In every age, there are a small number of men and women who are prepared to turn their backs on popular culture and personal gain to embrace heroically the life Jesus outlines in the Gospels. These people fashion Catholicism into a lifestyle, they listen attentively to the voice of God in their lives, and they passionately pursue their personal adventure of salvation. As a result, they capture the attention and the imaginations of everyone who crosses their path. Paradoxically, the modern world tends to pity these people, because it believes they are missing out on something. Never feel sorry for them. These men and women are the happiest people who ever lived. They are the heroes of Christianity; they are the saints. In Part Two of this book we will discuss how they managed to live such awe-inspiring lives, and we will discover how we can emulate their wisdom in our own lives. Whether the Church will thrive in this modern era depends on men and women like these.

I opened this book with a single thought. Perhaps you missed it. Maybe you read it but it didn't catch your attention. Consider again. The Church (like so many other things in life) is not so much something we inherit from generations past or take over from our predecessors as it is something on loan to us from future generations.

When making a decision, the Native American people used to ask themselves how their decision today would affect their people seven generations from now. One hundred years from now, none of us will be here. Let us always remember that in the whole scheme of things, the Church is on loan to us for a very brief time. And yet in that brief time we determine the Church our children and grandchildren will inherit. In this way, God has appointed us to take care of the vineyard—the Church. This is a responsibility we should take seriously. In Matthew's Gospel (Mt. 21:33–41) we are given a vision of what happens when servants are overcome with pride and arrogance.

The future of the Church is in our hands and you can be certain it will be what we make it.

• Let the Celebration Begin •

As Catholics, the one thing we do more than anything else is celebrate. Everything the Church does is centered around a celebration.

We celebrate life. We celebrate the changing seasons with the richness of the Church's calendar. We celebrate excellence by honoring as saints the heroes of our faith. We celebrate birth and eternal life with baptism and burial. We celebrate truth, beauty, and goodness by seeking them out wherever they are to be found and honoring them in our everyday lives. We celebrate Christmas and Easter. We celebrate pilgrimage—our common journey and our own individual journeys. We celebrate salvation. We celebrate forgiveness with Reconciliation. We celebrate total dedication to the service of God's people with Holy Orders. We celebrate education. We celebrate communion with God and community with the Mass. We celebrate unity by seeking to bridge the gap. We celebrate love with marriage. We celebrate . . .

The spirit of Catholicism is predominantly one of celebration, which is the genius and the fundamental orientation of our faith.

At this moment in history both life and faith are being attacked with the full force of a culture racing toward self-destruction. These are direct attacks on the essence of the human person.

I believe the best way to defend life is to celebrate life. I believe the best way to celebrate life is to live our own lives to the fullest—to embrace life with arms wide open, to lay our lives enthusiastically at the service of humanity, to love deeply the people who cross our paths, and above all, to embrace our God. Life should never be wasted—not one moment—because life is precious.

I believe the best way to defend the faith is to celebrate our faith. The best way to celebrate Catholicism is to live the faith more fully with each passing day, allowing it to reach into every corner of our lives. When Catholicism is the foundation of our family life, our social life, our intellectual life, our spiritual life, our community life, and our professional life, then we will have established an integrated life, a life of integrity. That unity of life will speak more powerfully than any words ever could. And if just a handful of people in one place and at one time will give their whole selves to seeking, discovering, embracing, and living this life, they will change the whole course of human history.

What are we celebrating as a culture? What are you celebrating? You have become the person you are because of the things you celebrate. Our culture has become what it is because of the things we celebrate.

You can celebrate anything you wish. You can celebrate life and faith. You can celebrate love and honesty, mercy and forgiveness, kindness and generosity. You can celebrate truth, beauty, goodness, and redemption. On the other hand, you can celebrate destruction and paganism. You can celebrate hatred and violence, selfishness and greed, contempt and disrespect. You can celebrate perversion, corruption, pride, deceit, and condemnation. But one thing is certain: We become what we celebrate. This is the one immutable truth found in the life of every person who has ever lived. We become what we celebrate. It is true not only of the life of a person but also of the life of a family. It is true of the life of a nation, and it is true of the life of the Church.

Let the celebration begin.

Part Two

THE AUTHENTIC LIFE

• • •

Several years ago, my brother Nathan was living in Japan for a year as an exchange student. During that time, I received a letter from him with a photograph he had taken of what seemed to be the courtyard of an ancient Japanese garden. In the middle of the courtyard was an almond tree in full bloom. Nathan has always been a talented photographer, but what really captured my attention was a quotation he had written on the back of the photograph. The quotation was from the writings of Greco, the famed Greek-born Spanish painter. It read:

> "I said to the almond tree,
> 'Sister, speak to me about God,'
> and the almond tree blossomed."

Only one thing is necessary for Catholicism to flourish—authentic lives. Throughout history, wherever you find men and women genuinely striving to live the Christian life, the Church has always blossomed. If we wish to speak effectively to the modern world about God, the Christian life, and Catholicism, we must be thriving, blossoming, and flourishing in that life.

The best way to speak about God is to thrive in the life he calls us to live.

• • •

Chapter Six

WHAT IS THE AUTHENTIC LIFE?

The authentic life begins with the simple desire to be who God created us to be and cooperate with God by playing the part he has designed for us in human history. The adventure of salvation begins when we stop asking, "What's in it for me?" and turn humbly to God in our hearts and ask, *How may I serve? What work do you wish for me to do with my life? What is your will for my life?*

Every generation turns its back on God in its own way. Our modern era has revolted violently against the idea of "God's will." Desperate to maintain the illusion of being in control of their lives, many modern Christians have either turned their backs on God or created a new spiritual rhetoric that allows them to determine selectively God's will for their lives. And yet, it is the very surrendering of our own will to God's designs that characterizes the whole Christian struggle. The spiritual life is primarily concerned with this single dynamic of turning our individual will over to God.

God calls each of us to live an authentic life. He has designed this life to perfectly integrate our legitimate needs, our deepest desires, and our unique talents. The more intimately and harmoniously these three are related, the more you become truly yourself.

God doesn't call you to live an authentic life in order to stifle or control you. He invites you to live an authentic life so that, from an infinite number of possibilities, you can become the-best-version-of-yourself. In a very beautiful way God wants you to be yourself. But not the self your ego wants you to be, and not the self the world wants you to be. Rather, the self God had in mind when he created you. By calling you to live an authentic life, God is saying, "Be all I create you to be."

• Fostering the Inner Life •

While we are each called to live an authentic life, the exterior qualities of this life can take many different forms and tend to differ substantially from one person to the next. Some people are called to live an authentic life as husband and wife, truly committed to love in marriage. Others are called as priests and religious, dedicated in a unique way to exploring the deep well of Christian spirituality and sharing the fruits of their efforts with the community. Still others are called to live as single persons, and use the versatility of their singleness to live and proclaim the Good News in ways that would be impossible for the married and ordained.

Professionally, some of us may work as doctors and lawyers, teachers and nurses, mechanics, bakers, and carpenters. Others may keep the home and dedicate the professional aspect of their lives to motherhood. Some may dedicate their professional energies to full-time ministry, which could include anything from counseling to volunteering at a local soup kitchen. These are all just different manifestations of the authentic life. Every honest human activity is compatible with the authentic life.

The external activity is less important than the internal transformation any activity is designed to achieve in our lives. Who we become is infinitely more important than what we do, and what we do only has value inasmuch as it helps us to become the-best-version-of-ourselves.

The authentic life is compatible with any honest human activity. All honest work can be transformed into prayer. You can transform your work into prayer one hour at a time, one task at a time.

A man's work may be to collect the trash, but if he does it well, and hour by hour turns to God in his heart and says, *Father, I offer you this hour of work as a prayer for my neighbor Karen, who is struggling with cancer . . . or in thanksgiving for my wife and children,* then he has truly discovered and is living the words "pray constantly." (1 Thessalonians 5:17) He has transformed an hour of work into an hour of prayer. Through his work he has grown in intimacy with God and neighbor, and he has become a-better-version-of-himself. The attitude with which we approach our work is crucial.

The transformation of ordinary activities into prayer is the very essence of the inner life. Every activity of our day can lead us to experience God. Learn to foster the interior life in this way and you will live a life uncommon in the midst of common circumstances.

Offer the actions of your life to God as a prayer, whether you are washing the dishes, repairing a car, or studying for an exam, and by your inner intention, you will transform ordinary daily activities into the noblest tasks. By doing so, you will elevate tedious tasks to spiritual exercises that draw you nearer to God. This is how modern men and women in the midst of busy lives can seek and find intimacy with God.

The role of work in the journey of the soul is firstly to provide an opportunity to grow in virtue, and secondly to provide for our temporal needs. When our primary focus is on providing for our temporal needs and those of our family, we lose sight of the true value and purpose of work. Consequently, work becomes less joyful and more of a drudgery.

Whether your work in this life is as a street cleaner or as a senator, remember that the interior effect that the work we do has on our soul is infinitely more important than the exterior fruits of our work.

• Modern Despair •

Toward the beginning of his reflections at Walden Pond, Henry David Thoreau observed, "Most men lead lives of quiet desperation." These words were penned and published more than 150 years ago, and yet they are words for our modern times. Ask yourself, "Is the quiet desperation Thoreau speaks of still alive in our society today?" Is it present in your own life?

Did you know that the number of people using prescribed medications for the treatment of depression is ten times greater today than it was ten years ago? Did you know that the suicide rate among teenagers and young adults has reached epidemic levels? Isn't it time we asked our culture and ourselves what is causing this great modern despair?

As I travel the world it is impossible not to notice how people's lives are becoming faster and busier every day. Caught up in the day-to-day drudgery of life, smothered by the hustle and bustle, many people are tormented by the feeling that their lives are moving so fast that each day they just get more behind. In this modern schema, most people are not thriving; they are merely surviving. And isn't that a life of quiet desperation?

• Our Essential Purpose •

When we separate the daily activities of our lives from our essential purpose, the very meaning of our lives, it is only a matter of time before despair and desperation take hold of us. And yet, the greatest casualty in this modern culture has been exactly that—our essential purpose.

What are we here for? What is the meaning and purpose of life? What is your essential purpose?

If you can distract a person from her essential purpose for long enough, she will become miserable. If you can prevent a whole generation from ever discovering their essential purpose, you will create an epidemic of misery and despair.

The greatest tragedy of modern Catholicism is the way we have become so distracted from the goal of the Christian life. My experience has been that the great majority of Catholics do not know the goal of the Christian life. Others have cast the ideal aside, saying it is not conducive to modern living. Tragically, a great many have never heard it clearly articulated.

Holiness is the goal of the Christian life.

Although I am too young to know from firsthand experience, it seems to me that after the Second Vatican Council, and perhaps before, a great many educators and priests stopped teaching, preaching, and speaking about this goal. It seems they felt it was an unattainable ideal or simply unrealistic in the changing context of the modern world. They thought it made people feel guilty. They apparently wanted to make it easier for people. So they threw away or watered down the great goal of the Christian life.

The result, of course, was exactly the opposite of what they had intended. They didn't make it easier for people; they made it harder for them. Have you ever tried to find your way to a place you have never been before with no directions, no map, and no clear description of the destination?

If you take away the goal of the Christian life, you don't make it easier for people—you make it harder. You don't bring them happiness; you start them along the road toward hopelessness and misery. People excel, thrive, and are ultimately happier when they have a higher standard to look to and strive for. I have never encountered a situation in which having a goal didn't flood my spirit with hope, fill my mind with determination, and generally bring out the best in me. It is true that our goals need to be achievable. But we make the great goals of our lives achievable by breaking them down into manageable portions, while at the same time keeping the ultimate end in mind.

Our times are plagued by a great deal of confusion regarding religious thought. This confusion exists both inside and outside the Church. The prophet Amos spoke of a famine of truth (cf. Amos 8:11). I believe his prophecy has its time in our own day and age. The loss of our essential purpose is the cause of the great modern madness.

The authentic life orients us toward the goal of the Christian life. We are called to live holy lives, every man and every woman without exception, regardless of our age, color, socioeconomic background, or state in life. Living holy lives is the goal of the Christian life and our essential purpose.

We are called to live holy lives and this is something we should strive for as Christians, but let me be very clear that this holiness is not something that we can attain for ourselves. In truth, holiness is something God does in us and not something we achieve. And yet at the same time, God is the perfect gentleman: He invites us to participate in his life, but never forces himself upon us. He wants our consent, he wants to be invited into our hearts and lives, but much more than consent and invitation he desires our loving cooperation. God yearns for us to be coworkers with him in this work of holiness. It is this dynamic collaboration between God and man that brings delight to God.

Modern man has simply become disoriented. We have lost our way. Perhaps that is why this idea featured so prominently in the writings of the

Second Vatican Council. By putting aside the goal of the Christian life, this call to live holy lives, we have lost our way in the modern world.

The North Star is the only star in the sky that never moves; it remains constant and unwavering, and therefore is a true guide. In the same way, God's call to live a holy life never changes. In a world of rapid and constant change, it is what is unchanging that allows us to make sense of change. The ideas you encounter may change, your emotions may change, but God's call to live a holy life never changes. The North Star of the spiritual life is the call to holiness. It leads us unfailingly to Jesus, who is "the Way, the Truth, and the Life," even when he seems distant or unknown. If we are to find our way as individuals and as a Church, it is vital that we rediscover this great spiritual North Star, so that in times of confusion or decision we can ask ourselves, "How is this situation an invitation to grow in holiness?"

Holiness and renewal are inseparably linked. Where there is holiness the Church has always thrived. If the Church is not thriving there is one primary reason for that... and when you and I begin to take God's call to live holy lives seriously, the Church will begin to thrive in new and exciting ways.

• What Is Holiness? •

The great confusion that is torturing the Church and weakening our faith surrounds one question: What is holiness? The falling attendance at church, the marginalization of the Church by our secular culture, and our failure to reach the youth are all caused by our inability to communicate clearly the answer to this question.

There are a lot of good people out there who want to walk with God. They want to know and embrace truth and live good Christian lives; they just don't know how to practically apply the principles of the Gospel to their everyday lives. The good people of every age cry out to their spiritual leaders, teachers, prophets, and priests, asking, "What does it mean to live a holy life and how do I live it in my everyday life?" They may not articulate the question with such clarity, but in essence all their questioning resolves itself if this question can be answered. If we can communicate powerfully and effectively what it means to live a holy life and how it is practically attained, people will walk that path.

What does living a holy life mean to you? We all have different ideas of who God is, and we all have different ideas of what it means to be holy. In your mind, does someone have to be a priest or a nun to be holy? Do people need to be poor to be holy? Can wealthy people be holy? Can married people be holy? Do you view sexual intimacy as a barrier to holiness or a path to holiness? Is it possible to have a good sex life and be holy? Can a businessman or -woman be truly holy? Can *you* be holy?

We all have a vision of what it means to be holy, and often our vision is distorted by prejudice or tainted by ignorance and past experience. God calls each and every one of us to live holy lives, without exception and in our own way. God calls you to holiness, as hard as that may be to get your heart and mind around.

Holiness is compatible with every state in life. Married people are called to live holy lives just as much as monks and nuns. Sexual intimacy is a profound gift from God and an instrument of holiness. The riches of this world have value only inasmuch as they help us fulfill our essential purpose. If we own them, they can be powerful tools that help us live holy lives. If they own us, they will prevent us from becoming the-best-version-of-ourselves. The rich are called to live holy lives by using their wealth in productive ways that foster their own growth and the growth of others.

Material possessions, marriage and sexual intimacy, work, money, and positions of authority are just some of the opportunities life presents to live holy lives.

History is full of examples of men and women who have become all they were created to be—we call them saints. Some of them were priests, monks, or nuns. Some were married and others were single. Some were rich; others were poor. Some were educated; others were uneducated. Some were young and some were old. Holiness is for everyone—no exceptions. Holiness is for you. Every day God invites you to be all he created you to be.

Many people falsely believe that if you want to be holy, you are not allowed to enjoy life. Some believe to be holy you have to run away from the world. Others think you have to be in church on your knees praying all day. Still others believe to be holy you have to walk around with a halo, that you're not allowed to smile, or have any fun, or enjoy yourself at all. They think to be holy you have to despise everything of this world and walk around with a long, drawn-out, stoic look on your face.

These are all the very unnatural and unattractive ideas that the world proclaims about holiness. The world ridicules holiness. The world pities the saints, saying, "Oh, he could have been so much more!" or "She had so much potential!" Let me assure you, it is not the saints who need our pity.

Holiness brings us to life. It refines every human ability. Holiness doesn't dampen our emotions; it elevates them. Those who respond to God's call to holiness are the most joyful people in history. They have a richer, more abundant experience of life, and they love more deeply than most people can ever imagine. They enjoy life, all of life. Even in the midst of suffering they are able to maintain a peace and a joy that are independent of the happenings and circumstances surrounding them. Holiness doesn't stifle us; it sets us free.

The surest signs of holiness are not how often a person goes to church, how many hours he spends in prayer, what good spiritual books he has read, or even the number of good works he performs. The surest signs of holiness are an insatiable desire to become all God created us to be, an unwavering commitment to the will of God, and an unquenchable concern for unholy people.

Living a holy life means letting our decisions be guided by the Holy Spirit. It means allowing each moment to be all it can be. Holiness is living with the goal of the Christian life in mind. It is allowing our decisions to be guided by the Holy Spirit. Holiness is surrendering to the will of God, and at the same time, it is grasping each moment and making it all it can be. Sometimes holiness means indulging yourself and sometimes it means renouncing yourself. Each event in your life is an opportunity to change, to grow, and to become a-better-version-of-yourself – and that grasping of each moment is holiness. Holiness is allowing God to fill every corner of your being; that is when we truly become the-best-version-of-ourselves. Holiness is being set apart for God. It is a desire to do the will of God, and yet, the desire for holiness is itself a gift from God. Holiness is as simple as knowing when to say yes and when to say no, but like so many things in this life, we complicate the pursuit of holiness unnecessarily.

In any moment when you surrender to the will of God and choose to be the-best-version-of-yourself, you are holy. Any moment that you grasp as an opportunity to exercise virtue is a holy moment. But as quickly as this holiness can be found, it can be lost, because in any moment that you choose to be less than the-best-version-of-yourself, you have become distracted from living a holy life.

This is what it means to be striving for holiness, to be continually answering God's invitation to grasp the moments of our lives and allow God to use them to transform us into all he has created us to be. In each and every moment of our lives God's transforming love is inviting us to choose to live holy lives.

When you see this holiness alive in a person, even for a moment, it is inspiring. The truth is, virtue is ultimately attractive. When Jesus walked the earth, people wanted to be with him. Whether he was speaking in the synagogue, walking down the street, or eating at someone's home, people wanted to be with him. They crowded around him, hung on his every word, grasped just to touch his cloak.

There is nothing more attractive than holiness. This attractiveness has not only been demonstrated in Jesus, but is constantly demonstrated here and now in our own place and time: whenever someone goes out of his or her way to ease the burden of a stranger; whenever someone is honest; whenever someone lays down his or her life by working hard to support his or her family; whenever someone rejects the premise of modern culture.

Not only is holiness attractive; it is inspiring and intriguing to the people of any era. It is also immensely practical. When you hear that the doctors and nurses at a local hospital are coaching the inner-city baseball teams, doesn't it fill you with hope?

What is holiness? Holiness is all the incredible things God will do in you and through you if you make yourself available to him.

• The-Best-Version-of-Yourself •

To live an authentic life is to become fully yourself. To be holy is to become fully the person God created you to be. The authentic life, responding to God's call to live a holy life, and our essential purpose are one and the same.

More than eighteen hundred years ago, Saint Irenaeus (c. 130–c. 200) wrote, "The glory of God is the perfection of the creature." We do not give glory to God by presenting ourselves at Mass on Sunday, sitting in the back, paying no attention, and believing that we will have our names ticked off in some divine attendance book that exists only in our minds. We do not give glory to God by falling before his altar helplessly and hopelessly to beg him to make right what we have set wrong, or what God has given us the ability and responsibility to make right ourselves. Nor do we give God glory by masking our rejection of his gentle but ever-present call with the occasional good deed, mindless prayer, or charitable contribution.

"The glory of God is the perfection of the creature." The human person is perfected by the grace of God through the conscious, disciplined, and persistent attainment of virtue. But the grace of God is never lacking, so it is our conscious, disciplined, and persistent effort that is the key to a richer and more abundant future for humanity. This disciplined striving for virtue is an indispensable characteristic of the authentic life.

It is important to understand that the perfection that God calls us to is not some type of robotic perfection. If you asked a kindergarten class to draw and color a perfect tree, they would use hard, straight lines and bright colors. No such tree exists. But there are lots of perfect trees. Their crookedness is part of their perfection. Your big ears and your bent nose are a part of your perfection, but the defects in your character are not part of your best self.

In the gospel of Matthew we read, "Be perfect as your heavenly father is perfect." What did Jesus mean when he spoke of perfection? The word *perfect* used here, in Matthew 5:48, means "whole and complete."

In his letter to the Thessalonians, Saint Paul writes, "This is the will of God: that you be saints." (1 Thessalonians 4:3) God wants you to be holy. Your holiness is the desire of God, the delight of God, and the source of your happiness. To embrace who you were created to be and to become the-best-version-of-yourself is God's dream for you. Therefore, holiness is for everyone, not just for a select few, for monks in monasteries and nuns in convents; it is for you and me.

Your daily tasks have spiritual value. You don't work just for money. When you work hard and pay attention to the details of your job, you cooperate with God as he transforms your soul. In this way your work helps you to become more fully yourself. It is also a way to love your neighbor and make a contribution to society. In the same way, washing the dishes can be as much a prayer as praying the rosary. Each task, each hour offered to God is transformed into prayer. And in all these ways you give glory to God through your daily work.

• Vatican II •

Ever since Vatican II, it seems we have been searching for new and modern ways to reach people with the Gospel, so that they might live richer, fuller lives. On some levels we have succeeded, but on a great many others we have done little more than provide another form of entertainment.

At this time, I think it is safe to say that Vatican II was grossly misunderstood by Catholics at large and misrepresented by a great many theologians. As I read and reread the actual documents of Vatican II, I find the overwhelming theme is not something new, but a reminder that we are all called to holiness. These documents are a life-based teaching that respects the classical sources and the richness of our Catholic tradition, while at the same time giving contemporary expression to these treasures. These teachings provide a worldview that is nothing short of awe inspiring to anyone interested in seeking answers to some of the questions that face the Church and humanity at this time in history.

If you have never read the documents of Vatican II, I would strongly encourage you to do so. Begin with *Gaudium et Spes (The Church in the Modern World)*. It is the last of the sixteen documents and by far my favorite. Read it slowly, reflectively, prayerfully. Take it with you to your time of prayer each day for a couple of weeks. Read one paragraph at a time, and from each paragraph, pick out a phrase, an idea, or a single word that jumps out at you. Use that as the beginning of a conversation with Christ. Speak to him in a gentle mental dialogue about what you have read and how it touches you, inspires you, upsets you, or offends you. Be honest with God. If you disagree, disagree. Speak to him about why you disagree. But try always to remain open to the spirit of truth. If you don't understand something, don't let it trouble you; just move on to the next paragraph, asking God to lead you to understand it in the future.

Reading the documents of Vatican II, it is impossible to ignore the prophetic nature of the Church. Take *Gaudium et Spes,* for example. In this one document about the Church in the modern world, we cover: fostering the nobility of marriage and family; human progress; the proper development of culture; the roles and challenges of the economic, social, and political dimensions of our lives; peace and war; and the fragile but indispensable bonds that exist between nations.

If we take time to read the writings of Vatican II, we will discover that the thrust of the Council's teachings was to remind us all, regardless of our age or vocation, that we are called to seek and live an authentic life—we are called to holiness. The Council sought to remind men and women in the modern world that regardless of the changes that take place in a culture we are all called to holiness. The cardinals and bishops who participated in the Council knew all too well that the only way Catholicism would thrive in the modern world was if we kept sight of our essential purpose.

I pray every day that I live to see Vatican II truly implemented in the Catholic Church.

• The Great Depression •

The great depression of our age is not economic; it is spiritual. There seems to be a pervading sense of purposelessness in many people's lives today. "Why are we here?" is a question many people have stopped asking and started avoiding. They have stopped asking this question not because they don't want to know the answer, but because they have seen nothing to make them believe that anyone has the answer. It seems those who have the answer have hidden it under a bushel (cf. Matthew 5:14). Remember, the human heart is on a quest for happiness; to believe that we can find happiness without discovering our essential purpose is foolish.

When the practice and preaching of Christianity are not clearly focused on the universal call to holiness, the activities pursued in the name of Christianity disintegrate into little more than a collection of social welfare initiatives. As the Church becomes more and more separated from this call to holiness, whether locally, regionally, nationally, or universally, it very quickly begins to resemble a social welfare organization rather than the great spiritual entity it was established to be for every age.

There is a great need to re-identify the essential purpose of the human being. Whenever brave men and women step forth and celebrate their essential purpose by striving to live holy lives, they do a great service not only to Catholics but also to people of every belief, because the search for meaning in our lives is universal. The Church, and indeed the whole world, desperately awaits a few brave souls who will stand up and remind us of our great spiritual heritage by redirecting us toward the goal of the Christian life: living holy lives.

We know all too well from our experience in other areas of life, whether it is business, science, or sports, that without clearly defined goals, little is achieved and most people grossly underachieve. This was Michelangelo's observation: "The greater danger for most of us is not that our aim is too high and we miss it, but that it is too low and we reach it."

I believe there is a direct relationship between happiness and holiness. This was my first serious observation of the Christian life as a teenager.

I must also confess it was the reason I first began to explore Catholicism seriously. As simple as it may sound, I was aware of my yearning for happiness. I had tried to satisfy this yearning in other ways and had been left wanting. I had witnessed a peace and purpose in the lives of a handful of people I knew who were striving to live their faith, and I knew they had something I was yearning for.

My experience of people and life continually teaches me that those who have no central purpose in their lives fall easy prey to petty worries, fears, troubles, and self-pity. I have also learned that those living authentic lives are not looking over some hill or around the next corner to some elusive future happiness. They simply try to be all they can be, here and now, and that brings with it a happiness all its own.

God calls each of us to holiness. He invites us to be truly ourselves. This call to holiness is in response to our deep desire for happiness. We cry out to God, saying, *Show us how to find the happiness our hearts are hungry for,* and God replies, *Walk with me, be all I created you to be, become the-best-version-of-yourself.* It is a natural and logical conclusion that we will never find happiness if we are not ourselves. Imagine if a bird tried to be a fish, or if a tree tried to be a cloud. No matter how hard a bird tried to be a fish, it would never succeed. The challenge life presents to each of us is to become truly ourselves—not the self we have imagined or fantasized about, not the self that our friends want us to be, not the self our ego would have us be, but the self God has ordained us to be from before we were in our mother's womb.

The authentic life manifests itself differently in every person through our needs, talents, and desires. Get in touch with your essential purpose—to live a holy life—and once you have found it, keep it always in your sight. This is the great spiritual secret of life.

Chapter Seven

THE PATH IS
WELL TRODDEN

I spent my childhood pursuing excellence on the sporting field. My seven brothers and I were constantly engaged in a variety of sporting endeavors and fiercely competitive. Each day when school was finished, we went to training: tennis, cricket, soccer, swimming, basketball, volleyball, golf, cycling, track, football. . . . On the afternoons when we didn't have training, we would test each other's skills in the backyard of our family home in suburban Sydney, Australia.

My father always encouraged my brothers and me to study the champions of each sport we played. Every good coach I have ever trained under, regardless of the sport, has encouraged me to do the same. My father and my coaches wanted me to study these great athletes for two reasons: firstly, to be inspired, and secondly, to learn the best techniques from the masters. "If you want to be good at something, study the best," they would say.

At the time, I thought I was just being trained to be competitive in the sporting arena. Little did I know how important these lessons would become in the arena of life.

Growing up, I went to church every Sunday, but I didn't begin to take an active interest in my faith until I was about sixteen. When I began to explore the riches of Catholicism, I quickly came to understand that God calls each of us to live a life of honesty and integrity—an authentic life. I discovered that when we pursue what is good, true, beautiful, and noble, with honesty and integrity, we are holy, yes, but this is also when we are most fully alive and most truly ourselves.

Being young and idealistic, I was immediately attracted to the concept of holiness. The discovery of this ideal was the single most important event of my life. It was not just the discovery of an idea; it was an awakening. It was the revelation of my essential purpose. It was an eclipse that brought focus and clarity to my life. By the grace of God, and with the direction that mysteriously emerges from the Scriptures and the Sacraments, in the months and years that followed, a transformation began to take place within me.

Today, I am still very much in the midst of that transformation. At times it seems as if I am progressing, while at other times I cannot help but feel that I am slipping back down a mountain I have struggled so hard to climb. All in all, I have learned that my feelings are a poor indication of the work God is actually doing in my soul. I have come to believe that at every turn in the road, God is drawing us along the path, whether we are aware of it or not. My courage to accept the present and my hope to look toward the future come from remembering how God has used the circumstances of my past to achieve his purpose in my life.

• In Search of Excellence •

Over the ten years since my original conversion experience, I have learned to apply the wisdom my coaches shared with me in the sporting realm to my pursuit of excellence in the spiritual realm. Our faith is rich with examples of great men and women who have trained tirelessly and perfected the art of firmly establishing virtue in their lives.

If you came to me and told me that you wanted to become a great basketball player, I would tell you to study the great players who have gone before you. Learn everything you can about Michael Jordan, Larry Bird, and Magic Johnson. Similarly, if you told me you wanted to be a great golfer, I would tell you to study Arnold Palmer, Ben Hogan, Jack Nicklaus, Tiger Woods, and that carefree swing of Fred Couples. Read books, watch videos, research their training techniques—find out what qualities led them to become extraordinary athletes. If you want to be a great violinist, study other great violinists. If you want to be a great artist, study other great artists. If you want to be a great business leader, study other great business leaders. And of course this same principle applies to those of us who want to become great Catholics.

Whom will you study?

There is a path that leads to the authentic life. It is not a secret path; the path to holiness is well worn. For two thousand years men and women of all ages, from all walks of life and every social class, have been treading this path. If you came to me and told me you were going on a journey to a place you had never been before, I would advise you to travel with a guide. If you had to choose a guide, you wouldn't choose someone who had never been to where you wanted to go. You would choose an expert, someone who has made the journey before.

The spiritual life is a long and difficult journey, and we are all pilgrims on this path. There are many men and women who have gone before us who are willing to serve as our guides as we make this journey. Their stories provide a living legacy of spiritual wisdom. If we seek their counsel in the wisdom of their life stories, we will discover that they have faced and conquered many of the snares and pitfalls that seek to trip us up along the way. If we open our hearts to their stories, we will learn from their successes and failures, and they will teach us and inspire us to become all we can be.

• The Saints •

As we live in the midst of this modern culture, the sweet deceit of secular humanism calls to us with an ever-increasing intensity. How can you and I muster the strength to resist the diabolical distraction of this call? The answer, I am certain, is no secret. The path Jesus invites us to walk, the path our age desperately needs someone to explore, has been walked before. This path may be covered with grass and leaves, and some shrubs may have even worked their way across it, but it is there. The path of true Christian spirituality has been well worn throughout the centuries. It may be sorely neglected of late, but for those who seek it with a sincere heart, it will not take much to rediscover—and the rewards are infinite.

If we sincerely wish to follow Jesus, it is only natural to ask: Who have been his greatest followers? Who has thrived by following Jesus? Who has walked this path successfully before us? Which men and women have made this perilous and difficult journey? Who has embraced the adventure of salvation? Are these people available to guide you and me along the path today?

The answer, of course, is the saints. But they have become unpopular among modern Catholics. We have stopped reading their stories to our children. We have taken their statues from our churches. And we have stopped reading the books they wrote.

As Catholics, we must ask ourselves an important question in relation to these spiritual ancestors of ours: Why have so many modern Catholics turned their backs on these great spiritual leaders? We would be fools to believe all this has happened in response to a handful of abuses and exaggerations that have at times found their way into our relationship with the saints.

• Common Objections •

It is true that from time to time some people have placed too much emphasis on the role the saints play in Catholic spirituality. It is also not uncommon for biographers of these holy men and women to portray them as if they were born saints. Many books about the lives of the saints completely ignore their very human struggles to overcome sinful tendencies and the great inner conflicts they experienced. Consequently, many biographies of these extraordinary spiritual champions end up reading like religious fairy tales. I suspect the authors thought they were doing the saints a favor by telling their stories without blemish. In fact, what they were doing was robbing the Church of a great treasure, namely, the wisdom these saints acquired in their struggles to overcome their faults, failings, and flaws. In addition to this distortion of the saints, and maybe because of it, we also find that the way some people approach the saints borders on superstition at times.

These and other similarly petty reasons are what many modern Catholics cite when justifying their lack of interest in the saints. I agree that these abuses should be discouraged, but the solution to the distortion or overemphasis of something that is good is never to abolish the good in question.

The saints have made the journey we are called to explore for ourselves. They serve as extraordinary examples of the Christian life, and after Christ, they are the best role models, guides, mentors, and coaches for those who truly desire to draw nearer to God and work out their salvation (cf. Philippians 2:12).

Some may object, saying that Christ is the only role model necessary. But the saints are living and practical proof that Christ's philosophy works. The saints show us that it is possible for a human person to be fully transformed in Christ. These rare men and women who emerge from time to time in Catholic history are proof that Jesus really has redeemed the world, and that he has sent his Spirit to empower us to make this great journey of transformation back to wholeness.

The truth is, the saints have lost their popularity in this modern era not because a handful of grandmothers prayed too much to Saint Anthony or Saint Joseph and neglected Jesus. The saints have lost their popularity and fallen from good grace among modern Catholics because the Church has been infected by common secular philosophy.

As we discussed in Chapter Two, the prevailing philosophies in the world at this time are individualism, hedonism, and minimalism. Sadly, these philosophies have also worked their way into the lives of most Catholics, and as Catholics we have carried these philosophies like a disease into the Church. It is therefore not uncommon for modern Catholics to judge Sunday Mass, the Church, and Catholicism by what they get out of it. This attitude is the fruit of individualism. Similarly, most modern Catholics have abandoned almost every Catholic tradition that is not self-gratifying or that requires any exercise of discipline. This attitude is the fruit of hedonism. It is also very common for people to think, *I go to church on Sunday, and I always say grace before meals. Isn't that enough?* This attitude is, of course, the fruit of minimalism. Consciously or subconsciously, we are often asking ourselves, "What is the least I can do and still be Catholic?" and "What is the least I can do and still get to Heaven?"

So, we shouldn't be surprised that many modern Catholics are uncomfortable with the saints. I suspect they are just as uncomfortable with Jesus— the real Jesus, that is, not the Jesus that they have conjured up in their minds.

The saints remind us of Christ's call to break with "the spirit of the world" and challenge us to reject the glamour and allure of sin and selfishness.

This break with the spirit of the world is real and difficult, but it is achievable. The saints are proof of that. They are also proof of the peace and joy that are born from this bold rejection. But as modern Catholics, many of us seem content to attend Mass on Sunday, send our children to Catholic schools (or not), and worship the gods of materialism and secularism for the other 167 hours of the week.

It is time for modern Catholics to rediscover the valuable contribution the saints make to all those who wish to live in harmony with God. Regardless of the abuses and exaggerations that have taken place in the past, it is time for us to find a genuine place in our spiritual lives for these heroes and champions of Christianity.

• The Pedestal Syndrome •

Much of the misunderstanding that surrounds the role of the saints in Christian spirituality is caused by our tendency to place them high on pedestals. We tell ourselves that they are different. Consciously or subconsciously, we subscribe to the myth that God has favorites, and that the saints are his favored few. Most of all, we convince ourselves that we are not like them.

This pedestal syndrome is not new. Men and women of every age place their heroes on high and tell themselves that these heroes are different, that they are the elite, the favored, the chosen. Why do we do this? We place them high on pedestals, far out of our reach, so that we don't have to strive to become like them.

When Jesus walked the earth he encountered the very same problem. Whenever he did something extraordinary, the people of that village wanted to put him up on a pedestal and make him a king. At those moments, he always left the town or region he was in. Why? Because Jesus didn't want people to fall down helplessly before him and worship him. He was, of course, worthy of worship, but he wanted the highest form of worship: Jesus wanted people to imitate him. He didn't come to solve all our problems; he came to show us the way. He came to show us that when we cooperate with God and with each other we become vessels of light and love.

If Jesus experienced this difficulty, this pedestal syndrome, we shouldn't be surprised that those who have been fully transformed in Christ experience a similar problem.

The great danger is that veneration can become more important than imitation. When this happens, our devotion to the saints becomes hollow and borders on superstition. There is also a temptation to simply respect the saints from a distance, instead of following their example, studying the wisdom of their lives, and applying their lessons to our own lives.

• The Rejection of Discipline •

The philosophy of Christ is based on discipline, and it is discipline that our modern culture abhors and has rejected with all its strength. It is true that Jesus came to comfort the afflicted, but as Dorothy Day, journalist, social activist, and Catholic convert pointed out, he also came to afflict the comfortable. The saints make many modern Catholics uncomfortable because they challenge us to throw off the spirit of the world and to embrace the Spirit of God. Like Jesus, by their example the saints invite us to a life of discipline.

Contrary to popular opinion, discipline doesn't stifle or restrict the human person. Discipline isn't something invented by the Church to control or manipulate the masses, nor is it the tool that unjust tyrants and dictators use to make people do things they don't want to do. All these are the lies of a culture completely absorbed in a philosophy of instant gratification.

Discipline is the faithful friend who will introduce you to your true self. Discipline is the worthy protector who will defend you from your lesser self. And discipline is the extraordinary mentor who will challenge you to become the-best-version-of-yourself and all God created you to be.

As loyal and as life-giving as discipline may be, its presence in our lives is dwindling. Whether we are aware of it or not we are becoming spiritually ill without it.

It may be of interest to you to know how we are passing this disease on to our children. In my travels, I have noticed that one element of our lifestyles that is propelling the modern madness is the number of activities that children are involved in today. Mothers have become taxi drivers. They go from school to tennis, to soccer, to ballet, to football, to piano lessons, to basketball, to the drive-through at McDonald's, to choir, to baseball . . . and on and on.

Perhaps it is time we stopped and asked ourselves why our children participate in these activities. Are they just another form of entertainment? Are they a measure of our children's social status? Or are they directed toward some meaningful contribution to the development and education of our children?

I propose that if these activities are to have any real value in the education and development of a child, it will be because a child learns the art of discipline through these activities. And I assure you, our children will never learn the art of discipline while they are switching from one activity to another with great regularity. The overwhelming number of activities our children are engaged in is serving only to distract them from acquiring any real discipline in their lives, and as a result they are being firmly grounded in the superficiality that is ruling our age.

The purpose of education and extracurricular activities is to provide opportunities for our children to develop discipline. Once discipline is learned, it can be applied to any area of life. Those who develop this discipline go off in search of excellence and live richer, more abundant lives. Those who do not find this grounding in discipline may do many things, but none well.

God has placed you here for some purpose, but without discipline, you will never discover that purpose. Without discipline, you will march slowly and surely to join Thoreau's masses leading "lives of quiet desperation."

Mozart was a great composer, but did he begin as a great composer? No. He began as a keen student, mastering the discipline of playing the harpsichord. Only then, from this mastery and discipline, did the individual style and genius emerge.

Did Picasso find his unique style on his first day at art school? No. First he learned to paint a bowl of fruit like a photograph. Only then, having mastered the discipline of painting, did the individual style and genius that we know today as Picasso emerge.

First discipline, then genius.

In the absence of discipline, man must content himself with superficialities and mediocrity. This is the spell that secularism has cast on modern man. Superficiality is the curse of the modern world.

Without discipline, we are confined to soulless living and must content ourselves with work, food, momentary pleasures, and anything that can help distract us from the misery of purposeless living. Without discipline, the soul dies. Slowly, perhaps, but surely.

The saints' lives were firmly grounded in discipline. In Part Three of this book we will explore seven disciplines that were almost universally part of the saints' lives and discover how we can apply them to our own. Today's culture rejects the saints for the same reason it rejects Jesus: because they remind us of the indispensable role discipline plays in the development of the human person.

• Keeping the Goal in Sight •

The goal of the Christian life is to live a holy life. Those who have attained this goal we call saints. They found their essential purpose, they pursued their essential purpose, and they celebrated their essential purpose. The saints responded to the universal call to holiness and followed that great spiritual North Star. They quietly chiseled away at the defects and weaknesses in their character. They became the-best-version-of-themselves. They have truly applied themselves to the Christian life. They have brought the Gospel to life, animating it with their own thoughts, words, and actions. They have lived authentic lives. I ask you to consider who has lived more fully than the saints.

The pursuit of holiness is our essential purpose; it is the core theme of the Gospel, the primary idea Vatican II sought to remind us of, and the only answer to the unquenchable yearning for happiness that preoccupies our hearts. But, as we have already discussed, modern Catholics have largely rejected the call to holiness.

A statue of a saint is a physical sign of a spiritual reality. We have taken them from our churches and from our homes because we don't want to be reminded of this great call to holiness. And above everything else, when all is said and done, the saints challenge us to become holy. Our discomfort with the saints is proof of our discomfort with our calling to live authentic lives. We have banished the saints from our modern practice of Catholicism because when they are present it is impossible to forget that we are all called to holiness.

If we, as Catholics, were genuinely striving to become holy, the saints and our devotion to them would never suffer the criticisms and blows that are endlessly hurled at them today. When veneration replaces imitation, the saints lose their genuine role in Christian spirituality.

The challenge is for me and you to open our hearts to the call of the Gospel, which is ultimately a call to holiness. If you open the ears of your soul and listen to God's gentle calling, you will discover that, just like the saints, you are called to holiness.

The Church has been carried throughout the ages by the personal holiness of a handful of her members in each place and each time. If there is to be "a new springtime," as John Paul II prophesied, it will be because we rediscover this indispensable principle of Christian spirituality. The great spiritual North Star hangs in the sky, calling each of us to become the-best-version-of-ourselves by leading lives of holiness, and what I love most about the saints is that they remind me that holiness is possible.

Chapter Eight

EVEN A BLIND MAN KNOWS . . .

People are always asking me three questions: What sort of books do you read? Who inspires you? Who are your heroes and role models? Most people are then surprised to hear that I don't read much. I love to read, but I am in fact a very slow reader. I rarely read for entertainment. I read to expand my vision of the world, myself, and God, with the hope that it will make me a better person. And while I do not read for hours at a time, I do read the Gospels every day. These four books are the foundation upon which I try to base my life more and more with each passing day. And so every day, even if only for ten minutes, I read from one of these great spiritual touchstones. Apart from the Gospels, I am usually in the midst of a good spiritual book, a novel of some type, a biography, and a business book.

There are a great many people living and dead whom I admire. My parents did a wonderful job of raising my brothers and me. As a teenager, I worked after school at a drugstore, delivering packages to the homebound elderly. Brian Brouggy, the owner of the drugstore, had an amazing mind, which fascinated me and helped me to develop some intellectual muscles that my formal schooling had clearly failed to develop in me. Over the years, he has become a good friend and has inspired me to strive to become the-best-version-of-myself.

My two eldest brothers inspire me. I am always impressed by Mark's incredible ability to deal calmly with people, whether it is in a crisis situation or in helping them to see all their unrealized potential. And ever since I was a child, I have always been in awe of Simon's generous spirit.

I cannot count the number of teachers who have inspired me and continue to inspire me, from Mrs. Western in first grade and Miss Hume in third grade, to Mrs. Rutter, Mr. McCullugh, Mr. Croke, and Mr. Wade in high school. I still hear their voices in different moments of the day, guiding me, encouraging me, challenging me. I have had the most incredible run of great teachers throughout my life, both inside and outside the classroom. The list of everyday people who are an inspiration to me goes on and on.

Apart from these, there are my friends in history: Abraham Lincoln for his perseverance; Van Gough, Picasso, and Mozart for their creative genius; Gandhi for his integrity and resolve; Michael Jordan for his ability to transform weaknesses into strengths; Tolstoy and Dickens for their mastery of thought and storytelling; Thoreau for his love of leisure and reflection; Aristotle and Plato for their love of wisdom; and again the list goes on and on.

These people inspire me, and I seek to gain wisdom from the lessons of their lives, but they are not my role models or heroes. Jesus is my role model. He is my hero. While I learn from many people, he is the one whom I wish to imitate. After Jesus, my greatest inspiration comes from those who have imitated him successfully, particularly Francis of Assisi, Mother Teresa, John Vianney, Thomas More, and John Paul II. I do not worship these people, but I do greatly admire them for their virtue and integrity.

History is full of examples of people who have lived authentic lives. If we learn to absorb the lessons their lives exude, it is possible to grow wise in our youth and prove wrong the saying "You cannot put an old head on young shoulders." You can and we should. There are very few people in the world who wouldn't say, "I wish I was younger and knew what I know now." Those who are willing to learn from other people's mistakes can live with the wisdom of the old from the earliest ages. It is not necessary to make all the mistakes yourself to learn about life, yourself, and others. Those who refuse to learn from the mistakes of others, those who refuse to study history, must content themselves to make mistakes that have been made before.

For as long as I can remember, I have observed and studied extraordinary people and tried to apply their wisdom and techniques to my own life.

I did this first as a child in the area of sports and later at business school in the areas of marketing, finance, and entrepreneurship. From the very beginning I have done this with my speaking and writing, and ultimately, I have observed those who have had remarkable success in the area of spirituality.

I would like to share with you now five stories that illustrate the wisdom and power of people who have opened their hearts to the will of God. They have lived in different places and at different times, but their lives are bound together by an inspiring commitment to seek and know God, an unrelenting effort to pursue their essential purpose, a deliberate and daily striving for holiness, and a hunger to celebrate and defend the-best-version-of-themselves.

People of all faiths have admired these men and women in every nation around the world. You may disagree with some of the things these holy men and women have said or done, but it is impossible for people of good will not to respect their desire to better themselves and leave the world a better place than they found it, by doing the will of God as they understood it.

Catherine of Siena wrote, "If you are what you should be you will set the whole world on fire." It is a strange thing, but I have noticed that even a blind man knows when he is in the presence of a great light. The world needs you to be such a light.

• Francis of Assisi •

At the dawn of the thirteenth century, the world was experiencing two problems that were very similar to those it faces today. First, coins were being mass-produced, and as a result were quickly becoming the primary medium of exchange. This general introduction of money was creating a greed and materialism that had not existed except among the elite under the bartering system. People had never hoarded eggs or grain or chickens, because they could not be stored for long periods of time without rotting or dying. But coins were cold and lifeless, and could be easily stored. Thus, the desire to amass wealth began to seduce the human heart more than ever before. The second problem of the day was that religion had become more of a habit and an empty tradition than a genuine conviction. Sound familiar?

In 1182, a child was born in the tiny town of Assisi, in the hills of Northern Italy. With his life, this child would address both the greed and the religious decay that plagued his day. His extraordinary example has never stopped inspiring us.

The boy's name was Francesco (or Francis); he was the son of a wealthy cloth merchant. While his parents hoped he would go on to great things, perhaps become a mayor or an influential businessman, Francis seemed to waste the first twenty years of his life indulging in parties and daydreams of becoming a great knight.

Francis was a leader and a favorite among the young people of his hometown. The life of every party, he spent endless nights in the frivolous pursuit of wine, song, and dance. Full of charm and wit, he was loved by all.

At twenty years of age, Francis decided he was ready to embrace what he believed to be his chance at greatness. He left Assisi in full armor, upon the finest horse, to take part in the battle between Assisi and nearby Perugia.

During the battle, Francis was knocked from his horse and later captured by the enemy. As the son of a wealthy man, he was held hostage for ransom. Only after several months was he released, and by this time he had become very ill.

His convalescence provided the necessary meeting ground for him to encounter God. Within this stillness and solitude his heart began to soften and transform. Though he recovered from his grave illness, Francis would never again be the frivolous fun-seeker the people of Assisi had come to know and love. All his glory seeking had revealed to him a profound dissatisfaction, a restlessness lurking in his soul that would not be ignored. While in his former life he wasted countless hours with crowds of rowdy friends, now he sought the solitude of time alone in the quiet fields that surrounded Assisi.

A turning point in his new life occurred one day when he visited the abandoned and dilapidated church of San Damiano, not far from Assisi.

Entering the weary structure, he knelt before the crucifix to pray. At that moment, Francis heard a voice speak to him, saying, "Rebuild my Church. As you can see, it is in ruins."

Believing he had heard the voice of God, Francis set about rebuilding the crumbling church of San Damiano. Using materials bought with his father's money or begged from the people of Assisi, Francis fully restored the little church with his own hands. He then set about rebuilding the abandoned church of Saint Peter, and finally restored the also dilapidated Portiuncula, which later became the center of life for Francis and his brothers.

Once the Portiuncula was completed, Francis again heard the voice of God, saying, "Francis, rebuild my Church. As you can see, it is in ruins." On this occasion, his heart was opened to understand that God was not calling him to a life of physical labor rebuilding churches. But rather, he was calling Francis to a spiritual mission.

Francis then turned his back on all worldly wealth to embrace a life of simplicity, humility, poverty, and prayer.

His spirit of uncompromising commitment to the Gospel has remained a force of renewal in the Church in every place and time for more than seven hundred years. Francis of Assisi has endured as one of the most intriguing figures in human history. Today there are more than one million Franciscan friars and brothers around the world. Have you ever tried to get people to volunteer for a couple of hours? Imagine inspiring more than a million people to give their whole lives for a cause.

During his lifetime, this little man of poverty became and continues to be a worldwide influence. He has inspired and influenced the great thinkers of every age. He is the subject of hundreds of books, thousands of studies, numerous motion pictures and documentaries, and a myriad of musical compositions honoring his life. If you travel the world, you will come upon countless rivers, mountains, roads, and even cities named after Francis, the most famous of which is, of course, San Francisco.

He has been hailed by historians, praised by religious leaders of all beliefs, and quoted by presidents. He has inspired artistic masterpieces including works by Rembrandt, who was by his own admission an anti-Catholic Protestant, yet he was enamored of the life and virtue of Francis. It was Francis who invented the crèche, or Nativity scene, to draw attention to the powerful paradox of God's son being born into the poverty of a stable. Every year, millions of families unconsciously honor the memory of Francis with the Nativity scenes they place in their homes. Recognized universally as a lover of nature, Francis is the statue most commonly placed in the garden.

He was all this in the past, and I believe he remains a powerful and trustworthy spiritual guide to the people of our own troubled times.

But what I delight in most about Francis is that the people who loved him honored him by remembering his story—all of his story, even his wild youth and his moments of impatience during the early days of his ministry. It is for this reason that biographers have been so successful at portraying Francis as a "whole man" rather than as a caricature of holiness. He was certainly saintly, but not sanctimonious. He loved God, but he also loved his neighbor and creation.

Francis was real. He was striving with all his heart to live an authentic life. And like the first Christians, he captured the imaginations and intrigued the hearts and minds of the people of his time and the people of times to come. Francis is a practical example of the power of one authentic life indelibly engraved upon history.

• Mother Teresa •

Mother Teresa was born Agnes Bojaxhiu in Serbia on August 26, 1910. Agnes grew up in Albania, surrounded by wealth and prosperity. Despite their wealth, her parents were models of virtue. They loved each other deeply, and that love overflowed to Agnes and her sister. At the age of eighteen, Agnes left home to join an Irish order of nuns. Later that year, in December 1928, she set sail for India to begin her work as a novice for the Loreto Order. Now Sister Teresa, she spent most of the next twenty years teaching. In 1937, she made her permanent vows of poverty, chastity, and obedience, and as was customary adopted the title of Mother.

By 1943, India was torn by war and famine. Mahatma Gandhi's great success in freeing India from British rule had become tainted by civil war between Muslims and Hindus living in India. More people than ever descended upon Calcutta. It finally became necessary for the Loreto Convent to move the children and the school outside the city. At this time, many nuns and whole orders decided to leave India and close their schools, but Mother Teresa stayed and worked tirelessly. As others left, she taught more and more classes, eventually teaching two subjects to eight grades.

She was happy in her work and well liked. By the mid-1940s, her mere presence already had a power that had been born through hours of prayer and reflection. Soon Mother Teresa was appointed headmistress, and she wrote to her mother, "This is a new life. Our center here is very fine. I am a teacher, and I love the work. I am also head of the whole school, and everybody wishes me well." Her mother's reply was a stern reminder of her original intentions for going to India: "Dear child, do not forget that you went to India for the sake of the poor."

Kipling described Calcutta as "the city of a dreadful night." Mother Teresa was in the capital of poverty, a poverty that most people never even witness firsthand, let alone personally experience. Have you been there? Have you seen it on television? Can you picture it?

This was the world that surrounded the school and this was the world that was crying out for help.

In 1946, Mother Teresa became very ill herself and was ordered by doctors to have bed rest for three hours every afternoon. It was very hard for her to rest and not do her work, but this period of enforced rest culminated in the directive to go away on retreat for a month. The intention was that in the interests of her health she should undergo a period of spiritual renewal and a physical break from the work.

On September 10, 1946, she boarded a train for Darjeeling, where she was to retreat. Aboard that train, Mother Teresa had a supernatural experience that changed the direction of her life forever. She referred to it as "the call within the call." Many years earlier she had been called to religious life (the call). Now she was being called to something more (the call within the call). The retreat provided the perfect period of silence, solitude, and prayer to follow the experience God had given her on the train.

The next couple of years were filled with dialogue between her spiritual director, the Bishop, and Rome. By 1950, at age forty, Mother Teresa had left the school and the Loreto Order, founded the Sisters of Charity, and was living among the poorest of the poor in Calcutta. At this time she began a new life, dreamt a new dream. She stepped into the classroom of silence, sat down with her God, and said, *How can I help?* Over the next twenty years she would capture the imagination of the whole world simply by living the Gospel. Such is the potency and spellbinding power the Gospel holds when it is actually lived.

When was the last time you stepped into the classroom of silence, sat down with your God, and asked, *How can I help?*

Over the next five decades, Mother Teresa emerged as an icon of modern holiness, capturing the imaginations and intriguing the hearts and minds of people from every nation on earth. Dedicated to a life of simplicity, she gave herself to society's most marginalized victims. Her love for people was tangible. You could see it. You could feel it. You could reach out and touch it. It was real and living. It wasn't a sermon or a speech. Each moment, she looked only for the next opportunity to love. For her, every individual mattered. "I believe," she once said, "in person-to-person contact. Every person is Christ for me, and since there is only one Jesus, the person I am meeting is the one person in the world at that moment." Those who spent time with her would often comment, "For the moment you were with her, there was only you and her. She wasn't looking over your shoulder to see what was happening around you. You had her full attention. It was as if nothing else existed to her except you."

Contrasted against the unbridled materialism of the modern world, Mother Teresa had an attraction that seemed impossible to explain. The contrast between the spirit of the world and the spirit of this woman was breathtaking.

Years before, the people of India had traveled hundreds of miles, often on foot, to catch a glimpse of Gandhi. Hindus believe that simply to be in the presence of a holy person brings with it a great blessing. Now they sought the company, the mere presence, even just a glimpse of Mother Teresa, a Catholic nun. Like a magnetic field, she attracted the rich and the poor, the weak and the powerful, irrespective of race or creed.

In time, Mother Teresa was awarded the Nobel Peace Prize, the United States Medal of Freedom, and the United Nations Albert Schweitzer Prize. Considered by many to be a living saint, she didn't allow all the attention to distract her and remained a soul wholly dedicated to a life of service.

Mother Teresa is one of the most beloved women of all time. She was a steadfast voice of love and faith, and yet her power didn't come from the words she used or the awards she received, and she never forced her beliefs upon anyone. Asked to speak about religion, she once said, "Religion is not something that you or I can touch. Religion is the worship of God— therefore a matter of conscience. I alone must decide for myself and you for yourself, what we choose. For me, the religion I live and use to worship God is the Catholic religion. For me, this is my very life, my joy, and the greatest gift of God in his love for me. He could have given me no greater gift."

When I reflect on the life of Mother Teresa the questions I ask myself are: Where does this power to love so deeply come from? Where does the strength to serve so selflessly come from? What is the source of this woman's extraordinary ability to inspire?

The answers to these questions are also deeply embedded in her life. Before everything else, Mother Teresa was a woman of prayer. Each day, she would spend three hours in prayer before the Blessed Sacrament. Her power to love, her strength to endure, and her gift to inspire the masses were all born in the classroom of silence. This woman believed in the centrality of Jesus Christ. She knew his centrality in history and eternity, and she trusted his centrality in her own life. There lies the source: She placed Jesus at the center of her life. In the depths of her heart, she knew that action without prayer was worth nothing.

Mother Teresa's story is remarkable, but the story within the story is equally remarkable. It would be a mistake for us to examine the life of Mother Teresa and not ask some simple questions: How did she learn to live, love, and pray the way she did? Who taught her? Whom did she take as her role model?

These questions lead us to a young Catholic woman Mother Teresa never met, another nun who lived in a Carmelite convent in southern France and died before Mother Teresa was born. Her name was Saint Therese of Lisieux. Therese believed that love is expressed through attention to the small things that fill our daily lives. Mother Teresa practiced "the little way" taught by Therese.

This connection demonstrates that every act of holiness is a historic event. Every time we choose to love God and neighbor we change the course of human history, because our holiness echoes in the lives of people in other places and other times. Therese entered the convent at the age of fifteen and died at age twenty-four, but her influence continues to resonate in the lives of more than forty-five hundred Missionaries of Charity (the order Mother Teresa founded) who work in 133 countries today. It is impossible to measure Saint Therese of Lisieux's impact on history, but it is vast. Holiness is deeply personal, but it is also communal and historic. Holiness is not something we do for ourselves; it is something God does in us if we cooperate. And it is something he does in us not for us alone, but for others and for all of history.

• John Vianney •

John Marie Vianney was born in the sleepy town of Dardilly, France, on May 8, 1786, three years before the storming of the Bastille. About five miles northwest of Lyons, Dardilly was home to fewer than one thousand people, and for much of the French Revolution remained a very peaceful place to live. At seven years of age, John knew little of the troubles that plagued his homeland. The son of a farmer, each day he drove the donkey, the cows, and the sheep down the valley to graze.

It was around this time that the violence of the French Revolution reached his hometown in a very subtle form. Catholicism had been outlawed. A price was on the head of every priest in France, and they fled. Church bells were silenced and Mass could not be attended without risking one's life, even if one could find a priest brave enough to celebrate it. Those who were found to be harboring priests were also in great danger.

This didn't stop Matthew Vianney, John's father. Priests were very often the secret guests of the Vianneys, and on other occasions, the whole family would set out in the middle of the night to attend Mass offered by a hunted priest in a nearby barn. John grew to admire these brave and holy men, and within that admiration grew the seed of his love for the priesthood.

In the early dawn of April 18, 1802, the bells of Notre Dame in Paris rang out and proclaimed the resurrection of Catholicism in France. Now sixteen, John already had his heart set on the priesthood, but as his brother Francis had been drafted and his sister Catherine was to be married, his father desperately needed him to help with the farm and refused to give consent. But by the time John was nineteen, his mother had pleaded with his father to let him go, and finally he entered minor seminary.

Despite his tireless efforts, John Vianney struggled in his studies, particularly with Latin. It was for his lack of knowledge of Latin that he was dismissed from major seminary in 1813 after only two months. But Father Balley, curé (meaning "pastor") of the church that the Vianney family attended in nearby Ecully, sent him straight back with a letter to the rector. Shortly after, John was dismissed again. This time, Father Balley went to the chancery and begged the Vicar-General on account of John's great devotion to prayer and the Church.

With much assistance, and his superiors' willingness to generously overlook his academic weaknesses, John was finally ordained on August 13, 1815.

Once ordained, John was sent to his old friend and mentor, Father Balley, in Ecully. Here, the old priest shared his wisdom and experience with the young priest. But late in 1817, Father Balley died. John wept like a child at the death of this good and holy priest and later wrote of him, "I have seen some beautiful souls, but none so beautiful!" From that day on, John mentioned Father Balley in his prayers at Mass every day.

In February 1818, John Vianney became the curé of a small parish in Ars, a tiny place twenty-two miles from Lyons with only sixty families. Most maps of France did not include it, and it was considered to be the Siberia of the diocese.

During those first weeks, John Vianney spent his time visiting each of the sixty families. He would talk to them about the crops, the children, the relatives, and every aspect of life. What he was really doing was making a moral assessment of his parish. He found that the people's spiritual lives were in great need of restoration. They cared little for the Church, as they had been seduced by the pleasures common to every age: slothfulness, drunkenness, blasphemy, lust, and impurity.

The new curé understood the meaning and value of the words "This kind can only be cast out by prayer and fasting." (Matthew 17:20) Father Vianney began a one-man campaign of prayer and fasting, offering all his sacrifices to God for the conversion of the people in his parish.

Many considered his penances too severe. He slept on the floor, went for days without food, and for several years ate nothing but a boiled potato each day. But the graces borne from his sacrifices brought clarity to his mind, and they flooded his soul and the souls of his parishioners with abundant grace.

The curé preached boldly and without reservation about the evils of his community. In the early days, he spoke out against the taverns and tavern owners who "steal the bread of poor women and children by selling wine to drunkards." One man closed his tavern at the urging of the curé, but seven more opened within a year. Father Vianney responded, saying, "You shall see, you shall see, those who open an inn in this place shall be ruined."

The people reacted violently at first, but in time the curé's prayer, fasting, and the example he set began to reap a tremendous harvest. It may have taken twenty years, but Ars was eventually rid of all taverns. And as the taverns began to disappear, other things began to disappear as well. By the 1850s, Ars was rid of destitution, and the wisdom of the curé's ways became evident. By suppressing the taverns, he had eliminated the main cause of poverty.

But the years between his arrival and the golden years of Ars were a time filled with tremendous trials and suffering for Vianney. Letters of false accusation flooded the Bishop's office, and inquiries were made into his behavior in the small rural parish. In speaking out against the evils of the village, he pricked the consciences of many, and they often became hostile. Ignorance and sin confuse us, and in our confusion we cause suffering to those who are truly holy. Late in his life, Vianney wrote, "If on my arrival in Ars, I had foreseen all that I was to suffer there, I would have died on the spot."

But the pain of his life was eased by a rare spiritual pleasure: He was seeing the transformation in the people's lives. Careless people were becoming good people; good people were growing better; and the men and women who had established the habits of virtue in their lives were practicing the heroism of saints.

For his own prayer, Father Vianney spent long periods in front of the Blessed Sacrament early in the morning and late at night. He encouraged his people to make regular visits to the church and sit before the Blessed Sacrament. The "good curé" (as he was affectionately called) knew that the Blessed Sacrament was the most powerful means of renewing the life of the parish.

Each morning, he would sit in his confessional, hearing the confessions of any who wished to come. At about the same time each day, he would hear a loud clanging noise at the back of the church. Five or ten minutes would pass and then he would hear the clanging again. He was always curious about this noise. One morning he came out of the confessional just as the second clang was ringing out. He hurried to the back of the church and found one of the farmers leaving the church with his tools. The curé asked the man, "Do you come here every morning?"

"Yes, Father," he replied.

"What do you do here?"

"I just sit a little and pray," said the simple farmer.

"How do you pray?"

The man was aware of his own simplicity and a little embarrassed. He bowed his head and said, "I look at the good God, and the good God looks at me."

Father John Vianney was a man of prayer and good living, and the people of his parish became people of prayer and good living. He was, first and foremost, a spiritual leader to his people, and took seriously the responsibility of guiding their souls along the path of salvation.

But his influence was not confined to the people of Ars. From his earliest days in Ars, the people from his hometown of Dardilly and the people of Ecully, where he had first served as assistant, came to him for spiritual direction. On their way to and from Ars, people would ask where they were going and why, and word would spread very quickly of the "Holy Curé," as they called him.

For more than thirty years, between 1827 and 1859, the church at Ars was never empty. At first, there were twenty visitors a day, but in time the floodgates opened and people streamed to this sleepy little village a thousand at a time. During the last year of Father Vianney's life, more than one hundred thousand people came to Ars. So many people were visiting Ars that a spur had to be added to the train line. Imagine how holy a person would need to be for a train line to be built to his doorstep in the middle of nowhere.

Within ten years of his death, that very same track was torn up, as it was used so infrequently. In the mid-1800s, Ars became the great focal point of spirituality in France, all because of one simple, humble, holy priest.

Why did the people come?

People of every era are hungry for God, whether they are aware of it or not. Whenever a man or woman emerges as an instrument of God's truth and goodness, people will beat a path to that person's door. The reason people flocked to see the Curé of Ars is no different. In his preaching, in his advice, and during confession, they sensed the truth, goodness, and guidance of God himself.

Above everything else, the Curé of Ars was a confessor. As the crowds came to Ars, Vianney simply increased the number of hours he spent in the confessional. Sometimes he would spend twelve, fourteen, sixteen, even eighteen hours a day hearing the confessions of pilgrims. His words were penetrating and challenging. He spoke to penitents with the same boldness and clarity with which he preached. As for the pilgrims, some of them waited in line for three days to have the curé hear their confession or to ask his advice on a matter. He served his God and God's people with the sublime monotony of routine.

As his popularity soared, so did the criticisms of him. His colleagues, the priests of France, remembered well his lack of education. And as the people of France began to speak of him as a living saint, great jealousy took hold of many. But the curé would not allow any of this to interfere with his work. The more he was exalted, the more he humbled himself.

On August 4, 1859, John Marie Vianney, the Curé of Ars, died. Many may look at his life and say he did a great many strange things. But the motives behind these seemingly strange actions were as pure as the fallen snow. If we can resist the temptation to cast his ways off as absurd and impractical, behind all of his actions we will find a profound and deeply moving love of God and neighbor.

John Vianney believed indifference toward religion and a lust for material comforts were the obstacles to true spirituality in his time. With his own life, he showed us all that there is another way. Is that "other way" calling you?

• Thomas More •

Thomas More was born in London on February 7, 1478. He served as a page boy to the Archbishop, who was so impressed that he sent Thomas to Oxford University when Thomas was only fourteen years old. During his time at Oxford, he became tutor to the prince who would later become King Henry VIII. As a young lawyer still in his twenties, Thomas was elected to parliament and there began his meteoric rise in the political world.

Thomas was monumentally successful. He was respectably but not nobly born. The son of a merchant-class family, he distinguished himself first as a scholar, then as a lawyer and judge, later as an ambassador, and finally, in the highest and most prestigious post in England, as lord chancellor.

Although Thomas was a man of considerable means, his lifestyle was often more akin to that of an ascetic monk even though he owned multiple homes, barns, and farming lands; employed live-in servants and private tutors for his children; and collected exotic animals and artifacts as a hobby.

A guest book at his estate in Chelsea would have read more like a who's who of the sixteenth century; Holbein, Erasmus, and Colet were among his noted guests. Thomas More corresponded with all the great minds of Europe and was himself considered a remarkable statesman and one of the great minds of his time. His home became known as a center of laughter, learning, and good conversation. He was a friend to the King, Henry VIII, who often called upon Thomas to advise him or simply to keep him company. On occasion and in unprecedented fashion, the King visited Thomas in his own home.

Thomas More adored his family, and they adored him. He raised his children in the disciplines of education and virtue, and was himself a worthy role model of both. In a time when education was considered to be wasted on women, he provided a fine education for his daughters.

He was a celebrated writer during his own time, and his writings continue to be widely studied today. Thomas's sociopolitical fantasy, *Utopia*, describes his dream of an ideal society, and gave a name to a literary genre and a new worldview.

Thomas More was a remarkable man. He loved and celebrated life. He was admired even by those who opposed him, he was unimaginably successful in numerous fields, and he was devoted to his family, but above all, he was a man who found the grace necessary to live with integrity when it would have been convenient not to.

When Thomas More parted with his life, he parted with more than most men, and that makes his actions even more powerful and meaningful.

In the spring of 1534, Thomas More was imprisoned in the Tower of London for refusing to sign the Act of Supremacy. King Henry VIII wanted to divorce his wife, Catherine of Aragon, and marry Anne Boleyn, so he petitioned the Pope for an annulment. But, as the Pope had already granted a special dispensation for Henry to marry Catherine, his deceased brother's wife, the request was denied. Accustomed to having his own way in all things, Henry became furious and set his stubborn mind all the more on marrying Anne. As a result, he decided to separate the Church in England from the Church in Rome, and by an act of parliament appointed himself the supreme head of the Church in England. It was this act that Thomas More refused to sign and support.

Thomas was an intelligent man. He knew that, by law, he could be imprisoned for not signing the Act of Supremacy, but not put to death. The law considers silence to be consent, but the silence of a man of virtue is louder than most men's words. Thus, England began to buzz, guessing at the opinions of Thomas More.

Henry didn't want to have Thomas put to death, and at any moment before his execution the king was willing to pardon him if he would simply agree to give public approval of Henry's marriage to Anne Boleyn. The King wanted Thomas's imprimatur. He had the signatures of dozens of leading officials and statesmen on the document, but the endorsement of immoral men is not worth having. The people of Europe paid no attention to who had signed the Act; they were fixated on who had not. Thomas was a man of virtue, and his character and reputation were undisputed. So naturally, the king wanted his approval.

All this presented a problem for Thomas. He could not in good conscience sign the Act, because his well-informed mind and his well-formed conscience told him clearly that parliament didn't have the authority to appoint the king as the supreme head of the Church in England. Parliament didn't have the authority because this was a spiritual office, not a political office.

Most men would have given in and signed the Act. Most men did. But Thomas was a man with a remarkable sense of self. He was not a stubborn, hardheaded man. He knew how to compromise in situations for his wife, his children, even his friends, but he refused to compromise his self. The greatest possession a person has is his own immortal soul; Thomas knew this truth with unwavering clarity.

A person takes an oath only when he wants to commit himself to a statement, and not just himself but his *self*—his immortal soul. In an oath, a man gives himself as a guarantor. He stands before God and joins his self with the truth, or in this case the lie, of the oath. The oath of a man willing to perjure himself is not worth having, because we sense that he has no self to commit, no guarantee to offer, for he has given his self away, compromised it, or sold it piece by piece along the way. This is why in the modern world we prefer people to guarantee their statements with cash and financial assets, rather than with their oath.

Since I was a child, I have heard the phrase "every man has his price." Thomas teaches us that this needn't be so. Life tests us all in this department, and Thomas More was no different.

Most men and women can be bought, and bought quite cheaply. Some can be bought with money, power, status, or possessions; others are bought with pleasure, land, bricks and mortar, knowledge, or fame. Men who are able to maintain possession of their self in the midst of these offerings are few. The world then tries to buy these rare souls with suffering, meaning not that you can buy a man by offering him suffering, but that you can impose suffering and offer him escape.

This is how Henry VIII, Thomas Cromwell, the Church of England, history, and the spirit of the world tried to purchase the soul—or self—of Sir Thomas More. They threw him in prison and threatened him with death. They tried to separate him from everyone and everything that he loved, hoping in that cold, dark, lonely cell, deprived of food, light, and human contact, he would break and give his self to their will.

But they had mistaken Thomas for themselves. They had forgotten that he was a man of prayer and virtue. His self was nonnegotiable, and had become so by the practice of temperance and long hours at prayer. In the midst of abundance, he hadn't allowed himself to get carried away, and now, in the midst of poverty, he was not disconcerted.

Thomas also proved that it is possible to be a politician and keep your character intact, despite the dishonest and self-seeking environment that surrounds you. He is one of history's most authentic models of selfless and virtuous leadership. Imagine what America would be like if we had a man of Thomas More's character and virtue as president.

On July 6, 1535, falsely accused of treason, Thomas More was executed.

Thomas More faced and overcame the enticements of this world. He was truly able to live among the world and yet not belong to the world. I pray you and I can develop the sense of self that Thomas More had.

I became fascinated with Thomas More for the first time when I worked as a stagehand for my high school's production of *A Man for All Seasons*. I was intrigued by this man who so obviously had his own life in his hands and yet chose to die. As the years have passed, I have grown more in awe of him. No one could accuse him of any incapacity for life. He embraced life, fully seizing every opportunity to explore its abundant variety. He loved deeply and was deeply loved. He was successful and admired. Thomas More was no plaster-cast saint; he was a man who loved life and was full of life. And yet, he found something within himself without which life is valueless. So when cruel and selfish men tried to take that something from him, he chose to embrace death rather than surrender to it.

I hope you and I can find that something within ourselves.

• John Paul II •

The great men and women of history are usually born in the most unexpected places and at the most unexpected times. Karol Wojtyla was born in the small provincial city of Wadowice, Poland, on May 18, 1920. Who would have known, who would have believed, that this Polish boy would become arguably the most influential figure of the twentieth century?

The life of Karol Wojtyla staggers the imagination. We all have great moments in our lives, and some men play a role in a significant event in history, but for one man to be so centrally involved in so many aspects of life and so many historical moments seems almost unbelievable. If it were fiction, we would dismiss it as simply too far-fetched.

And so, with the brief time I have to speak with you about his life, the most I can hope for is to sketch out some of his story. I do this with the hope that you will be inspired to learn more about this man we call John Paul II, and I have no doubt that in learning more you will be all the more inspired.

Karol Wojtyla's mother died before he turned ten, leaving his father, a retired military officer, to raise him. His father taught him the art of life—discipline—and firmly grounded him in the habit of prayer. These would become the pillars of Karol's life. In his youth, he was the best student in town, an enthusiastic athlete, and an amateur actor.

He later moved to Kraków with his father and entered Jagiellonian University. He continued to excel in the classroom and on the stage, but his promising progress in both was cut short by World War II.

It was then that he formed a bond with the worker. Toiling as a quarryman and blaster, he came to understand the plight of the worker and the value of manual labor in man's life. In defiance of his country's Nazi occupiers, he joined a cultural resistance movement. When parish priests were kidnapped and taken to Dachau, he received his first formal training in classic spirituality, under the guidance of a lay mystic.

After the death of his father in 1941, Karol began the internal struggle of discerning his vocation. He was torn between two worlds: the altar and the stage. After considerable prayer and anguish, he saw clearly, and joined the clandestine seminary run by the Archbishop of Kraków. He continued to work at a chemical factory, while studying philosophy and theology on the side. At night, risking his life, he made his way through the streets to attend classes at the Archbishop's residence.

After Poland was "liberated" by the Red Army, he was ordained a priest on November 1, 1946. He was immediately sent to Rome for graduate study in theology. The following year, he visited France and Belgium, where he was exposed for the first time to the way of the worker-priest. These were priests who, with the permission of their bishops, took up work in factories to experience the everyday life of the working class.

Having completed his studies in Rome, he returned to Poland and began an intense and very personal ministry to university students. It was there that he first developed his unusual patience with dialogue and his exceptional ability to listen even to those with whom he disagreed. He formed a number of innovative workshops and seminars, engaged the students in intense conversation, and spent thousands of hours in the confessional—all of which revealed a very different type of priest than the Polish people were used to. His style, which was received as a breath of fresh air, inspired the students to give him the nickname Wujek, which means "uncle."

In 1954, after receiving his second doctorate, Karol was invited to join the philosophy department of Catholic University of Lublin. He commuted via overnight train and was greeted by standing-room-only crowds in his classes. In 1960, he raised eyebrows everywhere with his first book, *Love and Responsibility,* in which he celebrates human sexuality as a gift from God for the sanctification of husband and wife.

In 1958, at the age of thirty-eight, he was consecrated bishop, and was named auxiliary bishop of Kraków. Between 1962 and 1965, he attended all four sessions of the Second Vatican Council. At the Council, he played a pivotal role in designing a new Catholic openness to the modern world and raised his voice in the Council's efforts to define religious freedom and basic human rights.

After he was named Archbishop of Kraków in 1964, he began a relentless battle for the religious and civil rights of his people. In 1967, at age forty-seven, he was named cardinal, but refused to act in the way senior prelates were expected to act. He continued to ski, hike, and kayak; he even vacationed with laypeople. In Kraków, he was the driving force behind the most comprehensive implementation of Vatican II. While more and more demands were made on his time, he continued to work as an intellectual, teaching, conducting seminars, writing, and delivering papers at international conferences.

On October 16, 1978, Karol Wojtyla was elected the 264th Bishop of Rome and took the name John Paul II. The world was shocked. He was the first non-Italian pope in 455 years and the first Slavic pope ever.

In 1979, Pope John Paul II visited his homeland for the first time as the leader of the Roman Catholic Church. Poland came to a standstill as millions neglected work and school to greet the man they had grown to love as Wujek. He drew the largest crowds in Polish history and single-handedly revitalized Catholicism in a land tormented by Communism. These enormous crowds became one of the many trademarks of his papacy. During that visit, he reawakened the conscience of Poland, and the nonviolent collapse of the Soviet empire in Eastern Europe began.

John Paul II breathed new life into the world's oldest institution, the papacy, in the context of the modern world. He traveled to every corner of the globe, preaching the Gospel to millions of people with each appearance. He wrote and taught endlessly, covering every aspect of Catholicism and every issue that faces humanity in the modern world. And not to be forgotten is the way he masterfully harnessed every modern means of communication to remind the world of the truth and light of God.

On May 13, 1981, Pope John Paul II was shot in Saint Peter's Square. He survived this assassination attempt and returned to his work with more vigor than ever. He redefined the relationship between the Catholic Church and Judaism, asked the Orthodox Catholics and non-Catholic Christians to imagine a papacy that could serve all Christians, preached to Muslim teenagers in Casablanca, and described marital intimacy as an icon of the interior life of God. During this same period he became a much-needed model of forgiveness to the modern world, by meeting with and befriending the man who shot him.

Over the years, under the weight of his relentless efforts to educate and unite Catholics, and indeed all of humanity, his health began to deteriorate. By late 1993 the international press begin to speculate about his health and television stations around the world commissioned documentaries in preparation for his departure from the world stage.

Defying all expectations in the next year, he preached to the largest crowd ever gathered in human history on the least Christian continent of the world and published a book that became an international best seller and was translated into forty languages.

In 1995, he defended the universality of human rights in his address to the United Nations. Two days later, celebrating Mass in New York City in Central Park, he joked with the crowd and delivered one of his characteristically challenging homilies.

Then, on the eve of the new millennium he urged Catholics to cleanse their consciences, both individually and collectively; and he single-handedly redirected an international gathering on population issues.

Who was this man? Where did his extraordinary strength and wisdom come from?

Let me ask you, did you ever see John Paul II pray? Each morning, he celebrated Mass in his private chapel with about twenty guests. Perhaps you were fortunate enough to attend. If not, perhaps you saw television footage of these Masses.

When this man knelt down to pray after Communion, he would close his eyes and go to a place deep within himself. Once he was there, nothing and no one could distract him. He would go to that place deep within himself, and from that place he brought forth the fruit of his life: wisdom, compassion, generosity, understanding, patience, courage, insight, forgiveness, humility, and a love so apparent you could almost touch it.

The amazing thing is, if you put this same man in a football stadium with a hundred thousand people and a million more distractions, he still knelt down after Communion, closed his eyes, and went to that place deep within him where he connected with God. He allowed nothing to distract him from his prayer. It was from that place that he lived his life.

Find that place within you. If you do nothing else in your life, find that place and start to live your life from there. I pray I can visit that place within me and go there more and more frequently.

Whatever name you give him, whether it be Wujek, Karol Wojtyla, Papa, John Paul II, or His Holiness, he was first and foremost a man of prayer. His primary concern was doing the will of God in his own life and encouraging others to do the same. To try to understand him separate from his spirituality is at best a waste of time.

He was a sign of hope and of contradiction. He was priest, prophet, and pope. John Paul II was a man perfectly suited to his era, and yet he was a man before his time. It will take centuries for the collective human consciousness to understand and truly appreciate his depth, insight, wisdom, and worldview.

He conducted and carried himself in such a way that you couldn't help but have ultimate respect for him, even if you disagreed with his point of view. Within him, he carried a truth and a wisdom that were so apparent that people of all religious beliefs and those of no religious belief were awed by his presence.

He was a living example of God's paradox at the dawn of the twenty-first century. Toward the end of his life, he was so old and so physically weak, yet God continued to use him as a powerful instrument of his love in the world (cf. 1 Corinthians 1:27).

At every moment of his life, from his earliest childhood, all those who encountered him were able to see his star rising. Those close to him knew it would happen, but when, where, and in what way, nobody knew. They waited with anticipation, and having waited so patiently, none were disappointed.

On April 2, 2005, at eighty-four years of age, Pope John Paul II died in Rome. He is universally acknowledged as one of the most influential leaders of the twentieth and early twenty-first centuries. He worked tirelessly to build a moral foundation in the modern world, played a critical role in overthrowing Communism and fostering peace, and was constantly reaching out to heal historic rifts. But more than this, he was a bright light in the midst of darkness. He was an expression of authenticity in a world filled with men, women, and children who yearn for the authentic.

Everywhere John Paul II went he captured the imaginations and intrigued the hearts of people of all faiths. In the days following his death the whole world turned its attention to Rome. People lined up in the streets for days just to pay their respects to his body for a moment. Even the secular media became enamored with the life and story of this great man.

The life that Jesus invites us to live has an overwhelming power to influence the world in every place and in every time. Karol Wojtyla demonstrated with his life that our age is no different.

• Taking the Gospel Seriously •

Francis of Assisi, Mother Teresa, John Vianney, Thomas More, and John Paul II are just five examples drawn from hundreds—no, thousands—of men and women who over the past two thousand years have taken the Gospel seriously. In their lives, you can catch a glimpse of how yours will unfold if you begin to take the life and teachings of Jesus seriously.

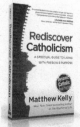

Chapter Nine

WHAT SETS THEM APART?

What is it that sets those who achieve extraordinary things apart from the rest of us? Some people would tell you it is mere chance, that they simply found themselves in the right place at the right time. Others will tell you that these favored few had better connections with people of power and influence. Some people believe that God has favorites and these men and women are his chosen ones.

Do not allow your heart and mind to be deceived. There are two great differences between the heroes, leaders, champions, and saints that fill the history books and the rest of us. In the first place, they tended to have a singleness of purpose that penetrated every activity of their lives. And in the second place, they formed habits that helped them to achieve their goal. These weren't the mindless habits that are acquired by choosing the path of least resistance and maximum pleasure, but the life-giving habits that lead to excellence and holiness.

• Singleness of Purpose •

As you study the lives of extraordinary people, you will discover that they are all marked by these two qualities. It doesn't matter if it is Bill Gates, Michael Jordan, or Mother Teresa; these characteristics can be found in each of their lives. Bill Gates wanted to dominate the software industry. He clearly defined his goal and thus had singleness of purpose. Then he developed habits in his life that would help him achieve his goal. Michael Jordan wanted to become the greatest basketball player in history. He had a clearly defined goal, a singleness of purpose. He did the things that moved him toward his goal and didn't do the things that didn't move him toward his goal. The same is true of Mother Teresa and of all the saints that honor the pages of Christian history. Mother Teresa wanted to love God with all her heart in every moment of every day. She clearly defined her goal and allowed this singleness of purpose to penetrate the everyday activities of her life.

It matters not whether it is in the field of business, sports, or spirituality. The same principles apply. They are the fundamentals of human excellence.

You may object, saying, "To dominate the software industry or be the greatest basketball player in history are not the noblest goals." This is true. The question now becomes, "What is your goal?" Do you even have a clearly stated goal? Do you have this singleness of purpose that gives focus to a person's life and allows him or her to excel beyond imagining?

This singleness of purpose will save you from wasting your life in shallow and superficial activities that mean almost nothing to anyone and will mean even less one hundred years from now. Imagine how many people wanted to distract Michael Jordan from practicing basketball. Imagine how many nights his friends wanted him to go out and party and he didn't, either because he had to practice or because he had to get up early the next morning for practice. Imagine how many people tried to distract Bill Gates from building Microsoft when he was in his late teens and early twenties. Similarly, imagine how many people tried to distract Mother Teresa from her prayer time or from her work with the poorest of the poor.

When you have singleness of purpose, everything else is embraced or discarded according to whether or not it moves you in the direction of your goal. When you don't have this singleness of purpose, you get lost in the tossing and turning of daily life.

The whole world will get out of the way for the man who knows where he is going. For the man who does not, the world becomes a playground filled with distractions and nothingness.

It was precisely with this in mind that Ignatius of Loyola established his First Principle and Foundation:

Man is created to praise, reverence, and serve God our Lord, and by this means to save his soul.

The other things on the face of the earth are created for man to help him in attaining the end for which he is created.

Hence, man is to make use of them in as far as they help him in the attainment of his end, and he must rid himself of them in as far as they prove a hindrance to him.

Therefore, we must make ourselves indifferent to all created things, as far as we are allowed free choice and are not under any prohibition. Consequently, as far as we are concerned, we should not prefer health to sickness, riches to poverty, honor to dishonor, a long life to a short life. The same holds for all other things.

Our one desire and choice should be what is more conducive to the end for which we are created.

So what will be your goal? Upon what will you fix yourself with singleness of purpose? All of Bill Gates's work and money have value only inasmuch as they help him to become the-best-version-of-himself. All of Michael Jordan's training and playing, fame and fortune have value only inasmuch as they help him become the-best-version-of-himself. Mother Teresa chose the better path and the ultimate goal. Her one desire was for union with God. She fixed her singleness of purpose on God and a life of sanctity. What does sanctity mean? To become a saint. What does that mean? To love God by seeking his will and becoming all God created you to be—the-best-version-of-yourself.

This singleness of purpose, this goal, is very important. Every day you and I make hundreds of decisions, some of them large and some of them small. If you have this singleness of purpose, decision-making becomes much easier. The saints simply asked themselves, "What is God's will for this moment?" If they concluded that something would help them draw nearer to God and the-best-version-of-themselves God desired them to be, then they embraced it. If they decided that it wouldn't, then they turned their backs on it regardless of how alluring the opportunity was. Singleness of purpose provides a rare clarity in a world of obscurity.

• The Will of God •

It sounds so simple to say, "Just do the will of God." It is simple and there is beauty and genius in simplicity, but simple and easy are not the same. In many things, perhaps in most things, the will of God is easily known. If we accept that we should love God and neighbor, a great many of life's choices become clear: We should not steal, murder, or covet our neighbor's husband or wife. If we accept that God has not created us to be some second-rate version of ourselves, but that God yearns for us to become the-best-version-of-ourselves, then a great many more of life's choices become very clear—perhaps clearer than we would like. Should we work out or watch endless hours of television? It is easy to see God's will in the context of his desire for us to become all he created us to be.

But there are some decisions, often the most important ones, that do not fall into either of these categories. And often, these are the biggest decisions of our lives. Perhaps you are deciding whether to be a nurse or a teacher. You can love God and neighbor in both of these professions. You can become a-better-version-of-yourself in both of these professions. But which is God calling you to? In *The Rhythm of Life* I explained that God speaks to us all in what I call the three ordinary voices of God. They are legitimate needs, deepest desires, and talents. God has given us legitimate needs, dreams and desires, and talents and abilities to help us understand how we might best make a unique contribution. But even after thoroughly examining these it may still not be clear what God's will is for our lives.

A priest once asked Mother Teresa if she would pray that God would give him clarity in a choice he had to make. She told him, "God may never give you clarity. All you can do is trust."

Sometimes we think we know for sure, sometimes we think we are pretty sure, and sometimes all we can do is trust. We can know that we are trying to love God and neighbor. We can know that a choice can help us become a-better-version-of-ourselves. We can know that a certain choice is a good fit for our legitimate needs, our unique talents, and our deepest desires. But we won't necessarily know that something is the will of God. Then, all we can do is trust.

The saints tried in each moment to align themselves with the will of God. It was this synthesis and the surrender of their own individual will to the will of God that made them saints. In this modern era, people have been seduced by the dark lie that it is impossible to know the will of God. This is a diabolical lie of unfathomable proportions, because it separates us from our essential purpose and leads us down the road to misery and despair. The bright truth is that God sent the Holy Spirit to guide us toward his will in every moment of every day.

The will of God in the broadest sense is that you become the-best-version-of-yourself, that version of you that most perfectly allows God to come into the world through you. God doesn't want to control you, or manipulate you, or stifle you, or force you to do things you don't want to do. If that were God's desire, then he would not have given you free will. God wants you to become all you can be, and in the process he wants you to experience the greatest mystery of them all: love. God invites you to embark on the adventure of unveiling and actualizing your unimagined potential. The challenge is to come before God with open hands as Henri Nouwen invited us to, and say, *Lord, this is what I have. Take whatever you want to take from me and give me whatever you want to give me.* God invites you to empty yourself so that he can fill you up. This is the adventure of salvation, and we make this journey by learning to love God, neighbor, self, and, indeed, life. This is the journey of the soul and the quest for love. This is the great task life lays before us.

The will of God is not as mysterious as many make it out to be. You come home from work and you have a choice: You can sit on the couch in front of the TV with a large bag of potato chips and some beer, or you can go for a run. Which will help you become the-best-version-of-yourself? Every situation can be approached with this question.

In his first letter to the Thessalonians, Paul addresses this same question, writing, "This is the will of God: that you be saints." (1 Thessalonians 4:3) God wants you to be a saint and it is critical for modern Catholics to hear this call to sanctity. We all need to be reminded that holiness is possible. The will of God can be discovered and embraced, and this is a truth that both encourages and challenges us at the same time. But in order to allow this truth to animate our lives, we need to set aside our prejudices against the idea of holiness and embrace a new vision of what it truly means.

The caricatures of holiness that modern society has created are not authentic models of holiness. Men and women listening to the voice of God in their lives, allowing the Spirit to guide them, seeking God's will, becoming the-best-version-of-themselves—that is holiness. The world and the Church are desperately in need of this authentic striving for holiness.

As we discussed earlier, holiness is as simple as knowing when to say yes and when to say no. But in order to say no to anything, you have to have a "deeper yes." It is this deeper yes that most of us lack. The spiritual life, among other things, gives us clarity about what matters most. Defining our goal—to live a life of holiness by becoming the-best-version-of-ourselves and helping others to do the same—creates a singleness of purpose and the deeper yes necessary to turn our backs on so many of the self-destructive and superficial activities of this modern culture.

This is precisely what sets the saints apart from the masses of humanity marching through history. They fixed their gaze on God. They listened to the voice of God in their lives. They resolved to cooperate with God in the fulfillment of his will on earth. They discovered their essential purpose and they fixed the attention of their thoughts, words, and actions on leading a life of holiness. They saw each moment as an opportunity to do the will of God. They knew that what God did in them was more important than anything they could ever do themselves. And as a result of these defining characteristics they blossomed and became all God had created them to be. That is the value of singleness of purpose in the Christian life, and it is written on each of their lives.

One of my favorite passages from the Bible affirms my belief that the will of God is not as much of a mystery as we make it out to be. It comes from the book of Micah, "You have been told what is good and what Yahweh wants of you. Only this, that you live justly, love tenderly, and walk humbly with your God." (Micah 6:8)

In my own life, I know justice from injustice. I suspect you do also. We may not always act justly, but we know the just path even when we do not choose it. We know what is just and what is not in the circumstances of our own lives. We may not know what is just and right in matters of international politics, but few of us are in positions that require us to make those decisions. And the same God who shows you what is just and unjust in your life also shows presidents, kings, and commanders what is just and unjust. The challenge is not in the knowing—our hearts are faithful in directing us when we listen; the challenge is in surrendering our prideful and selfish wills to the will of God.

The second directive from this passage in Micah is that we love tenderly. In the same way that you and I know what is just, we also know how to love tenderly. In every situation, we can choose love or selfishness, love or pride, love or gluttony, love or jealousy, love or lust. . . . We know how to love tenderly.

Finally, the prophet speaks of walking humbly with God. It is cited last, but it is in fact primary, because it is walking humbly with God that makes justice and love possible in our lives. Without God alive within us and working through us, you and I would not be capable of love or justice. Walking humbly with God means allowing God your Father to take you by the hand and lead you. But too often we want to race off ahead of our loving Father, tearing our hand from his and running frantically in all directions. We don't want to miss anything. We want to experience everything that this life has to offer, so we run here and there in search of happiness—but we are always left yearning for something more. If we will walk humbly with our God, he will lead us by the hand to exactly who and what we need, to those people, things, and experiences he has designed and intended just for us, and this alone will be the cause of our deep fulfillment and happiness.

But this walking humbly with God is difficult. To achieve it, it is essential that we acquire the habits of recollection and self-possession. Let me use another illustration to further our understanding of this point. How hard is it to walk humbly with God? It is as if I lit a candle and gave it to you to hold, and told you to take it everywhere you go and never let it be blown out. You would have to protect it, wouldn't you? You would have to move slowly, thoughtfully, and deliberately. It would require conscious living: thoughts, words, and actions that spring from an awareness of who we are and what we are here for.

This is what is required to walk humbly with God. The candle is within you. When you have learned to carry and protect it, then you will be able to live justly—to choose what is good, just, true, and noble in every situation—and love tenderly.

The candle is within you. Protect it. Don't let the world blow it out.

The will of God is that you become the-best-version-of-yourself, or in classical spiritual language, that you live a life of holiness and become a saint. This is your essential purpose and the more you allow your life to center on this purpose the more you will experience the joy that is the aroma of holiness.

• How Would You Like Your Life to Change? •

Apart from this singleness of purpose, there is one other sign that separates men and women of extraordinary achievement from those who get devoured by mediocrity and superficiality. While some may still be arguing that the difference between those who excel and those who don't is luck or chance, I can tell you with absolute certainty that it is not. The difference is that those who excel just have better habits. If you dissect their lives, you discover that they fill their days, weeks, and months with habits that are helping them to excel in their chosen field and become the-best-version-of-themselves. Most people fill their lives with habits that are self-destructive and that cause them to become less than God created them to be.

It is interesting and important to note that the habits that diminish us can be acquired with virtually no effort and are usually the result of acting without any real thought, while the habits that allow us to celebrate and defend the-best-version-of-ourselves require real effort and an openness to the grace of God. These habits could include eating foods that respect and fuel the body, working out on a regular basis, being patient with people when they frustrate you, and making time for prayer and reflection each day.

What are your habits? What are the things you do every day, every week, every month? Are your habits helping you become a-better-version-of-yourself or are they self-diminishing?

If you can tell me what your habits are, I can tell you what sort of person you are. Socrates, Aristotle, Thomas Aquinas, and Ignatius of Loyola established that habits create character. Good habits create good character, and bad habits create poor character. From a person's habits it is easy to deduce what his or her future will be like, because habits create character, and your character is your destiny. The good character created by good habits in turn creates a prosperous future. The bad character created by bad habits in turn creates misery in your future. Your character is your destiny in the workplace, in relationships, and in eternity. What are your habits?

The good news is we can change our habits.

What new habits are you trying to form in your life right now? If you can tell me, I can tell you how your future will be different from your past, because our lives change when our habits change.

How would you like your life to be different this year than it was last year? How will this change come about? Most people live in the misguided fantasy that one day they will wake up and suddenly their lives will be magically different. It doesn't happen. These people grow old and die waiting. Others live in the illusion that if they make more money, get a new car, buy a bigger house, get a promotion, or vacation in the Bahamas, then their lives will change. This doesn't work either.

Our lives change when our habits change.

Take a few minutes right now. Put this book down. Find a piece of paper and write down your habits. Think about it. What are the things you do every day, every week, every month? Now go down the list and ask yourself, "Which of these habits are helping me to become the-best-version-of-myself? And which of the habits are self-destructive?"

Now, you tell me: What sort of person are you? What does your future look like?

If you want your future to be different from your past, there is only one way: Change your habits. Our lives change when our habits change. Think about all the heroes, leaders, champions, and saints. What set them apart from their peers? They just had better habits. Theirs were not the self-destructive type that we effortlessly pick up by traveling the path of least resistance. Their habits were helping them to become the-best-version-of-themselves, and they were acquired intentionally through the effort of discipline.

Chapter Ten

THEIR ATTRACTION AND INFLUENCE

There is nothing more beautiful in this life than a good friendship. When I was a teenager, my father held out his right hand, spread his five fingers wide, and said to me, "If you find five true friends in your lifetime, you will have lived a life infinitely blessed." At the time, I thought it was a little strange, because I had so many friends, but as the years have passed, my father's wisdom has become more and more apparent.

• Friendship •

This is a question I have pondered for years: What constitutes a true friend? Perhaps it would be helpful for you to pause for a moment and reflect. Who are your true friends? What makes them good friends?

As a child, I thought friendship was about hanging out together all the time and sticking up for each other when others were critical or cruel. In my adolescence, I thought a true friend was someone who liked everything you liked and never did anything to upset you. But as an adult, I have learned that the defining characteristic of true friendship is someone who encourages you to be all you can be and challenges you to become the-best-version-of-yourself. It is these people who tend to energize and invigorate us. What types of people do you like being with? What types of people energize you?

Throughout my years of travel there have always been certain people I have looked forward to seeing in different cities. Some days as I am walking through the airport I look at the list of flights departing and the cities they are going to. Each city brings with it memories of people who energize and inspire me, and often I find myself wishing I was going to a city where I have a great friend. One of the biggest challenges of my life is that my friends are spread all over the world, and many of them I get to see very rarely.

I love being around people who are striving to love God and better themselves. They energize me. They inspire me. They challenge me. They make me want to be a better person.

This is true friendship. A true friend brings the best out of his or her friends. You cannot convince me that someone who is not helping you to become the-best-version-of-yourself is a good friend.

For this reason, when I have time to spend with friends, I try to surround myself with people who make me want to be a better person. I admit they are not easy to find, but when you do find them, they are more precious than any treasure or pleasure this world has to offer.

If you want a litmus test for choosing friends, use this question: Will spending time with this person make me a better person?

• Spiritual Friends and Loneliness •

I try to apply this truth not only to my social life but also to my spiritual life. This is why the saints are such good friends. They encourage us to love God and neighbor more fully and challenge us to use the daily events of our lives to become a-better-version-of-ourselves. But the real beauty is found in their method: They don't preach endless sermons, and they don't try to impose their views on others—they challenge, inspire, and encourage us simply by living their own lives to the fullest. That is the social dynamic of holiness. It is attractive and it is contagious.

If you and I sit down at lunch and you order soup and a salad, it makes me think twice about ordering a double bacon cheeseburger and fries. If my friends are going to the gym after work, I feel that inner nudge to work out myself. If a colleague is honest and humble about a mistake he has made, I am humbled by his example.

Goodness is contagious. The problem is, so is evil. The challenge for you and me, as Christians in the midst of the modern world, is to be examples of good living.

None of us realize how much we influence others. Everything you do, people are watching, and everything you say, people are listening to. The influence of your words and actions is contributing to the way they live their lives. In *A Call to Joy,* I wrote, "You will learn more from your friends than you ever will from books. Choose your friends wisely."

This is why the saints are such treasures. They may have lived in other places and times, but they can be true friends to you and me today. I'd rather spend a couple of hours with Francis of Assisi and Teresa of Avila than with some of my contemporaries getting drunk on a Friday night. I'd much rather spend time with dead people who inspire me to celebrate the-best-version-of-myself than with living people who lead me to be just a shadow of all God created me to be. I promise you, it is better to spend time with dead people who bring you to life than with live people who lead you to death.

From time to time, I meet people who are dating a person they know they don't want to spend the rest of their lives with. If you ask them why, they say it is because they don't like being alone. I have learned it is better to be alone than to be with the wrong person.

Don't be afraid of your loneliness. Use it as an opportunity to befriend people who inspire you. Harness your loneliness as a chance to befriend the saints.

• Foster This Spirit •

Let us begin today to develop this striving to love God and better ourselves. Each morning when I am showering, I ask myself the same question: What will it take today for me to become the better person I know I can be? Then I go through the four major areas of life: physical, emotional, intellectual, and spiritual. In each of these areas, I try to focus on one thing I can do that day to grow.

It is the transformation that energizes us and fills our lives with passion and enthusiasm. We are most fully alive when we are becoming a-better-version-of-ourselves.

Focus on developing the spirit of transformation in your life. When you are choosing friends, choose those who are striving to better themselves. And if you are young and single, and sense you are called to marriage, seek a soul mate, a spouse, a companion for the journey who has this quality.

• Bright Lights •

The saints were remarkable men and women, but surprisingly what made them remarkable was rarely anything too spectacular. What made them extraordinary was the ordinary. They strove to grow in virtue through the ordinary things of everyday life. If they were caring for the sick they were growing in humility. When they were educating children they were growing in patience. As Saint Therese of Lisieux. said, "Do the little things with great love."

There is something ultimately attractive about holiness. When holiness emerges in any place and time, all men and women of good will are inspired. What is it that makes them so attractive? Perhaps it is their humble surrender to the will of God and the joy that emerges from that surrender. Perhaps it is the many virtues that they acquire along the way: patience, kindness, humility, gentleness, forgiveness, and love. Or is it their desire to explore their God-given potential? This quality is incredibly attractive and ultimately inspiring. Or perhaps it is that they are not proud and arrogant about who they are and what they have done. Or maybe it's just that they are focused on loving God and neighbor by becoming the-best-version-of-themselves. I suspect it is some combination of all of these.

I walked into a bookstore recently and sitting on the shelves in the front of the store were several large coffee-table books. One in particular caught my eye, so I walked over to have a look. For the next ten minutes, I flipped through the pages of two books, glancing at the pictures, and a great fire was fanned in my heart. One was about the life of Mother Teresa and the other about the life of John Paul II. The world has a great need for the example of authentic lives because we all need to be inspired. We need to be reminded of what is possible. These people have allowed God to fill them with his love, and the glow of that love alive in them is blinding. The power of their lives and the greatness of their spirits cannot be adequately put into words. But occasionally, in the memory of an event in their lives, or in the story a photo tells, we catch a glimpse.

Just passing through those pages, glancing at the pictures, elevated my heart and made my spirit soar. Just looking at those pictures made me want to be a better person—I didn't even read a word. That is the power of these great lives.

They are the personification of that phrase from Matthew's Gospel: *luceat lux vestra,* "let your light shine." (Matthew 5:16) And because these men and woman have allowed God to shine so powerfully through them, people of all faiths gasp in awe in their presence.

Even a blind man knows when he is in the presence of a bright light.

There is nothing more attractive than holiness. Throughout history, wherever men and women of holiness have lived, the Church has blossomed. This is the answer to all of our questions and the solution to all of our problems: holiness of life.

Chapter Eleven

WHO WILL BE NEXT?

The stage is set. The modern world awaits the emergence of a handful of spiritual heroes who will inspire and mobilize enormous numbers of people toward a more Christ-centered way of living.

The fruit is ripe on the vine. The question is not: *Will* God raise up great saints in our own day and age? The question is: *Whom* will God raise up? It will be those you least expect and those who make themselves available to him.

Throughout history, the great transformations and movements within the Church have always come from outside the expected channels. First man creates a problem, and then God, in his infinite wisdom, provides a solution. If the problems today are greater than ever before, then God will raise up saints greater than ever before.

You can be certain of one thing: As dark and as grim as things may seem for the Church at times, these circumstances will conspire to produce a group of modern saints. God will use these circumstances to call forth men and women who will shadow the saints of ages past.

The Church and the world need saints—people willing to acknowledge God's will for their lives, men and women dedicated to prayer and striving for virtue. We need great spiritual masters to teach us the way of holiness.

Beyond the Church, our whole culture is desperately in need of a return to virtue. But apart from striving for virtue in our own lives, how can we help God raise up this next generation of spiritual leaders?

• To Whom Does the Future Belong? •

As we look at where we are and where we are going, both as a Church and as a human family, we should ask ourselves: Who and what will be the greatest influences in determining the future? To whom does the future belong? What will our society be like twenty, fifty, or one hundred years from today?

The most powerful and influential position in any society is that of the storyteller. Storytellers are not just the mythical cultural icons who dress up on Thursday afternoons and read stories to your children in local libraries and bookstores. Musicians are storytellers; politicians are storytellers. Screenplay writers and business leaders are storytellers. Teachers, preachers, nurses, lawyers, priests, scientists, salespeople, artists, mothers, fathers, poets, philosophers, brothers, sisters, babysitters, grandparents . . . we are all storytellers.

The future belongs to the storytellers and it belongs to us. What will it be like? Well, that depends very much on the stories we tell, the stories we listen to, and the stories we live.

Stories have a remarkable ability to cut through the clutter and confusion and bring clarity to our hearts and minds. Stories remind us of our hopes, values, and dreams. They sneak beyond the barriers of our prejudices to soften our hearts to receive the truth. Great periods in history emerge when great stories are told and lived. Stories are history that form the future; they are prophecies set in the past.

Never underestimate the importance of stories. They play a crucial role in the life of a person and in the life of a society. They are as essential as the air we breathe and the water we drink. Stories captivate our imaginations, enchant our minds, and empower our spirits. They introduce us to who we are and who we are capable of being. Stories change our lives.

If you wish to poison a nation, poison the stories that nation listens to. If you wish to win people over to your team or to your point of view, do not go to war or argue with them—tell them a story.

All great leaders understand the persuasive and inspirational power of stories. When did you last hear a great speech that didn't contain a story?

A story can do anything: win a war, lose a war, heal the sick, encourage the discouraged, comfort the oppressed, inspire a revolution, transform an enemy into a friend, elevate the consciousness of the people, build empires, inspire love, even reshape the spiritual temperament of a whole age.

Sixty-five percent of the Gospels are stories, or parables. One hundred percent of the Gospels is the story of Jesus Christ—and it is the most influential story ever told.

The future belongs to the storytellers, and we are the storytellers. What type of stories are we telling? Because I can promise you with absolute certitude that the stories we tell today are forming the future.

• Shame on Us •

If we wish to raise up a new generation of saints, there are two indispensable ingredients. First, and always first, we must strive to grow in holiness, to become more perfectly the person God created us to be. And second, we must tell the stories of the champions and heroes of Christianity who have gone before us.

There is no medium more powerful than stories to convey a message. We have the stories, but we are not sharing them. Our two-thousand-year Catholic history is full of extraordinary stories about ordinary people who opened their hearts to God and allowed the life, teachings, and person of Jesus Christ to transform them. These men and women are the heroes and heroines of our faith; they are a rare gift of inspiration, and we have failed as a Church to tell their stories. Shame on us.

Pick up a photo book about Padre Pio. Don't even read the words; just look at the pictures, and you will have goose bumps. Pick up a book about Mother Teresa or Fulton Sheen and flip through the photos, and you will have a tingling sensation up and down your spine. Read George Weigel's biography of John Paul II and you will have a life-changing experience. Read Robert Bolt's *A Man for All Seasons,* or watch the movie, and you will be challenged to become the-best-version-of-yourself.

Read your children stories of the saints.

It is true our modern culture is guilty of telling horrific and disdainful stories that promote violence, sexual promiscuity, and every manner of sin known to man. It is true that the modern media has launched an attack on Catholicism at this time in history. It is also true that in this age of anti-prejudice, the only socially acceptable prejudice is to be anti-Catholic. But we have contributed to all these problems because, as a family of faith, we are guilty of not telling the great stories of our spiritual ancestors, the saints.

The lives of the saints are stories of virtue and character, and if we would read them, tell them, and listen to them over and over again, our lives would become examples of that same virtue and character.

We become the stories we listen to.

• What Are You Willing to Give Your Life For? •

I once heard a story about Abraham Lincoln during the Civil War. He had called for one of the men under his command who had an excellent reputation. Lincoln needed the soldier to deliver a message to another battalion that was dangerously positioned on the other side of the enemy. If both battalions could be coordinated to attack the opposition at the same time, their position would become a strategic advantage.

When the young man arrived, without disclosing the nature of the assignment, Lincoln explained that he had a very dangerous mission and asked the soldier if he would be willing to take on such a commission.

The soldier said, "I am willing to die for our cause."

Lincoln replied, "I have twenty-five thousand men who are willing to die for the cause. What I need is one who is willing to live for it."

Throughout the history of Christianity men and women have died for their faith. Even today there are many parts of the world where members of our Catholic family are politically persecuted, physically tortured, and sometimes executed just because they are Catholic. So it is important for us not to set martyrdom aside as something that took place only in early Christian times. But you and I, here in America, in Australia, and in the United Kingdom, are not called to die for our faith. We are called to live for it. The modern Church desperately needs men and women who are willing to live for the faith.

What are you willing to live for?

Just before her death, Joan of Arc wrote, "I know this now. Every man gives his life for what he believes. Every woman gives her life for what she believes. Sometimes people believe in little or nothing, and yet they give their lives to that little or nothing. One life is all we have, and we live it as we believe in living it and then it's gone. But to surrender what you are and to live without belief is more terrible than dying—even more terrible than dying young."

What are you willing to give your life for? There are two ways to interpret the question, but I am not asking what you are willing to die for. I am wondering what you are willing to live for. What are you willing to give your life for? Not in death or martyrdom, but in life. What great cause are you willing to support with the moments of your life?

On September 11, 2001, we learned a lesson that history has taught us many times before: The most powerful people in history are those who are willing to give everything. The nineteen hijackers were willing to give everything to complete their mission. In every age, on both sides of the fence of good and evil, the most powerful agents of change are those people willing to give all their time, effort, and energy without reserve to the cause they deem worthy of their lives. We saw this in the hijackers and we saw this in Hitler. But we also see it in Francis of Assisi and Mother Teresa, in mothers who selflessly raise their children, in fathers who work tirelessly each day to support their families, in the priests who serve in our parishes, and in countless other heroic men and women throughout history who have given their lives to the service of God, humanity, and the Gospel. The question I ask again is: What are *you* willing to give *your* life for?

Perhaps a better place to start is with the question "What are you giving your life to today?" When you examine the way you spend your days and weeks, to what are you contributing your time, efforts, energy, and talents?

As a teenager, I used to play a lot of golf at a club not far from where we lived. I remember how some men would spend their whole lives at the golf club. There were one or two in particular whose lives seemed to revolve around the life of the club. They would play, but they were also on the board.

They would hang around in the clubhouse, and from time to time I would even see them pulling weeds or trimming the plants that surrounded the first tee. Even as a child, I remember thinking that there must be something lacking in them to spend their lives this way. But I suppose we all need something to live for, something to get out of bed for each day, and for them it was the golf club.

Do you ever think about dying? Whenever I am confronted with the reality and inevitability of death it heightens my awareness of how brief and precious my time here on earth is. Sometimes it is the death of a friend, at other times it is a news story, or perhaps it is just a bumpy ride on a plane. These events help me to treasure my own life more and more with each passing day. But they also challenge me to reassess the way I am spending the time, effort, and energies that are my life. I am more intimately aware than ever before that we all waste life. We waste it one day at time—a day here and a day there—or an hour at a time. We waste time drowning in unforgiveness. We waste time immersed in frivolous or irresponsible activities. We waste time being lazy and procrastinating. We waste time. Life is passing us by.

Life is wonderful but brief. Each day is filled with unimaginable potential. The life God invites us to allows us to live each moment consciously and with vibrant enthusiasm.

Within each of us there is a light. It is the light of God, and when it shines it reflects not only the wonder of God but also the greatness of the human spirit. We live in difficult times. I pray that we never become fearful, but rather we turn our focus to nurturing the light within us. I hope we allow that light within us to be nourished and to grow. Darkness has one enemy that it can never defeat, and that is light. Let your light shine!

As we reflect on our brief and precious lives, let us also remember that they are but a transition to a long and blissful eternity. Teresa of Avila encourages us, "Remember you have only one soul; that you have only one death to die; that you have only one life, which is short and has to be lived by you alone; and there is only one glory, which is eternal. If you do this, there will be a great many things about which you care nothing."

• Finding Your Place •

It is for you now to find your place in the history of humanity. Nobody can do it for you. It is a work that will be left undone unless you do it yourself. The world doesn't need another Mother Teresa. The Church doesn't need another Francis of Assisi. The world needs you. The Church needs you. Mother Teresa had a role to play in God's plan, and she played it. Francis had a mission to fulfill in God's plan, and he fulfilled it. Now it falls to you to find your role, your place. Who will be next? You. You will be next if you make yourself available to God.

Find your place in salvation history. Be a saint. Be yourself. Perfectly yourself.

The best thing you can do for yourself is to become the-best-version-of-yourself. The best thing you can do for your spouse, your children, your friends, your Church, your nation, and God is to become the-best-version-of-yourself.

Catholicism is not a lifeless set of rules and regulations; it is a lifestyle. Catholicism is a dynamic way of life designed by God to help you explore your incredible potential.

• Where Do We Start? •

We are at a turning point in human history. Most people do not recognize it because they are so consumed with their own selfish desires and the trivial happenings of their daily lives. Nonetheless, we are at a turning point. What is needed is a handful of great spiritual leaders to direct the human family during this critical period of transition. The modern western empire is in decline. It will soon die. It's not the end of the world. It's not the end of humanity. It's just the beginning of a new era. A new civilization will emerge. And what will this new civilization be like? That is entirely up to the stories we tell, listen to, and live.

Pope Benedict XVI wrote, "The crucial question is whether there are saints who . . . are ready to effect something new and living." As Christians, we are called to holiness, a life of prayer and virtue. We are called to be saints. I pray God will grant us generous spirits.

This commission is certainly a great task. A little self-reflection signals to us clearly how far we have to go. But don't allow yourself to become discouraged. Familiarize yourself with the lives of the saints. They were not born saints. They did not become saints overnight. In most cases, they didn't set out to do anything extraordinary, and they didn't set out to change the world. These extraordinary souls were very much focused on the ordinary. They allowed the everyday activities of their lives to transform them. They saw every event as an opportunity to grow in virtue. And as a result, they lived extraordinary lives that inspired the people of their time and the people of centuries to come. They may seem larger than life, but most of them found their greatness by performing simple daily tasks with love.

Who will be next? You. You and I, I pray. Where do we start? At the beginning, with ourselves, today. Francis of Assisi shared the secret with his brothers and sisters: "First do what is necessary. Then do what is possible. And before you know it, you will be doing the impossible."

If not you, then who? What will your excuse be? What are you afraid of? What is holding you back from being all you can be? Whatever it is, allow these words from Marianne Williamson to give you courage to struggle anew and overcome whatever it is that holds you back:

Our deepest fear is not that we are inadequate. Our deepest fear is that we are powerful beyond measure. It is our light, not our darkness that most frightens us. We ask ourselves, Who am I to be brilliant, gorgeous, talented and fabulous? Actually, Who are you not to be? You are a child of God. Your playing small doesn't serve the world. There is nothing enlightened about shrinking so that other people won't feel insecure around you. We are born to make manifest the glory of God that is within us. It is not just in some of us, it is in everyone. And as we let our own light shine, we unconsciously give other people permission to do the same. As we are liberated from our own fear, our presence automatically liberates others.

If you could change anything about the world, what would it be? The world is the way it is today because of people like you and me. Our thoughts, words, actions, and inaction have all contributed to create the world of today.

What would the world be like if we multiplied your life by seven billion?

To have a global and historic impact, act locally. Whatever change you desire for the world, create that change in your own life. You are here for a purpose. Seek it out. Hunt it down. The greatest misery is to be purposeless. The great depression of our age is not economic, but spiritual. Our spiritual poverty is rooted in our purposelessness.

As I have written the pages that make up this chapter, the words of John Henry Newman have echoed in my heart:

God has created me to do him some definite service. He has committed some work to me which he has not committed to another. I have my mission. I may never know it in this life, but I shall be told it in the next. I am a link in a chain, a bond of connection between persons. He has not created me for naught. I shall do good—I shall do his work. I shall be an angel of peace, a preacher of truth in my own place while not intending it, if I do but keep his commandments. Therefore I will trust him, whatever I am, I can never be thrown away. If I am in sickness, my sickness may serve him. In perplexity, my perplexity may serve him. If I am in sorrow, my sorrow may serve him. He does nothing in vain. He knows what he is about. He may take away my friends. He may throw me among strangers. He may make me feel desolate, make my spirits sink, hide my future from me—still, HE KNOWS WHAT HE IS ABOUT.

Only one thing is necessary for Catholicism to flourish: authentic lives. Throughout history, wherever you find men and women genuinely striving to live the Christian life, the Church has always thrived. If we wish to speak effectively to the modern world about God, the Christian life, and the Catholic Church, we must be thriving, blossoming, and flourishing in that life.

Part Three

THE SEVEN PILLARS OF CATHOLIC SPIRITUALITY

• • •

Yesterday I was visiting a friend in Atlanta. He lives in a beautiful neighborhood and as we drove past these magnificent homes, one after another, I began to ask myself, "If your spiritual life were a house, what would it be like?"

I would like to place the question before you now. If *your* spiritual life were a house, what would it be like? What street would it be on? What part of town would it be in? What would it look like? Would it be a house or a home? Is it in need of renovations? Is it peaceful, noisy, distracting, well organized, messy?

I must admit, these questions make me a little uncomfortable, but at the same time, they ignite a desire deep within me to begin the spiritual renovations that are necessary at this time in my life. Wherever you are in your spiritual journey, it is my sincerest hope that the next seven chapters will help you to begin the work you need to do on your spiritual life. Whether you are in need of a complete spiritual overhaul or some minor renovations, or you are just beginning to build your spiritual life, I hope these pages help you to begin that work.

When I read the Bible it strikes me with alarming importance that in the course of the entire Gospels, the disciples make only one request of Jesus as a group: "Lord, teach us to pray." (Luke 11:1)

The people of every age yearn for God. I yearn for God, though for the longest time I did not recognize it as such. Even now I often confuse my yearning for God with a yearning for other things and experiences. I suspect you have also come to recognize your yearning for God. We have a longing to draw nearer to God, a desire to be in communion with him.

My favorite passage from the *Catechism of the Catholic Church* appears as the first line of the first chapter, and it reads, "The desire for God is written in the human heart, because man is created by God and for God; and God never ceases to draw man to himself. Only in God will he find the truth and happiness he never stops searching for."

The request modern Catholics have of Jesus alive in the Church today is the very same request the disciples presented to the Master: "Teach us to pray."

One of the greatest tragedies of modern Catholicism is that as Catholics we are no longer considered a spiritual people. If you polled people on the streets of any city in America today and asked them to list five words to describe Catholics, I suspect only a small percentage would say *prayerful* or *spiritual*. The tragedy, however, is not how people perceive Catholics, but the possibility that the perception may reflect the reality. It is a generalization, but as Catholics in this modern climate, we tend not to take our spirituality seriously.

The seven pillars of Catholic spirituality that we will discuss in this section combine two thousand years of spiritual wisdom into a handful of spiritual exercises. They may be ancient practices, but don't let that fool you into believing that they are not relevant to your life in the modern world. These practices are dynamic and ever fresh. I don't think it is a coincidence that you find these seven pillars so common in the lives of the saints. Is it not, then, a logical and reasonable conclusion that if we apply these practices consistently to our own lives we will grow in holiness?

Every now and then we read about a natural disaster devastating a city in some part of the world with enormous waves. Watching the television footage, I am always amazed that some trees are able to withstand the wind and waves, while everything else is blown away. How do they do it? With strong, deep roots.

A tree with deep roots can weather any storm. In your life and mine it is only a matter of time before the next storm gets here: an illness, the death of a loved one, unemployment, financial difficulties, a troubled child, a natural disaster, marital strife, or any number of other things. The storms of life are inevitable. The question is not whether there will be another storm. The question is: When will the next storm get here? And when the next storm gets here, it's too late to sink the roots. When the next storm gets here, you either have the roots or you don't.

Sink these roots, the Seven Pillars of Catholic Spirituality, deep into your life and you will weather any storm. But more than that, so much more than surviving the storms of life, you will come to know the abundant life that Jesus invites us to experience here in this life and in eternity.

Our spiritual heritage is rich in wisdom and practice. If we can embrace this heritage and adapt it to the modern context, we will begin again to thrive as the spiritual people God intended us to be—individually and as a Church.

• • •

Chapter Twelve

CONFESSION

In the 1990s I was amazed at the emergence and dominance of two great sporting legends. Michael Jordan and Tiger Woods are arguably the greatest sportsmen in history. Although these icons of modern sport may seem to have nothing to do with Catholicism, I promise you, I intend to explain the connection.

What intrigues me about the success Jordan and Woods have experienced is that the one quality that makes Michael Jordan the greatest basketball player in history is the same quality that makes Tiger Woods the greatest golfer. They play two very different sports that require very different skills and disciplines, yet their extraordinary success can be linked to a singular quality. Let me explain.

As a teenager growing up in North Carolina, Michael Jordan couldn't even make his high school basketball team, yet today he is the greatest basketball player in history. How does that happen? Some people would tell you it was mere luck or freak talent. Others would say he was in the right place and had opportunities others didn't have. Still others would suggest that he had an incredible growth spurt after high school. All of these would be wrong.

Jordan trained harder and longer in high school than anyone else on the team or on the bench. When he didn't make the team he pressed the coach for a reason. Jordan's coach explained that his free throw record was weak. So what did Jordan do? He practiced his free throw. He made five hundred free throws every day for ten years. He didn't *shoot* five hundred free throws; he *made* five hundred. He wouldn't let himself go to bed each night until he had made five hundred free throws. When would you next sleep if you didn't go to bed until you made five hundred free throws?

Jordan increased his skill and earned his place with hard work. Did he have talent? Yes. But he also worked harder to develop his talent than anybody else. When he made it to college basketball, he realized that his fadeaway jump shot was a weakness. So he focused his practice on his fadeaway jump shot until it became one of the high points of his game. By the time he entered the NBA he had mastered it—so much so that it was as if Jordan had invented the shot.

When was the last time you identified a weakness in any area of your life and then systematically set about eradicating it?

Similarly, in 1997 Tiger Woods won the Masters by a record number of strokes. In the world's most prestigious golfing event, in which young players are known for losing their nerve, the twenty-one-year-old demolished a world-class field in such fashion that many began to wonder whether golf would be competitive anymore.

Only weeks later, Woods and his coach announced at a press conference that he was going to take some time off to work on his swing. The press laughed; they thought it was a joke. Woods and his coach then proceeded to explain that they intended to completely deconstruct and reconstruct his golf swing. Baffled, the international press asked why. Woods explained that, with the help of his coach and video footage of his swing, they had discovered a flaw in his swing, which they believed would not stand up under the pressure of a tight match. Before too long, Woods returned to the tour with his new swing to completely dominate the sport like no one else in history.

Now, some people have suggested that I shouldn't speak about Tiger Woods anymore because of the struggles he has had in his personal life. And while he has certainly demonstrated a lack of character in some areas of his life, my reason for writing about him here is unchanged. I would like to be as good at being a Catholic as Tiger Woods is at playing golf. I would like you to be as well. And if Tiger Woods can teach me something about living my faith more fully, I want to learn it. I think every parish could use more parishioners who approach their practice of the faith with the discipline and commitment that Tiger Woods approaches golf with.

Both Michael Jordan and Tiger Woods have an incredible ability to look at their game and identify both their strengths and their weaknesses. Once they have done this, they work tirelessly to make their strengths impenetrable and transform their weaknesses into strengths. A world-class athlete would never even consider the idea of ignoring a weakness. World-class athletes want to know their weaknesses better than anybody else. Where did they get this idea?

Do you think it is the fruit of twentieth-century sports psychology? Do you think Michael Jordan came up with the idea and handed it on to Tiger Woods? Is it an idea that has just been born in the last twenty-five years? The answer to all of these is no.

This process of identifying strengths and weaknesses and transforming weaknesses into strengths is classic Catholic spirituality. For two thousand years, the champions of Christianity, the men and women we call saints, have been going into the classroom of silence, taking a humble and honest look at themselves, and assessing their own strengths and weaknesses. Then, armed with this knowledge, they have bravely set forth to transform their weaknesses into strengths, their vices into virtues. In the classroom of silence, they don't reflect on their basketball game or their golf swing; they reflect on their character. Their search for excellence is the most important of all: the quest for holiness and inner transformation. They understand that who we become is infinitely more important than what we do or what we have.

What are your weaknesses? Do you know? Most people don't want to know. We don't want to think about our weaknesses. We don't want to talk about them, and we certainly don't want anyone else to point them out. This is a classic sign of mediocrity, and this mediocrity has a firm grip on the Church and humanity at this moment in history. The proof is our collective attitude and approach toward Confession, and most people's inability or unwillingness to admit when they are wrong and then apologize. Great men and women want to know their weaknesses. They see those weaknesses as the key to a richer, more abundant future. Wouldn't you rather have God deal with your weaknesses in private than have them dealt with in public?

Your weaknesses are the key to the unimaginable bigger future that God has envisioned for you. Your strengths are probably already bearing all the fruit they can. They will continue to bear those good fruits in your life, but at some point they will begin to plateau. Your richer, more abundant future is intimately linked to your weaknesses.

In order to understand, imagine you are a farmer with one thousand acres of land. Five hundred acres is producing wonderful fruit and an abundant harvest. You have a variety of crops and a small orchard of fruit trees. But the other five hundred acres is completely neglected. This land is overrun with weeds; there are rocks in the field and a couple of abandoned old cars that have grass growing up through them.

Now consider how you want your future to be bigger than your past. You cannot plant your crops an extra time each year. The first five hundred acres is already producing all the fruit it is capable of producing. You could slave on the first five hundred acres and squeeze a little more out of it, increasing the crop size by a fraction. And if that were the only five hundred acres, I would encourage that. But that is not the pathway to your bigger future.

If you genuinely want to build that bigger future, you need to get into that neglected second five hundred acres of land and transform it into producing land. You need to get those old cars out of the field and remove the rocks. You need to pull out the weeds and till the soil. In this way you can almost double the harvest that you are producing.

The first five hundred acres is your strengths. Our culture obsesses over these and encourages us to focus on these alone. But that is because our culture does not have a vision for the human person. The culture has no interest in you becoming whole. Far from wanting you to become the-best-version-of-yourself, the culture is driven by productivity and consumption. To the culture, you are just a consumer and a cog in the global economic wheel. But God has a much greater vision for you. And it is for this reason that he gently encourages you to explore that other five hundred acres of your farm—your weaknesses.

More than that, God wants to get down in the dirt with you. He wants to work with his children. God is willing to do all the heavy lifting. He yearns for our cooperation, but he will not go where he is not invited.

It is this second five hundred acres that we come to Confession to explore and begin to work on.

• Turning to God •

I have spent much of my adult life speaking to groups around the world about the Seven Pillars of Catholic Spirituality. One of the questions I am asked most often is, "Why do you put Confession first?" Others will say, "You should let people warm up and get comfortable before you drop Confession on them." But there is a reason I placed Confession as the first of the seven pillars.

When John the Baptist first appeared in the desert of Judea, this was his message: "Repent, prepare the way of the Lord." (Matthew 3:2) Later, when Jesus began his ministry, he led with this message: "Repent, for the kingdom of heaven is at hand." (Matthew 4:17)

Repent is a powerful word. But what does it mean for you and me, here and now, more than two thousand years later? It means the same as it did to the people walking around the dusty pathways in their sandals, trying to inch closer to Jesus as he passed through their town or village. *Repent* means "to turn back to God."

I find myself needing to turn back to God many times a day, in ways small and large. It is not a matter of guilt and it is not a shameful thing. It is simply that at his side I am a better person—a better son, husband, father, brother, friend, employer, and citizen. Over time, I have also come to realize, quite painfully, that when I turn away from God I am also turning my back on my true self. Do you need to turn back to God today? Do you need to repent?

If we are honest with ourselves, if we can stomach a moment of truth, if we are willing to give truth a place in our lives above all our excuses and jus-tifications, I think each of us discovers for ourself that we need to turn back to God. We often turn away from God, sometimes in small ways, just for a moment, and at other times in much larger ways. Turning our backs on God is an inner action. It is quite possible for people to turn their backs on God and still go to church every Sunday. The external actions don't guarantee the internal disposition. Have you turned your back on God?

Very few people turn their backs to God completely. Most of us just turn our backs on him in one or two areas of our lives. Most of us turn our backs on God in one corner of our hearts. In what area of your life have you turned your back on God?

Every journey toward something is a journey away from something. If we need to turn back to God at this moment in our lives, we also need to turn away from whatever led us away from God and keeps us away. It may be that certain people have led you to stray from God—perhaps possessions have distracted you from your true and authentic self, or maybe pleasure has seduced you into walking a wayward path. Whatever has distracted you, it is important to realize that you cannot journey to a new place and at the same time stay where you are. This is why Confession is first. Walking with God demands that we bring order to our lives and put first things first. Sometimes it is just as important to know what you are journeying away from as it is to know what you are journeying toward.

The journey toward the-best-version-of-yourself is a journey away from the defects of the-present-version-of-yourself. The question that really presents itself to you, me, and this modern age collectively is: Are we willing to turn back to God? Are you willing to be more attentive to what God is calling you to be?

If you are, I think you will find that Catholic spirituality is rich with tools and insights that are astoundingly helpful. If you are willing to pursue truth wherever it leads you, I know you will discover there is genius in Catholicism. But it is not always apparent on the surface. You have to delve into it. I hope you will.

• I Am a Sinner •

Every day I find myself doing things that are self-destructive and that make me a lesser person. I say things that hurt others, or I hurt others by not saying things. When that happens, you can be sure the things I am thinking are giving birth to those words and actions. These are the thoughts, words, and actions that deviate from the natural order and separate me from the peace of knowing I am contributing positively to the common good of the unfolding universe.

The strange thing is, deep within I don't want to think, say, and do these things. I don't want to be the lesser person; I want to be the-best-version-of-myself. I want to live by contributing to other people's happiness, not their misery. In each moment of each day, I find myself caught in a struggle. I am divided. No different from you, I find myself experiencing what Paul described: "The good that I would I do not, and the evil that I would not it is that which I do." (Romans 7:19)

I am a sinner and I need to be saved. I need to be saved from myself and from my sin. There are many people who love me deeply—parents, siblings, friends, colleagues, and neighbors—but they cannot save me. I need a savior. It is the clarity of this realization that is life changing. This is what makes me eligible for membership in the Catholic Church. Jesus didn't come for the healthy; he came for the sick, and he established the Church to continue his work (cf. Mark 2:17). I am imperfect, but I am capable of change and growth. We are all imperfect but perfectible. The Church holds me in my weakness, comforts me in my limitations, endeavors to heal me of my sickness, and nurtures me back to full health, making me whole again. And throughout this process, the Church manages to harness all my efforts and struggles, not only for my own good, but for the good of the entire Church and indeed humanity. This is just a tiny part of the incredible mystery of the Church.

• The Drama of Life •

Since my late teens I have been speaking and writing extensively about what I like to call "the journey of the soul." In *The Rhythm of Life*, I described it as a journey from point A to point B, with point A representing the person you are today and point B representing all God created you to be (the-best-version-of-yourself). The great spiritual North Star is God's unchanging invitation to holiness. Point B is where you experience an intimate union with God. This journey is the adventure of salvation. The whole drama of a person's life can be understood by examining the tension between the-person-I-am and the-person-I-ought-to-be. This is the tension of life. And it is the resolution of this tension that Paul spoke of when he suggested we must each work out our salvation (cf. Philippians 2:12).

Everything has its meaning in relation to the goal, and when we forget the goal, nothing makes sense. When we forget that God wants us to live holy lives, we become disoriented. When we lose sight of the great spiritual North Star, we become lost and confused. This is why Catholicism means so little to so many today, because they have forgotten—or in some cases have never been introduced to—the goal of the Christian life.

Everything should be weighed with the journey in mind and the goal in sight. The question that should be a consistent part of our inner dialogue is, "Will what I am about to do help me to become the-best-version-of-myself?"

This is the drama of life—the struggle to become the-best-version-of-myself, the quest to bridge the gap between the-person-I-am and the-person-God-calls-me-to-be and created me to be.

• A Sacred Encounter •

It is within this context that I wish to speak to you about the beauty and genius of the practice of Confession. In my own personal journey, Confession has played a very powerful role, helping me to strive to become the-best-version-of-myself. I find Confession to be a humbling experience, but not a humiliating one. Above all, I find that it is an experience of liberation that enables me to reassess where I am in the journey, helps me to identify what is holding me back, and encourages me to continue along the way. The sacrament of Reconciliation is much more than just confessing our sins and asking for forgiveness (though that in itself can be tremendously powerful both spiritually and psychologically). Confession is an integral part of the genius of Catholicism, which seeks to nurture the whole person and transform the entire world into a place where all men and women can live in the peace and joy of God.

While any spiritual exercise can be helpful in our journey, I find regular Confession to be a particularly powerful tool. As I have traveled the world, it has become apparent that this sacrament has been abandoned during our own time. I believe this has happened because a tragic mediocrity has gripped the Church.

People striving to excel in any area of life want to know their weaknesses so they can work to overcome them. This striving for excellence is precisely what needs to be re-ignited in Catholics today. Confession is the perfect spiritual practice to rekindle our passion for excellence in the spiritual life.

When I close my eyes in prayer, I see the-person-I-am and the-best-version-of-myself side by side, and I am challenged to change. This is what takes place in Confession. We prepare by asking ourselves some soul-searching questions in an examination of conscience. Those questions give birth to the dual vision of the person we are at this moment and the person we are capable of becoming. We then bring our faults, failings, and flaws to God. Through this process we open ourselves up to God and the mysterious gift of grace. This grace often takes the form of a stronger desire to become a-better-version-of-ourselves.

Grace is the power of God alive within us. It heals the wounds that our sins have created and helps us to maintain moral balance. Grace helps us to persevere in the pursuit of virtue. It enlightens our minds to see and know which actions will help us become all God has created us to be. Grace inspires us to love what is good and shun what is evil. Grace is not a magical illusion. It is mystical and real.

I come to this sacrament to reconcile with myself, with God, and with the community. Confession is not just a cleansing experience; it is also a strengthening experience. Confession is an opportunity for you and God to work together to form a-better-version-of-yourself. It also increases our desire for holiness, and that is a desire we should fan with all our energy.

• Common Objections •

There are, of course, some common objections to the practice of Confession. The secular culture propagates the myth that there is no such thing as sin or evil, no objective truth, and no universal right and wrong. They tell us that these are just ideas the Church invented to control and manipulate people. I assure you, sin and evil are real. This truth should require no proof or explanation. If you feel it does, turn on your television tonight and watch the evening news, or take a casual walk through history.

This idea is strengthened by the fact that most people don't identify with sin because we see ourselves and others as generally good. This allows us to overlook the deeply rooted nature of sin in our attitudes, our habitual ways of thinking, and our orientation to life. But Jesus did not come simply to heal us of our external behaviors. He wants to reorient our attitudes, behaviors, and the way we think. Sin is obvious in the external actions of humanity throughout history, but beyond our external behaviors it is also deeply psychological and emotional.

Once we consciously recognize that sin and evil exist in our world, we are faced with the problem of history: What do we do about sin and evil? It would be lovely if we could gather up all the evil people and put them together on one island, leaving them to self-destruct in their collective sinfulness. That is not possible because the line that separates good from evil is not out there somewhere. This line does exist, but not with some people on one side and others on the other side. The line that separates good from evil is cast down the center of my heart and yours; the battle is within. So the question is, are we willing to fight the battle?

The secular view of sin and evil seems almost absurd the moment it is removed from the self-centered, pleasure-seeking environment that sustains and encourages it. The objections of our non-Catholic Christian brothers and sisters to the practice of Confession require considerably more discernment.

The catchcry of modern Christians has become, "I don't need to confess my sins to a priest. I can confess them straight to God." You *can* do anything you want; that is the nature of the freedom with which God endows us. But if you are serious about being Christian, then it follows that you are serious about seeking and doing the will of God.

The tradition of Confession is deeply rooted in the life and teachings of Jesus, as seen in the Gospels. I have often wondered how non-Catholic Christians are able to ignore or explain away some of these central passages; for example, John's account of Pentecost: "'Peace be with you. As the Father has sent me, so I am sending you.' And when he had said this, he breathed on them and said, 'Receive the Holy Spirit. Whose sins you forgive are forgiven them, and whose sins you retain are retained.'" (John 20:21–23)

But perhaps the biggest danger with the direct-to-God approach is that it becomes all too easy to deceive ourselves, and then we begin to create God in our image. When it is "just me and God" it is all too easy to project my own qualities and biases upon God. Then, rather than being created in the image of God, we begin to create God in our own fallen image.

There are two truths of self-knowledge for us to consider here. The first is that as human beings we all have an incredible ability to deceive ourselves. The second is that we almost never see things as they really are.

We all think we have 20/20 vision in most things, but it simply is not the case. To prove this point I often ask groups at seminars and retreats to write down on a small piece of paper whether they think they are an average, above-average, or below-average driver. More than eighty percent of participants consider themselves to be above-average drivers. However, the statistical reality suggests that this is not possible. So, we are presented with two options: Either some of us don't see our driving ability as it really is, or my seminars attract a disproportionate number of above-average drivers. I think we all know which it is.

We almost never see things as they really are. When I go to Confession, half the time I need the priest to say, "You are being too easy on yourself." The other half of the time, I need him to say, "You are being too hard on yourself." I almost never see things as they really are. This is just one small part of the genius of Confession.

Excellence in any field requires coaching. Coaches see things we don't, and they are able to hold us accountable. I remember once I had my golf swing recorded. When I went home and watched it on my television I couldn't believe that was my golf swing. In my mind my swing was smooth and graceful. In reality—and recordings don't lie—it was quite erratic. Just like I needed coaching in golf and tennis as a child when I was keen to excel, I need spiritual coaching. I am so grateful for all the priests who have given their lives to provide us with invaluable spiritual coaching. Who is your spiritual coach?

A similar dynamic exists in our relationships. God gives us husbands and wives, brothers and sisters, parents, colleagues, and friends to help us to see things as they really are. And there is no relationship more precious in this world than the friendship of people we love, trust, and respect enough to allow them to correct us when we are not seeing things as they really are. We need to be constantly mindful of our ability to deceive ourselves and our tendency to distort the way we see things in our relationship with God and our relationships with others.

Today, many Catholics subscribe to the Protestant and Evangelical view that they don't need to confess to a priest. I will point out that while many Catholics claim the *right* to confess directly to God, my research suggests that, unlike many of our non-Catholic brothers and sisters, Catholics who use this argument tend not to be in the habit of confessing directly to God either. Too often it is used not to justify a different form of confession, but as an excuse to avoid confession altogether.

Another objection that has been raised is that Confession (or Reconciliation, as it is known in some parts of the world now) was only instituted in 1215 at the Fourth Lateran Council, and therefore was not part of Christian tradition from the beginning. This is clearly not the case. While the earliest Christian writings, such as *The Didache,* from the first century, are not clear on the form or procedure to be used for the forgiveness of sins, in the second century Father Irenaeus makes it clear in his writings that the sacrament goes back to the beginning of the Church. Christian writers of the third and fourth centuries such as Origen, Cyprian, and Aphraates clarify that confession is to be made to a priest, and we have no reason to believe that this was not the practice from the beginning. In *Leviticum Homiliae,* which was written around 244, Origen refers to the person who "does not shrink from declaring his sin to a priest of the Lord." Seven years later, in *De Lapsis,* Cyprian writes, "Finally, of how much greater faith and more salutary fear are they who . . . confess to the priests of God in a straightforward manner and in sorrow, making an open declaration of their conscience." Writing to advise priests, Aphraates says in *Demonstrationes,* "If anyone uncovers his wound before you, give him the remedy of repentance. And he that is ashamed to make known his weakness, encourage him so that he will not hide it from you. And when he has revealed it to you, do not make it public."

The Fourth Lateran Council didn't invent the practice of Confession as we know it today. The Council sought only to reaffirm what it understood to have been the constant practice of Christians since the beginning, and to emphasize the advantages of this practice for all men and women who desire to draw nearer to God.

Among Catholics who still hold a place for Confession in their spiritual life, there are some who consider the practice necessary only in the case of serious sin (according to the minimum obligation set out in canon law). This argument makes me wonder what type of relationships these people have with their spouses, siblings, children, employers, colleagues, and close friends.

Let us take as our example a relationship between a husband and a wife. Would it be good for their marriage if they never apologized to each other for anything? In 1970, the movie *Love Story* was a huge hit and went on to win an Academy Award and three Golden Globes. The most famous line from the movie proclaims, "Love means never having to say you're sorry." I wonder what impact that one line has had on viewers' relationships with the people they love and their relationship with God? The screenwriter has clearly confused love with pride.

Would it be healthy for a relationship if a husband and wife apologized only for serious offenses? How healthy would your key relationships be if you never apologized? I would suggest that they would not be healthy at all; rather, they would be massively dysfunctional and woefully inadequate. I also suspect that we all know at least one person who refuses to apologize— ever—for anything. Even when it is blatantly obvious that this person has done some wrong, filled with pride, he or she stubbornly refuses to apologize. Sometimes these people will not even admit any wrongdoing. Do you see God in them? Are they the light in the darkness? Do they represent hope and goodness to everyone around them? Are they becoming the-best-version-of-themselves?

If we apply this guidance of never apologizing to our relationship with God, that relationship will suffer the fate that so many modern human relationships are suffering.

After the cultural objections and non-Catholic Christian objections, there are, of course, Catholic objections and excuses. People say to me all the time, "I cannot go to Confession with my priest." When I ask them why, they reply, "Because he knows me." The priest is supposed to know you. It helps that he knows you. The more he knows you, the more helpful he can be to you in your inner journey. You don't go to a different doctor every time you are sick. Your doctor knows you—your medical history, your allergies, and the circumstances of your life. All this makes him or her infinitely more effective. Similarly, you can go to Confession with a priest who does not know you, or you can go to a different priest every time, but there is an additional advantage to having a regular confessor: Because he knows you and the various aspects of your life, he is able to provide unique insight and continuity to the experience.

Others will say, "I couldn't go to Confession to a priest I know." When again I ask why, they reply, "Oh, if he knew my sins he would never talk to me again." This is absurd. When we reveal our faults and failings, most people don't love us less; they love us more. Besides, it is not as if you are going to tell him anything he has not heard before.

You are not that original. The ways men and women sin are remarkably unoriginal and similar.

One thing that we have lost sight of is that the priest is there to help you become the-best-version-of-yourself. He has given his whole life to serve the people of God, so at that moment the only thing he is concerned with is helping you in your journey to become all God created you to be. He may not say it in this way, but as you approach the experience of Confession keep in mind that everything the priest says is designed to help you live a life of holiness.

These represent the common objections that the people of our present age have toward the Catholic experience of Confession. But with all that said, I would like to affirm once again that God is not an unjust dictator trying to rule humanity with an iron fist. God doesn't want to control or manipulate you, he doesn't want to force you to do things you don't want to do, and he doesn't want to make you feel guilty and bad about yourself. God wants you to become the-best-version-of-yourself, and in turn he sends you out into the world to help others to do the same. We all have faults and failures, and we all have inner tensions. Prayer, the Sacraments, and the Scriptures are all wonderful gifts designed to help us to understand and manage our inner tensions and take one step closer to God each day.

• Behold the Beauty •

We all have spiritual disease. We all have sins. Some people like to pretend that they don't, but over time their sins spread through their lives like cancer in the body. Like cancer, if our sin is not addressed and arrested, in the end it will devour us. Other people try to justify their sins with all types of explanations, none of which will ever satisfy their own hearts. Then there are those who go to "experts" with the hope that such people will help them overcome their troubled consciences.

The truth is, I do things every day that are contrary to the ways of God, things that stop me from being the-best-version-of-myself, and so do you—every day. Then we carry all this baggage around with us and it affects us in ways that we are often not even aware of. Our sins affect us physically, emotionally, intellectually, spiritually, and psychologically. They affect our relationships, our work, our health, our intellectual clarity, and our ability to genuinely embrace and experience all of life. Sin limits our future by chaining us to the past. Yet, most people are able to convince themselves either that sin doesn't exist, that they don't sin, or that their sins are not affecting them. But if we take an honest inventory of our thoughts, words, and actions, it becomes abundantly clear that every one of us does things that are self-destructive, offensive to others, contrary to the natural laws of the universe, and in direct conflict with the ways of God. If we really think we can carry all this around inside us and that it is not affecting us, then we are only deceiving ourselves.

If you want to spend the rest of your life arguing for your weaknesses, so be it. If you want to keep losing your temper and telling yourself, "it's my character," go ahead. If you want to have someone try to explain away or justify the sins of your life, go to a psychologist or a psychiatrist. But if you want peace in your heart, I want to personally invite you to come to Confession. There is no treasure in life like a clear conscience. If you want the joy of a clear conscience, come to Confession.

The mystery of grace can never be adequately described by cold words on cold pages. It must be experienced. So if you haven't been to Confession for a while, maybe now is your time. Perhaps it has been ten years, or twenty years, maybe even longer. Jesus says to you, "Do not be afraid." (Matthew 14:27) Bring the sins of your life and place them at the feet of Jesus in this sacrament of Reconciliation. Do not think of it as confessing your sins to a priest; think of it as confessing your sins to God your heavenly Father.

God sees your unrealized potential. He sees not only who you are but also who you can be. Ask him to share that vision with you.

Our faults and failings have a tendency to eat away at us inside, but great freedom is born from bringing our darkness into the light. Darkness cannot survive in the light. While we hide our faults and failings, they grow larger and develop a power over us. Before we know it, we are planning our days around our self-destructive habits, much like an alcoholic plans his day around when he will drink. And the more we try to hide these faults and weaknesses, the more power they tend to have over us. If they are serious enough and left unattended for long enough, they can begin to control our whole lives. But when we bring them into the light, they lose their power over us.

I assure you, if you approach this sacrament with a sincere and humble heart, you will experience the flow of grace in your life. Listen to those words of absolution: "By the ministry of the Church, may God grant you pardon and peace, and I absolve you from all your sins in the name of the Father, and of the Son, and of the Holy Spirit. Amen." As the priest speaks these words the floodgates of grace are opened and your soul will be filled with a deep peace. You will experience an inexplicable lightness and an intoxicating sense of joy and liberation.

Confession is a gift. Behold the beauty. Embrace the treasure.

• Self-Knowledge •

In the spiritual life, it is very important to grow not only in our knowledge and understanding of God but also in knowledge and understanding of ourselves. Both knowledge of God and knowledge of self are necessary to make the journey of the soul. These two are inextricably linked, and one without the other is useless.

Confessing our sins in the sacrament of Reconciliation helps us to develop this self-knowledge. The saints hungered for it. They developed it from hours of self-examination and consistent practice of Confession. They knew their strengths and weaknesses, their faults, failings, and flaws, their talents and abilities, their needs and desires, their hopes and dreams, their potential and their purpose. They were not afraid to look at themselves as they really were by the light of God's grace in prayer. They knew that the things of this world are passing, and that when this brief life is over, we will each stand naked in the presence of God. At that moment, money, power, status, possessions, and worldly fame will mean nothing. The only thing that has value in that moment is character—the light within you. Who we become is infinitely more important than what we do or what we have. As Francis of Assisi once said, "Remember, you are what you are in the eyes of God, and nothing else."

Get to know yourself. The gifts of self-knowledge include freedom from the world's image of who you are (and who you should be) and an unquenchable compassion for others. The more I get to know myself (and my own brokenness), the more I am able to accept and love others. Furthermore, the more I get to know myself and my sinfulness, the more I am able to understand others and be tolerant of their faults, failings, flaws, addictions, and brokenness. Self-knowledge breeds the ultimate form of compassion.

Self-knowledge also deflates all the false pride and egotism in our lives. Genuine self-knowledge is humbling, and two humble people will always have a better relationship than two prideful people. Not sometimes. Always.

Get to know yourself and every relationship in your life will improve.

• A New Habit •

Our lives change when our habits change. I have been convinced of the power of the habit of regular Confession in my own life, and I would like to encourage you to make it a spiritual habit in your life.

Is once a year during Lent enough? Well, it's enough to fulfill your obligation, but that would be minimalism. Becoming the-best-version-of-yourself and loving God are not about obligations and minimalism. When we are dedicated to these matters our aspirations soar far beyond the rules and regulations of our faith. These rules and regulations define only the lower limits of our quest, but God invites us to explore the optimum possibilities.

Consider this analogy. How often do you wash your car, or have it washed? Perhaps once every two or three weeks, maybe once a month, but it is probably not ten years since you had your car washed! And when your car is all shiny and clean on the outside and clean and tidy on the inside, you feel pretty good about that. Driving a clean car feels different than driving a dirty car.

When you are driving home from the car wash with your clean car, what do you pray? You pray it doesn't rain, right? Or you at least think it, hope it! As if God doesn't have better things to worry about. There are fifty thousand people dying every day in Africa from extreme poverty and preventable disease, but you just got your ten-dollar car wash and you want that at the top of his list. In any event, it doesn't rain, but the next day you are driving down the road and there is a big puddle of mud right in the middle. What do you do? You go around it, of course; you just got your car washed.

The day after that you think to yourself, *It might get cold later; I better take a jacket.* You take a jacket with you but you don't need it. So you say to yourself, *I'll put this in the backseat; I'll get it later.* Do you get it later? No. The next day you think to yourself, *I have to go to the doctor today; I better take a book or a magazine with me, because they never seem to have any good magazines.* Besides, what type of people go to a doctor's office? That's right, sick people. Then they all gather together in a little room with six magazines and they touch those magazines with their sick fingers. When you get to the doctor's you pick up that magazine and look at the cover and it reads, "Issue 137, February 1983," and you think to yourself, *How many sick people have been here since February 1983?* You bring your own magazine and once you get done with your doctor's visit you put that magazine on the backseat of your car. You say to yourself, *I'll get it later.* But you don't.

The next day you are going somewhere and it's getting late, you are hungry, and you don't know when you are going to have a chance to eat. So you go to the drive-through and get whatever it is you get when you go to the drive-through. Now you are driving while eating, and you're talking on your cell phone, so you are steering with your knees. When you get done eating you say to yourself, *I won't put this trash on the backseat; I just got my car washed.* So you get all the trash from the meal and you stuff it back into the bag the food came in and say to yourself, *I'll just put this trash neatly on the floor in the backseat. I'll get it out as soon as I get home.* Do you? Probably not.

The following day you throw another little piece of junk into the backseat and the day after that you toss another piece back there. Before you know it, it's Sunday again, and you're coming home from Church, and what do you have now? That's right, you've got the bulletin, which you probably read while Father was giving his homily. So, you think to yourself, *I've already read this,* as you throw it over your shoulder into the backseat. The next day it's a gum wrapper or some other small bits of trash and the day after that it's one or two little bits of junk that you are moving from home to work or vice versa.

The next thing you know, two or three weeks have passed since you got your car washed. The car is quite messy on the inside and dirty on the outside, and you become less careful with it. You just throw another little piece of trash in the backseat because there is already so much that you won't notice the extra piece. And then, before long, you are throwing big bits of trash back there. Do you know why? Because you have lost your sensitivity, and once you lose that sensitivity a big piece of trash doesn't look that bad among all those little bits!

We lose our sensitivity to sin in exactly the same way. After a while, a big self-destructive behavior doesn't look that bad among all those little self-destructive behaviors.

When you get your car washed you are sensitive to the things that make it dirty. In the same way, after you have been to Confession you are sensitive to the things that stop you from being the-best-version-of-yourself. When you come out of Confession you are sensitive to the thoughts, words, actions, people, and places that will not help you to walk with God. I don't know how long that sensitivity lasts for you, but after a while it wears off and you become indifferent to the things that will not help you to live a life of holiness and be true to yourself.

Haven't you ever noticed the way people living good lives have a glow about them? They don't seem to be carrying the weight of the world on their shoulders. When you go to Confession your soul is cleansed and an inner beauty shines from within you. But after a few weeks, the little sins begin to pile up, and before you know it, a big sin doesn't look so bad on top of a pile of small sins. And once you add the big one to the pile, you figure you've made a mess already so you might as well really make a mess. Little by little, you begin to lose your sense of sin. Before you know it, you are very unhappy, and you don't really know why. You don't feel at peace with yourself and you find yourself becoming impatient and irritable with the people around you. You begin to experience a certain restlessness and anxiety, but you don't know what is causing it.

How long does this desensitization take? I suspect it is different for different people, and even different at various times in our lives. There have been times when I have struggled with habitual sins, even while trying to rid my life of them. During those times I have gone to Confession as often as every week. But now, at this time in my life, I lose that sensitivity after a month, so I have made a habit of going to Confession once a month. If I don't, I find I become inattentive and desensitized to the things that separate me from God, my neighbor, and my true self.

Another interesting lesson I learned is that I have to pick a specific time each month. Otherwise, one month started turning into two or three. Now I go to Confession the first weekend of each month. That way, there is no confusion and I don't open the door to procrastination, laziness, and all those other lurking traits that want to steal me away from God and my best self.

How often should you go to Confession? No one can tell you. The Church requires that you go at least once a year, but encourages regular Confession. Some people go once a week, others go once a month, and there has long been a rumor that Pope John Paul II used to confess daily.

Once a month works for me, but if you haven't been in a while, at first you may wish to go every week to reawaken your spiritual senses. This weekly Confession may be particularly helpful if you are caught in some habitual sins. But as the weeks pass, most people should be able to apply the rhythm of monthly Confession to their spiritual life.

There is still nothing quite as wonderful as a clear conscience. Nothing fills us with joy in the same way. Ah, a clear conscience—it is the ultimate simple pleasure.

• Temptation •

Once we have turned back to God and embraced him again, like the prodigal son embraced his father (cf. Luke 15:20), we still have to live in the world. Here we face all the distractions and temptations that have drawn us away from the path of peace so many times before.

Temptation is real. Every day I am tempted to do things that do not lead me to become the-best-version-of-myself. I suspect the same is true for you. I am tempted by lust, gluttony, greed, anger, envy, laziness. . . .

It seems to me that if we can master the moment of temptation, we can master the Christian life. There should be whole books about the moment of temptation. There should be courses we can take to study it and learn how to respond to it. But we almost never talk about it.

There are some immutable truths when it comes to our struggle with temptation. The first is this: Don't dialogue with it. When temptation whispers in your ear, turn away. Temptation will say things like, "Everybody is doing it," or "It won't matter just this once," or "You deserve it," or "Nobody will know." Don't surrender the peace in your soul. Keep yourself busy. The temptation will pass. Learn to prize the peace in your soul above all else.

But it is not enough for me to advise you not to dialogue with temptation. That would be like me saying, "When you get home tonight there will be a small crystal container filled with a magical purple potion on your front doorstep. Anything you pour that purple potion on will turn instantly to solid gold—as long as while you are pouring it you don't think about a herd of purple hippopotamuses!"

You have probably never thought of a herd of purple hippopotamuses, but as soon as you go to pour that potion, what is the first thing that you are going to think about? A herd of purple hippopotamuses. As hard as you may try, you will not be able to get that image out of your mind. The same thing happens when we try not to dialogue with temptation by thinking about not dialoguing with temptation. We end up in a dialogue with temptation. What we focus on increases in our lives. We have to turn our focus away from what stops us from experiencing our full potential in Jesus and place our focus on what will cause us to experience the life Jesus invites us to in him.

It is not enough not to dialogue with temptation. We have to replace the dialogue of temptation with another type of dialogue. What do we call that other type of dialogue? Prayer. In order to overcome temptation we have to pray unceasingly in the midst of it. But the truth is, most of the time we don't pray when we are being tempted. Do you know why? Because we are people of faith! This may sound strange to many, and it may appear to be a contradiction, but let me explain.

As men and women of faith, we believe that God is all powerful. We know this instinctively, and often we don't want God and his all-powerful self getting in the way of our sins. We love some of our sins. This is the first truth we discover on the path to conversion. We love some of our self-destructive behaviors, especially the habitual ones.

It is important that we recognize and acknowledge this truth. Then, as it is with all truth, we have to respond to it. We don't have a choice; truth demands a response. We can choose how we respond, but we cannot choose not to respond. You cannot take the Fifth with truth. Once you discover it you are required to respond. You can, of course, ignore the truth you discover, but that in itself is a response.

One response may be to turn to God and beg him to free you from a certain habitual sin. Then, next time you are tempted to entertain that sin, call out to God unceasingly in prayer, asking him to deliver you from the temptation.

Another very real possibility is that you don't want to give up a certain habitual sin. If that is the case, and you genuinely have no desire to give up a certain self-destructive behavior, then I encourage you to go to church and sit in the presence of God and ask him to give you the desire to give up that sin. That prayer might sound something like this: *Lord, I know [my sin] is stopping me from becoming the-best-version-of-myself, and that it is stopping me from loving you and the people in my life. But I love this sin. Please give me the desire to give it up.* This is an honest prayer, and all true growth in the spiritual life begins with this type of raw honesty.

Temptation is real and we all experience it every day. The best way to spend your time while you are waiting for temptation to pass is to pray. Replace the dialogue of temptation with a dialogue of prayer: *God, I know what is good and true, but I am still attracted to what is self-destructive. Give me strength. Be my strength.* Sometimes the temptation is so great that you are not even able to formulate your own words in your head. It is then that you will learn the value of those simple prayers that the modern world despises so much: "Our Father, who art in heaven . . ." (Matthew 6:9) or "Hail Mary, full of grace . . . " (Luke 1:28).

Whatever you do, don't dialogue with the devil. He always has more questions than you have answers. He will suggest one thing and you will reply in thought with a rebuttal. This will go on, over and over again: He raises a thought and you reply. But the back-and-forth will wear you out. Eventually you will give in to the sin out of sheer exhaustion or just to end the dialogue. Sin is exhausting; avoid the dialogue that precedes it. Temptation is real; get to know how it takes place in your life, and avoid those people, places, and situations that create moments of temptation for you. When the tempter whispers in your ear, turn your back on him. Why complicate your life? Don't dialogue with the tempter. Turn to God and pray. You will be happier and you will have the peace of Christ in your heart.

To know your strengths and weaknesses is a great advantage in any field. In the spiritual realm it is of ultimate importance. The proud basketball player doesn't notice the faults in his game. The proud businesswoman doesn't notice the weaknesses in her leadership style. A proud artist doesn't notice the defect in her style. The proud man doesn't notice the weakness in his character.

The proud must content themselves with mediocrity; excellence belongs to the humble. Humble yourself to know who you really are and God will respond by revealing the incredible person you are capable of becoming.

• The Touch of the Master's Hand •

In her wisdom, my fourth grade teacher, Mrs. Rutter, introduced my classmates and me to the following poem. After reciting it one day, she announced that over the next week, we were all to learn the poem by heart. Then every day for about a month someone would recite the poem for the class. It was just one example of her many moments of genius. At the time, our understanding of it was shallow, perhaps because one must experience some of life's hard knocks to truly appreciate the full meaning. The piece is titled "The Touch of the Master's Hand" and is by Myra B. Welch. Amazing things are possible if we allow the Master to lay his hands on our lives.

'Twas battered and scarred, and the auctioneer
Thought it scarcely worth his while
To waste much time on the old violin,
But held it up with a smile.
"What am I bidden, good folks," he cried,
"Who'll start the bidding for me?"
"A dollar, a dollar," then, two! Only two?
"Two dollars, and who'll make it three?"
"Three dollars, once; three dollars twice;
Going for three . . ." But no,
From the room, far back, a grey haired man
Came forward and picked up the bow;
Then, wiping the dust from the old violin,
And tightening the loose strings,
He played a melody pure and sweet
As a caroling angel sings.

The music ceased, and the auctioneer,
With a voice that was quiet and low,
Said, "What am I bid for the old violin?"
And held it up with the bow.
"A thousand dollars, and who'll make it two?
Two thousand! And who'll make it three?
Three thousand, once; three thousand twice;
And going and gone," said he.
The people cheered, but some of them cried,

"We do not quite understand
What changed its worth?" Swift came the reply:
"The touch of a master's hand."

And many a man with life out of tune,
And battered and scarred with sin,
Is auctioned cheap to the thoughtless crowd
Much like the old violin.
A "mess of potage," a glass of wine;
A game—and he travels on.
He is "going" once, and "going" twice,
He's "going" and almost "gone."
But the Master comes and the foolish crowd
Never can quite understand
The worth of a soul and the change that's wrought
By the touch of the Master's hand.

Chapter Thirteen

DAILY PRAYER

Almost every day I meet people who tell me they are writing a book. Others tell me they have always wanted to write a book. I always encourage them, but in my heart I know that very few will actually ever write the book they tell me about. Most people like the idea of writing a book because it intrigues them. They get caught up in the idea of losing themselves in the creative process. But the reality is writing a book is just hard work. The beginning, when you conceive the idea for the book, is wonderful and exciting. But that doesn't last very long and then the hard work begins. Throughout the process there will be times when you catch a wave of inspiration, but if you wrote only when you felt inspired you would never finish your book.

Writing a book requires daily discipline. You have to work at it every day, even if some days all you do is read over what you wrote yesterday to keep it fresh in your mind. Writing a book requires the discipline to write when you feel like it *and* when you don't. Most people don't have this discipline, which is why many who start writing a book never finish it. When we think of writing a book we conjure romantic images of the artist at work in an inspirational setting, effortlessly penning page after page. The truth is, as already mentioned, writing a book is mostly hard work, and we are still just talking about writing a book. We have not spoken of writing a good book or even a great book yet.

Prayer is similar in many ways. Many people fail to establish a daily habit of prayer in their lives because they approach it with the wrong expectations. Consciously or subconsciously, most people approach prayer expecting it to be easy. The truth is, prayer is perhaps the most difficult thing we will ever do. From time to time, we may get carried away by a moment of inspiration in our prayer, but for the most part prayer is hard work—work well worth doing, but hard work nonetheless.

You don't become a great athlete by training only when you feel like it. You don't become a great writer by writing only when you feel inspired to write. And the saints did not become such fine ambassadors of God on earth by praying only when they felt like praying. In each case, a daily discipline is required.

Many years ago I saw a violinist interviewed. At the time he was considered the best in the world. He explained to the interviewer that he practiced for eight to ten hours each day. The interviewer implied that surely at this stage in his career he could ease up a little with the practice. The violinist smiled and said, "If I miss practice one day and perform the next night, I am the only person who can tell. But I can tell. My performance is off. If I missed practice every day for a week and then performed, there would only be a handful of people in any audience who would be able to tell that my performance was off. But if I missed practice for two weeks, or three weeks, almost every person in the audience would be able to tell that I was not performing at my best."

The same is true of prayer. If you neglect prayer for a day, you are probably the only person who can tell. But you can tell. You have less patience and you are less focused. If you neglect prayer for a week, several people around you will notice the change in you. But if you neglect prayer for two or three weeks, almost everyone around you will recognize that you are not at your best.

Prayer is central to the Christian experience. A Christian life is not sustainable without it, because growth in the Christian life is simply not possible without prayer. Growing in character and virtue, learning to hear the voice of God in our lives and walking where he calls us—all require the discipline of prayer. And it is not enough simply to pray when we feel like it. Prayer requires a daily commitment.

• Why Pray? •

A few months ago I was visiting a grade school, and a child, perhaps seven years old, asked me, "Why do you pray?" Sometimes a question is so simple and yet so striking that it causes you to pause time and time again to ponder the answer. This child's question was just such a question for me.

I know all the right answers to the questions. The catechism tells us that the purposes and forms of prayer are adoration, petition, intercession, thanksgiving, and praise. But I knew this answer would not satisfy my curious young friend.

Therese of Lisieux, one of the great teachers of Christian prayer, wrote, "For me, prayer is a surge of the heart; it is a simple look turned toward heaven, it is a cry of recognition and of love, embracing both trial and joy." But I am fairly sure if I had used that as my answer, the seven-year-old student would have just looked at me with a blank stare.

Dozens of thoughts and answers flashed through my mind, all of which may have suited an adult or a theologian, but I couldn't find the words to express them to a child. So, I asked him a question instead of answering his. I asked him the same question he had asked me: "Why do you pray?"

He didn't have to think about it. Spontaneously and casually he said, "Well, God is my friend, and friends like to know what is going on in each other's lives."

Sometimes I pray for very selfish reasons. Perhaps I am stressed and overwhelmed, and I go to prayer hoping God will calm my heart and mind and bring peace to my soul. Sometimes I pray for completely altruistic reasons. When some region of the world is torn apart by natural disaster or war, I often find myself driven to prayer. And sometimes I pray for very holy reasons. There are times when I pray not because I want something from God, but just to express my gratitude for all the things, people, and opportunities he has filled my life with. And when I am at my best, I pray simply to be with God and seek his ways.

Most of the time I pray for more practical reasons—three in particular. First, I pray to make sense of things. Life is often complex and confusing, but in the midst of all that, God always seems to present a simple path. The ways of the Lord may not be easy, and at times may be tremendously difficult, but they are almost always simple.

I also pray because I want to live life deeply and deliberately. I am not confused about how precious a gift life is, and I want to fully experience that gift. In high school these words of Thoreau became engraved on my heart: "I went to the woods because I wanted to live deliberately, I wanted to live deep and suck out all the marrow of life, to put to rout all that is not life and not when I had come to die discover that I had not lived." I go to the woods of prayer each day for the same reason.

The third of the very practical reasons I pray is to build up the kind of inner density required to prevent the culture from swallowing me up.

We live in a time of tremendous cultural pressure. The spirit of the world is powerful and unrelenting, and there is little societal support for those who choose to reject the spirit of the world and embrace the Spirit of God. This is not a popular choice, and as a result, it can often lead to a certain loneliness in our lives.

Osmosis is the scientific theory that essentially states that what is more dense will filter through to what is less dense. If we are going to be true to our values, if we are going to celebrate and defend the-best-version-of-ourselves, we need to build up a certain density within us. This inner strength, or density, will allow us to resist the cultural pressure to abandon our values, our true selves, and God.

If we are going to walk with God and become the-best-version-of-ourselves, we need this inner density, which seems to be created by a combination of grace and discipline. This inner density is not something we can attain for ourselves; it is a gift God freely gives us when we cooperate with his plan for our lives. When we have this density within us, we will have a Christian effect on our environment. When we don't have this density, our environment has an effect on us. What is more dense filters through to what is less dense, and the cultural density all around us is intense. The most powerful way to build this density, this inner strength, is through prayer and the sacraments. I pray to gather density to survive and thrive in a culture that is often hostile and sometimes violent toward what is good and true and noble.

It is almost twenty years now since I began a serious habit of prayer in my life. Now I cannot imagine a life without prayer. I don't know how people survive in our crazy, noisy, busy world without the sanctuary of prayer to renew and refresh them. There are many reasons to pray and many ways to pray—what is critical is that we make an effort to create a daily habit of prayer in our lives.

• Thought Determines Action •

To contemplate is to ponder something deeply. As Christians we are called to think on a deeper level, and to live on a deeper level. Daily prayer makes this possible. It is in our prayer that we move beyond the fleeting thoughts of life and begin to lead meaningful lives of contemplation.

Contemplation is not just for monks and nuns. In truth, we all lead lives of contemplation, but we spend our lives contemplating very different things. What do *you* contemplate? Is it the riches of the world? Is it every woman who passes you in the street? Do you ponder the latest fashions? The local gossip? Or do you contemplate the wonders of God, the glory of his creation, and the joys of the spiritual life?

It is not necessary to go away to a monastery to live a life of contemplation. We are all contemplatives because we are all thinking all the time, and what you contemplate will play a very significant role in the life you live.

The reason prayer and contemplation are so integral to the Christian life is because thought determines action. If you send your thoughts down one road, your actions will follow your thoughts. Thought determines action, and so the actions of your life are determined by your most dominant thoughts.

For a moment, imagine you are a basketball player. It's game seven in the NBA playoffs. There is one second left on the clock. The scores are tied. You have just been fouled, and you have one shot from the free throw line.

Between the moment the foul is called and the time you shoot the ball, everything moves in slow motion. There are millions of people watching you, but really there is just you and your thoughts. During those moments before shooting, if you imagine yourself missing the shot, you will miss the shot. If you imagine yourself making the shot, you will make the shot. But what if, in that brief time, you have forty-seven thoughts of missing the shot and only thirteen thoughts of making the shot? What will happen then? You'll miss it. Why? Because the actions of your life are determined by your most *dominant* thought.

Consider the heroes of Christianity, the men and women we call saints. They have lived in every place, in every time, and in every culture. Some of the saints were young and some were old. Some were rich and some were poor. Some were educated and others were uneducated. Some had positions of power and authority and others did not. My point is that you cannot find a more diverse group of people in history than the saints. And yet, the people of their time say exactly the same thing about every single one of them: They brought Jesus to life for us. What did they say about Francis of Assisi? He brought Jesus to life for us. They said the same about Therese of Lisieux, Ignatius of Loyola, Catherine of Siena, and Dominic. What did they say about Mother Teresa and John Paul II? They brought Jesus to life for us in our own place and time.

For two thousand years men and women have been saying exactly the same thing about each and every one of the saints. Why? Because the saints all spent their post-conversion lives pondering the life and teachings of Jesus Christ—the Gospel—and they simply became what they thought. Human thought is creative. What we think becomes.

Some of the saints were converted from other faiths and others were converted from incredibly wayward lives, but most of them were converted from a very common complacency toward God's will for their lives. Are you ready to begin your post-conversion life?

When I was in middle school, we went away on retreat. At that time, I was more or less disinterested in things of a spiritual nature, yet I seem to remember vaguely that the theme of the retreat was placing Christ at the center of our lives. For three days every speaker shared about living a "Christ-centered" life.

Since that time, I have discovered that this is not just a nice phrase or idea, but that it is, in fact, the very core of our Catholic spirituality. The centrality of Christ in human history and in our individual lives is no small discovery, nor is it just an idea. It is an idea that has been tried and tested, and the results are awe-inspiring.

But if I am honest with myself, despite my deep desire, it is a constant struggle to keep Christ at the center of my life. There are moments when there is no question he is at the center of my life. Sometimes there are days at a time when I am able to place God and his will at the center of my life, but then I get distracted by the many conflicting desires of my heart and all the things of this world that lure me away from God and the-best-version-of-myself.

My thoughts always wander before my actions do. Thought determines action, and before too long, you will be living out what has already happened in your mind. Human thought is creative. What we think becomes. What you allow to occupy your mind forms the reality of your life. Good or bad, almost everything happens in your mind before it happens in time and space. There are accidents and things beyond our control, certainly. In these cases we can only control how we respond to such unexpected circumstances. If you can direct what happens in your mind, you can massively influence what happens in your life and completely direct how you respond to what happens in your life.

So, what are you thinking? What do you think about all day long? What do you think about in the car on the way to and from work each day? What do you think about while you are waiting in line at the supermarket?

Whatever you place your mental attention on will increase in your life. If you place your attention on money, you will have more money. If you place your attention on how much you are loved (or not loved), you will have more love (or not) in your life. If you place your attention on virtue, you will have more virtue. And if you place your mental attention on the life and teachings of Jesus Christ, he will increase in you (cf. John 3:30).

Paul gives us this advice: "Whatever is true, whatever is honorable, whatever is just, whatever is pure, whatever is lovely, whatever is gracious, if there is any excellence, if there is anything worthy of praise, think about these things." (Philippians 4:8) And to my mind while Paul could have been speaking about many things of this world and the next, his description of what we should think about is at the same time a description of the Gospel and an invitation to ponder Christ and his teachings.

Earlier we said that the difference between the saints and those who have been less successful in living the Christian life was that the saints affixed their singleness of purpose on doing the will of God and that they had better habits. These habits were not only external habits but also internal habits. One of those critical internal habits was the habit of the mind we call contemplation. Too often we just let our thoughts wander. God invites us to focus our thoughts, and the discipline of daily prayer teaches us how to direct those thoughts toward the higher things.

As you move from one activity to the next in your day, become aware of what you are thinking and how different thoughts make you feel. Become aware of the thoughts that encourage you to love God and those around you more, and those thoughts that don't. Then consciously try to focus more and more of your thinking on those that do. When you realize that your mind is wandering toward negative, self-destructive, or gossip-ridden thoughts, steer your mind in another direction.

You cannot grow an oak tree with an apple seed. You cannot grow a good life with bad thoughts. Certain thoughts give birth to certain actions. With each passing day God invites you to change, to grow, and to become a-better-version-of-yourself. God loves you as you are, but he loves you too much to let you stay that way.

• The Classroom of Silence •

If I asked you to conduct a search for some suitable candidates to be leaders and prophets in the modern world, where would you look? You probably wouldn't immediately start looking for shepherds. I have always found it interesting that the most common profession among the prophets and leaders of the Old Testament was shepherding. Why do you suppose God called so many shepherds to occupy positions of authority and influence? What made them uniquely suited?

It seems to me these shepherds spent long hours in silence and solitude. They were immersed day after day in God's cosmic temple. This produced in them a unique understanding of nature and creation, making them worthy stewards of the earth and all that is in it. But these long days spent immersed in the classroom of silence also provided them with plenty of time to think, reflect, and contemplate. And most importantly, this silence and solitude gave them more opportunity than most to hear and listen to the voice of God in their lives.

When we read the Bible it seems the most common preface to any sentence is "God said." "God said to Adam . . . ," "God said to Noah . . . ," "God said to Abraham . . . ," "God said to Moses . . . ," and on and on. Throughout the history of God's relationship with humanity he has constantly been communicating with us. I am convinced that in this modern time it is not that God has stopped speaking to us, but rather that we have stopped listening. And while I believe that God can communicate through anyone and anything at any time, his preferred venue is still silence and solitude. In the silence God speaks. Or perhaps it is just that in the silence, away from the hustle and bustle of the world, we are able to hear him.

If I live to be a hundred and write for my whole life, I will never be able to emphasize enough how important silence is as an ingredient of the spiritual life. In *A Call to Joy* I wrote, "You can learn more in an hour of silence than you can in a year from books." In *Mustard Seeds* I wrote, "It is in the classroom of silence that God bestows his wisdom on men and women."

I will make two promises to you: In the silence you will find God and in the silence you will find yourself. These will be the two greatest discoveries of your life. But these discoveries will not be moments of epiphany; they will be gradual. You will discover a little at a time, something like a jigsaw puzzle being put together. I cannot imagine how miserable life would be without the adventure of discovering God and self. It is this process of discovery that allows us to make sense of life.

In the silence things start to make sense. Consider this example: You are taking a road trip and you get lost or a little turned around. What do you do? Do you tell the people you are traveling with to talk louder and turn the music up? No. You ask everyone to be quiet and you turn the music off. Why? Things start to make sense in the silence.

Now, applying this to our personal lives, we are all trying to make sense of something in our lives right now. We are all constantly trying to make sense of something in our lives. You are trying right now. What is that something? Are you giving yourself the silence you need to make sense of it?

Our modern world is spinning out of control, and one of the chief contributors to the chaos and confusion of our modern age is noise. Our lives are filled with noise. We are afraid of silence.

During the 1940s, C. S. Lewis wrote a series of letters that appeared in a London newspaper called the *Guardian*. These letters were the humorous and insightful correspondence between a senior devil, Screwtape, and an apprentice devil, his nephew Wormwood. The thirty-one letters were later published in the form of a book titled *The Screwtape Letters*. In the letters, Screwtape is advising Wormwood about the procedure for winning a soul away from God for the devil. At one point, Wormwood is trying to think up all kinds of exotic ways to tempt the man who has been assigned to him, and Screwtape rebukes him, explaining that their methods have long been established. One such method, he explains, is to create so much noise that men and women can no longer hear the voice of God in their lives. In one letter, the senior devil Screwtape announces, "We will make the whole universe a noise in the end." Can you hear the voice of God in your life?

I believe the writings of C. S. Lewis were operating in a prophetic capacity when he expressed this idea more than sixty years ago. Today, we wake up to clock radios, we listen to the radio while we shower, and we watch television while we eat breakfast. We listen to the radio in the car on the way to work or school, we listen to music all day over the intercom, we get put on hold and we listen to music. We have Game Boys, pagers, cell phones, Walkmans, Discmans, portable DVD players, iPods, and iPhones. Most homes have multiple televisions, and we leave them on even when nobody is watching them. We have so much noise we can't even hear ourselves think.

How do you imagine that in the midst of all that noise you are going to work out who you are and what you are here for? The reality is, you won't. Unless you withdraw from all the noise of your life and the world for a few minutes each day, you will most likely just become another cog in the global economic wheel, consuming and being consumed.

Our world has been filled with noise, and as a result, we can no longer hear the voice of God in our lives. It is time to enter into the classroom of silence.

• Getting Started •

This is how my commitment to daily prayer began. At the time I was in high school. Everything at school was going very well—I had a great group of friends, a wonderful girlfriend, and a good part-time job. On the outside everything seemed fine, but on the inside a growing restlessness was building up.

My heart was restless. I sensed something was missing in my life. I knew something was wrong, but I couldn't pinpoint it. I sensed there must be more to life, but I didn't know what it was, or where to find it. I tried to ignore these feelings, but the nagging restlessness persisted.

Several weeks later I bumped into a family friend and he asked me how school was going. "Fine," I replied. He is a doctor, so he knows how to ask the right questions, and for five or ten minutes he gently probed the different areas of my life. Each question and each answer led us a little closer to his diagnosis. Then he paused briefly, looked deep into my eyes, and said, "You're not really happy, are you, Matthew?"

He knew it and I knew it, but I was ashamed to admit it at first. But our lives seem to flood with grace at unexpected moments, and I began to tell him about the emptiness and restlessness I was experiencing. After listening to me carefully he suggested I stop by my church for ten minutes each morning on the way to school.

I listened, smiled, nodded politely, and immediately dismissed him as some sort of religious fanatic. As he expanded on his idea and how it would transform my life, I wondered to myself, *How is ten minutes of prayer each day going to help me?* Before he had finished speaking I had resolved to completely ignore everything he said.

In the coming weeks I threw myself into my studies, my work, and my sporting pursuits with more vigor than ever before. I had done this to appease my restless heart at other times in my life. But achievement in these areas no longer brought the fulfillment it once had.

One morning about six weeks later the emptiness had become so great that I found myself stopping by church on the way to school. I crept quietly into the church, sat near the back, and began to plan my day. Just planning the day ahead of me lifted the clouds of hurried confusion. For the first time in my life I tasted a few drops of that wonderful tonic we call peace—and I liked it.

The next day, and every day, I returned. Each morning I would simply sit toward the back of the church and move through the events of the day in my mind. With each passing day a sense of peace, purpose, and direction began to fill me.

Then one day as I sat there it occurred to me that "planning my day" wasn't really prayer. So I began to pray: *God, I want this . . . and I need this . . . and could you do this for me . . . and help me with this . . . and let this happen . . . and please, don't let that happen. . . .*

For the next few weeks, this is how it went. Every morning I would stop by church, sit toward the back, plan my day, and tell God what I wanted.

For a while this was the depth of my prayer life. And then one day I had a problem. That morning I came to the church and with a simple prayer in my heart, I looked up toward the tabernacle and began to explain, *God, I've got this problem. . . . This is the situation. . . . These are the circumstances. . . .* Then I stumbled onto the question that would change my life forever: *God, what do you think I should do?*

With that question my life began to change. Asking that question marked a new beginning in my life. Up until then, I had only ever prayed, *Listen up, God, your servant is speaking.* But in that moment of spontaneous prayer the Spirit that guides us all led me to pray, *Speak, Lord, your servant is listening.* It was perhaps the first moment of honest and humble prayer in my life. Before that day, I had only been interested in telling God what *my* will was. Now for the first time I was asking God to reveal his will.

God, what do you think I should do? I call this the Big Question. It is the question that changed my life forever, and the question that continues to transform my life on a daily basis when I have the courage to ask it.

This question should be a constant theme in our spiritual lives. When we are attentive to it we are happy regardless of external realities, because we have a peace and contentment within. It is the peace that comes from knowing that who we are and what we are doing makes sense regardless of the outcome, and regardless of other people's opinions. This peace comes from taking into account the only opinion that truly matters: God's.

Every day you make dozens of decisions, some of them large and some of them small. When was the last time you invited God into the decisions of your life?

I *try* each day to let God play a role in my decision making, but often the allure of this world distracts me. Sometimes I simply forget to consult him. Sometimes I block his voice out because I want to do something I know he doesn't want me to do. Sometimes I foolishly believe that I know a shortcut to happiness. These decisions always lead me to misery of one form or another.

There is only one question and one course of action that leads to lasting happiness in this changing world: *God, what do you think I should do?* To think that we can find happiness without asking this question is one of the grandest delusions.

Ignatius asked the question. Francis asked the question. Benedict asked the question. Dominic asked the question. Joan of Arc asked the question. Theresa asked the question. But will you? We need saints today. These men and women began by asking a very simple question: *God, what do you think I should do?* And as a result of constantly asking this question they became giants of their age. Our age needs its own spiritual giants.

Sometimes when we talk about the saints we make the mistake of thinking that they were different from us. They were not. To be a saint is to decide for God and with God. You and I make decisions every day. Some of them are large but most of them are small. But when was the last time you sat down with the Divine Architect and asked, *God, what do you think I should do in this situation with my spouse?* When was the last time you sat down with the Divine Navigator and asked, *God, what do you think I should do in this situation at work?* When your kids come to you to talk about what they are thinking of doing with their lives, do you just ask them what they want to do? Or do you ask them what they feel God is calling them to?

I've known happy people and I've known miserable people, and I can tell you without any shadow of a doubt that the difference between the truly happy people in this world and the miserable people is one thing: a sense of mission.

People who are passionate, energetic, and enthusiastic about life have a sense of mission in their lives. They are not living their lives in the selfish pursuit of pleasure or possessions. They are living out a mission, and through that mission, they are making a difference in other people's lives.

What's your mission? How will you discover your mission? Perhaps the first realization is you don't choose a mission—you get sent on a mission.

"Most men lead lives of quiet desperation." If you don't ask the big question, you won't discover your mission, and sooner or later you will be numbered among Thoreau's masses. You won't plan to live a life of quiet desperation; nobody does. You'll just wake up one morning and wonder how you got there.

If you are already living a life of quiet desperation, you don't have to stay there. Just start asking the big question. *God, what do you think I should do?* In the moments of the day ask the question. In your daily prayer, ask the question. Make this one question a constant part of your inner dialogue, and I promise you, your life will start to change.

Life is vocational, meaning it is about seeking, finding, and living out your mission, your vocation. We talk a lot about vocation, but I don't get the sense that the average person really knows what it means. With the current shortage of vocations to the priesthood, our discussions about vocations tend to be focused on priesthood. We acknowledge that marriage, religious life, and the single life are also vocations, but our discussion, education, and prayer for vocations seem to be focused almost exclusively on our need for priests. All this leaves many people thinking that some have a vocation and others don't.

The idea of vocation in general has nothing to do with priesthood. Vocation is about finding what you are best suited to. It's about finding your mission in life, discovering who God has created you to be and what tasks he has created you to carry out in this world. Everyone has a vocation, and finding it truly is the single event that will create more happiness in our lives than anything else. Life, therefore, is about vocation. It is about seeking and finding what God has created you for—and then doing it. It is through this process that God will transform you into the-best-version-of-yourself and the world into the place he intended it to be.

Some people are best suited to marriage, some are best suited to priesthood, some to religious life, and others to being single. These are the vocations we tend to speak of, but every one is different. Some priests work in parishes and others in universities. There are a thousand ways to live out the vocation to priesthood. The same is true for marriage, religious life, and the single life.

Each of us is created for a reason. The important thing to remember is that *you* have a vocation. Everyone has a vocation, and unveiling it is critically important to our experience of life, because life is vocational. For this reason, when we speak, teach, or pray about vocations we should personalize it for each individual. Vocation is deeply personal.

In the opening chapters of this book I discussed our overwhelming desire for happiness and the different ways we respond to this desire. In the end, it seems it all comes down to deciding how long you want to be happy. If you are willing to trade happiness for moments of pleasure, I suspect sex, drugs, food, alcohol, and gambling will be your things. But I want more than that. How long do you want to be happy for? If you just want to be happy for an hour, take a nap. If you want to be happy for a whole day, go shopping. If you want to be happy for a weekend, go fishing. If you want to be happy for a month, take a vacation to Australia. If you want to be happy for a whole year, inherit a fortune. If you want to be happy for a decade, find a way to make a difference in other people's lives. But if you want to be happy for a lifetime and beyond, seek the will of God for your life. Don't overwhelm yourself. Seek it one day at a time, one moment at a time, one decision at a time.

Several months after I first began visiting our local church for ten minutes each morning, a very wise old man said to me, "You are unhappy. Think to yourself: 'There must be an obstacle between God and me.' You will seldom be wrong."

Years later I was on a plane just about every day and I got into the habit of writing one small passage each day. I would then use these passages to guide my thoughts, actions, and reflections for that day. A collection of those passages was later published as *Mustard Seeds*. This is one of my favorites: "When you know you are doing the will of God, that alone is enough to sustain your happiness. When you don't have that, all the possessions in the world cannot sustain happiness in the depths of your heart."

The will of God is a mysterious thing. In my own spiritual journey I have learned that God reveals His will one step at a time. This creates a great deal of uncertainty, and we don't like that. We want to know where we are going and when we will get there. In this modern age we try to control all the elements so that we can have security and stability. If only we could learn to enjoy uncertainty. Uncertainty is a sign that all is well. God is your friend; he will take care of the details.

Our lives change when our habits change. My life changed when, encouraged by a friend, I began to pray for ten minutes a day. In those quiet moments of reflection I stumbled upon the big question: *God, what do you think I should do?*

For many years I have been traveling around the world speaking to different groups of people. I cannot remember a time when I have not urged my listeners to enter into the classroom of silence for ten minutes of prayer and reflection each day. As these years have passed, millions of people have attended my talks, seminars, and retreats, and sometimes I cannot help but wonder how many of those have actually formed the habit of spending ten minutes in prayer each day. Often people dismiss the message as too simple. It is the simple things that have a tremendous ability to transform our lives. I have experienced the power of simplicity in my own life and I invite you to do the same.

So now it is your turn. Before you go to bed tonight, take a small piece of paper and write these four words on it: TEN MINUTES A DAY. Stick that piece of paper on the mirror in your bathroom where you brush your teeth. Tomorrow morning when you are brushing your teeth decide a time during your day when you will spend ten minutes in the classroom of silence with your God in prayer. If at all possible, stop by your church. It is probably empty and quiet for most of the day. I know we can pray anywhere, but there is something mystical and powerful about God's presence at Church.

I challenge you to make daily prayer a priority in your life, and to make it an indispensable part of your daily schedule. Enter into the classroom of silence. Sit with the Divine Architect and together design something wonderful. Visit with the Divine Navigator and plot a course to uncharted territories. Sit with God and dream some dreams.

Ten minutes a day. If you are confused, angry, tired, frustrated, happy, excited, grateful . . . come to the silence. Stick a note on your bathroom mirror. TEN MINUTES A DAY. And every day as you brush your teeth, ask yourself, "When will I spend my ten minutes in the classroom of silence today?" Don't be deceived by the simplicity of this message. You will be amazed how much ten minutes each day in a quiet church can change your life.

In time you may decide to spend more than ten minutes each day, and that is wonderful. There may be days when you are able to sit with God for an hour or two, and it is wonderful to have this carefree timelessness with him from time to time. But regardless of how busy you are, defend and celebrate your ten minutes every day.

It would be nice if our souls growled when they were hungry, like our stomachs do. But they don't. Your immortal soul is the most valuable possession you have—feed it, nurture it, celebrate it. The saints realized the value of their immortal souls, so they made it a priority to nourish and nurture them. I hope one day soon you will realize this too, not only in your mind, but in your heart and deep within your being. And I hope that, having come to this realization, you will begin to nourish and nurture your soul. Only then will you truly thrive.

Ten minutes a day. Begin today. The beginning of anything is the most difficult; getting started is the tough part. Recognize it so that you don't get discouraged. The space shuttle uses ninety-six percent of its fuel at takeoff, but then it virtually glides through space and back to earth. Get started.

• Do I Have to Go to Church to Pray? •

I hope in these past few pages I have convinced you to begin (or renew) the discipline of daily prayer—not just when you feel like it, or when it is convenient, but every day. The next question for us to consider is where you should pray.

Whenever I tell people the story of how I started spending ten minutes a day at church, I get the question, "Do I have to go to church to pray?" The short answer is no. You can pray anywhere, and spontaneous prayer should be something that accompanies you wherever you go. We can pray while we are driving to work and while we are exercising, while we are doing the shopping or washing the dishes, the moment we learn that a friend is sick or as a speeding ambulance passes us on the road. Prayer should spring forth from the daily events of our lives. But we also need a time of focused prayer each day, a time set aside from everything else, when we give our undivided attention to God. Does this time have to be spent at church? The short answer is no. But allow me to pose another question: Where is the best place to spend your daily prayer time?

There are many days when I don't pray at church, but I always yearn to. When I am able to get to a church for my daily prayer time, my prayer seems more focused and fruitful. I have thought long and hard about why this is and I have reached two conclusions. One is a very natural reason. The other is the most astonishing spiritual reality our faith has to offer.

The first is that our churches are quiet and designed for prayer. They lend themselves easily to the spiritual, and provide a place set apart. In the Scriptures we read over and over again about Jesus going alone to a quiet place. He would go to a place set apart from everyone and everything else so that he could pray. If Jesus needed to do this, I know how much more I need it.

The second reason I think my daily prayer time seems more effective when I am able to spend that time in a church is the supernatural reason. I believe that Jesus Christ is present in the Eucharist, and that he is present in a very unique and powerful way in every tabernacle, in every Catholic church around the world. I think his presence makes a difference. How could it not?

There are many people who do not believe that Jesus is present in the Eucharist. In John's Gospel Jesus says, "I am the living bread . . . whoever eats this bread shall live forever," (John 6:51) "Unless you eat my flesh and drink my blood you do not have life within you," (John 6:53) "Whoever eats my flesh and drinks my blood remains in me and I in him." (John 6:56) Many of Jesus' followers at the time left him because of these statements, just as many of Jesus' followers today have left his Church because of our belief that he is present in the Eucharist. In the Gospel after Jesus speaks of this we read, "This saying is hard, who can accept it?" and "As a result many of his disciples returned to their former way of life and no longer accompanied him." (John 6:66)

I can understand how those who don't believe in the true presence of Christ in the Eucharist would discount the power of praying at church. But once you believe that Jesus is present, how could you believe that the presence of the Eucharist would not make a difference?

Years ago, I received a letter from a priest who had worked as a lay missionary in China before he returned to his homeland of America and became a priest. He shared many stories about the Church in China, but there is one that made a huge impression on me. It is a story I have told hundreds of times and one that always humbles me.

Many years after being ordained a priest, he returned to China, incognito, for a brief visit. Even today, there are priests and bishops in prison in China for nothing other than refusing to let the Communist government control their churches. For this reason, nobody in China knew that he was a priest.

On the second night of his visit, he was awakened in the middle of the night by the noise of people moving around the house. A little scared, he got up and went to his door. Opening it, he asked one of the men living in the house what was going on.

His Chinese host replied, "We're going to the wall."

He inquired further, "What is the wall?"

His host replied, "Come with us and we will show you."

There were more than twenty people living in the small house, and while none of them knew he was a priest, they knew he could be trusted.

Not satisfied with the answers he had received, he went downstairs and found one of the older women whom he had known many, many years earlier and asked her, "What's going on? Where are you all going?"

She gently replied, "We're going to the wall."

He persisted, "Yes, but what is the wall?"

She replied with the same gentleness, "Come with us and we will show you."

He got dressed and ventured out into the night with the group. They walked for miles and along the way other groups joined them. Now, all together, they numbered almost 120 men, women, and children. Soon they came to a forest and as they began to walk into it, he noticed that some of the men in the group were climbing trees.

Several minutes later they came to a clearing in the forest, and in the middle of the clearing was a small wall about four feet tall, from an old, derelict building. The old woman turned to him and smiled with all the love in her heart, and though he sensed an incredible excitement in her he did not know what to make of it. The people seemed excited, but he was scared.

Looking up into the trees, he noticed that there was a circle of men in the trees surrounding the clearing. And now, as the group came close to the wall, they fell down on their knees before it.

Moments later, one man got up and walked toward the wall, then, reaching out with one hand, he took a single brick out of the wall. Behind the brick was a tiny monstrance holding the Eucharist. The group spent one hour in silent prayer before the Blessed Sacrament, and then the same man got up, approached the wall, and replaced the single brick. The men came down from their lookout positions in the trees and the group went quietly home.

The next day he told the people that he was a priest and they told him that they had not had Mass in their village for ten years. Once or twice a week they would go to the wall in the middle of the night, risking their lives, to spend an hour with Jesus, truly present in the Eucharist.

The following night, the priest said Mass at the wall and replaced the host. It was one of the highlights of his priesthood.

I am not sure we appreciate the power of God present among us in every tabernacle in every Church. If this priest had been discovered that night he would have been imprisoned and tortured, and the rest of the group would have been imprisoned and quite possibly executed. They knew this all too well, and it was a risk they were willing to take.

There is something very powerful about spending time in a quiet church. I would like to invite you to explore this experience. Over the years, I have visited many churches, but there are a few that I go back to time and time again. When I was growing up in Sydney, my family and I belonged to St. Martha's Parish, and it is there that I first started spending my ten minutes each day in prayer. I always look forward to spending time there when I am back in Sydney visiting my family and friends. Below the tabernacle it reads, "My Lord and My God," and this simple phrase had a profound effect on me. These days, when I am at home in Cincinnati, I like to spend my prayer time in the chapel at a Franciscan monastery not too far from my home. The friars have a series of chairs gathered around the tabernacle, and I like to sit there close to it and talk to Jesus about what is happening in my life.

Experience has taught me time and time again that all the answers are in the tabernacle. I can go to many people in my life and ask them what they think I should do in a given situation, but nothing compares to sitting before Jesus in the tabernacle and placing my question before him.

Beyond the power of silence in the lives of individuals and the power of Christ's presence in our tabernacles, I can attest also to the power of silence and his presence in a community. There is a phenomenon reemerging in the Catholic world known as Eucharistic adoration. There are more and more parishes that have adoration chapels, and many of them are open twenty-four hours a day. It may be considered old-fashioned and overly pious by some, but my experience has been that wherever you find Eucharistic adoration in a parish, those communities are more vibrant. The people are more spiritually focused, more involved, more generous with God, and the communities tend to be thriving.

When are we finally going to stop casting these signs aside as if they were merely coincidence? It seems that adoration chapels draw people closer to God, deeper into the spiritual life, and provide something people desperately need at this time.

It can be very hard to find a quiet place in this world. But this quietness is essential to the growth in the Spirit. Your soul needs silence like you need air to breathe and water to drink. I pray that as the noise of the world becomes louder and more constant we will continue to dedicate ourselves to providing places set apart for people to experience God in the silence they so desperately need.

While modern man is filling his life with more and more noise and trying to absent God from more and more areas of his life, God is inviting us into the silence and into his presence. Here, in the presence of God, we will find rest for our weary hearts and minds. In the great classroom of silence we will develop resolute hearts and peaceful spirits. If you listen, you will hear Jesus speaking to you with a clarity that is unmistakable: "Come to me all you who labor and are heavy laden, and I will give you rest." (Matthew 11:28)

So, returning to the question at hand, do you have to pray at church? No, but if you are able, why wouldn't you? I realize that for some it is impossible. They are homebound or live in rural areas where the nearest church is fifty miles away. But for most of us it is simply a matter of making it a priority. Is it convenient? Probably not. But I don't think you and I do anything more important on any day than spending a few minutes with our God. Our daily commitment to prayer deserves to take priority in our lives, but too often we find ourselves caught up in all the urgent things. The problem with that is that the most important things are hardly ever urgent. Prayer allows us to work out what matters most and place it at the center of our lives.

All I ask of you is this: If at all possible, try what I describe here. Stop by your church for ten minutes each day for the next couple of weeks. If you can, do it first thing in the morning. I think you will find that your days are more fruitful and focused, and that you are filled with a passion that is invigorating and a joy that is intoxicating.

Come into the silence.

• Begin Today •

Perhaps your last concern is that you don't know how to pray. It is much simpler than you suppose. Step into the silence, and in your heart, say to God, *I don't know how to pray,* and already you will have begun to pray. Just talk to him. Simply open your heart to him in a gentle dialogue. Speak to him as you would a great friend, mentor, coach, or teacher.

When you leave your time of prayer, continue the dialogue with God in your heart throughout the moments of your day. Share with him your joys and your disappointments, your questions and your doubts. Speak to him about everything.

Tevye, from *Fiddler on the Roof,* is a great example. He is always talking to God, about everything. This constant dialogue is perhaps part of what Paul had in mind when he wrote, "Pray constantly." (1 Thessalonians 5:17)

So, begin today with ten minutes. In time you may feel called to spend more time. If that is the case, I encourage you to increase the time you spend in prayer gradually and consistently. If it is going to be ten minutes a day, make it ten minutes a day—not six and not fourteen.

I would also like to encourage you to keep track of what days you do it, what days you don't, and how long you spend in prayer each day. In my work as a business consultant I have had the privilege of working with many Fortune 500 companies. One of the greatest lessons I have learned from the very best companies is that they measure everything. They have a fundamental understanding that if you don't measure it you won't change it. This lesson has led me to conclude that we measure very little in our lives the way the best companies measure everything in their business.

As a result I started measuring several things in my life. I started measuring how much time I spent in prayer each day, how much time I spent exercising each day, and what I ate each day. I wrote all of this down on a piece of paper throughout the day and at the end of each week I tallied it up. I was amazed how much I ate and how little I exercised. I was also surprised to see how little time I spent in prayer.

So I would like to encourage you to measure how much time you spend in prayer each week. Visit DynamicCatholic.com to download a card that you can print and carry with you as an easy way to keep track of the time you spend in prayer each week. You will be amazed how measuring this time allows you to focus and grow in your prayer life. You may also want to visit the site to discover what happened when a whole parish did this.

• Cast into the Deep •

When my soul is hungry I often think of the passage in Luke's Gospel. Simon and his friends have been fishing all night without catching anything. Jesus says to him, "Put out into the deep water and lower your nets for a catch." (Luke 5:4) You can imagine what Simon is thinking to himself. He has been fishing all night and this is his profession and he has caught nothing, and now Jesus, who has no knowledge or experience of fishing, is telling him to get back out there and lower his nets. If they were fishing all night you can be sure they are tired. If they caught nothing you can be sure they are frustrated. And it is important to note that putting out into the deep water and lowering the nets is not a five- or ten-minute exercise. Jesus is making a significant request.

Perhaps at this time in your life you are tired and frustrated—with your career, with your marriage, with your children, with society, with your spiritual life—but Jesus is saying to you, "Put out into the deep water and lower your nets for a catch."

In the story we know that Simon and his friends listen to Jesus and do what he suggests, and they catch so many fish that their nets begin to tear and they need help from fishermen in other boats to haul in the catch.

Over and over in life, God challenges us to abandon our doubts and fears and cast our nets into the deep waters of the spiritual life. It is never convenient, it is almost always difficult, and it is sometimes quite painful, but if we heed the Lord's direction we will always bring in a huge catch. Don't be afraid of the deep places.

As I have written this chapter my mind has time and time again been drawn back to a story that highlights the power and the purpose of daily prayer:

Once upon a time on a glorious summer's evening, in an ancient English castle in the hills on the outskirts of London, there was a banquet.

More than six hundred guests had traveled from all over the world to attend this lavish affair. There were movie stars and musicians, artists and politicians, princes and princesses, fashion designers and beautiful models, men and women who owned businesses large enough to be small countries, and a handful of others, of no particular note, who had endeared themselves to the host over the years.

The evening was to be celebrated not with music, or speeches, or dancing, but with a presentation by a famous Shakespearean actor.

The castle was radiant, adorned with a springtime of flowers and perfectly lit with a myriad of candles. The people enjoyed a sumptuous meal and a wonderful selection of the finest wines the world had to offer.

When the guests had finished their dinner, but before dessert was served, the host stood up and welcomed them. He then explained, "This evening, instead of music, and speeches, and dancing, I have invited England's most celebrated Shakespearean actor to perform for us." The people graciously applauded, and the actor stood, moved toward the center of the banquet hall, and began to speak.

He spoke eloquently and powerfully. For thirty-five minutes he moved about the banquet hall, brilliantly reciting famous passages from the writings of William Shakespeare.

"Oh, I am but fortune's fool . . ."

"To be or not to be—that is the question:
Whether 'tis nobler in the mind to suffer
The slings and arrows of outrageous fortune
Or to take arms against a sea of troubles . . ."

"Shall I compare thee to a summer's day?
Thou art more beautiful and more temperate . . ."

"Neither a borrower nor a lender be,
for loan oft loses both itself and a friend.
And borrowing dulleth the edge of husbandry.
This above all, to thine own self be true,
And it must follow as night follows day
Thou canst not then be false to any man."

After each brief episode the audience erupted in applause, and their applause echoed up through the castle and spilled out into the moonlit courtyards.

"'Tis but thy name that is my enemy: Thou art thyself . . . What's
in a name? That which we call a rose by any other name would
smell as sweet;
So Romeo would, were he not Romeo call'd,
Retain thy dear perfection which he owes . . ."

"If we shadows have offended,
Think but this and all is mended,
That you have but slumbered here
While these visions did appear . . ."

With this, the closing passage from *A Midsummer Night's Dream,* the actor took a bow and announced that he was finished. The guests clapped and cheered and called for an encore. The actor rose to his feet once more to oblige his eager audience. "If anyone has a favorite Shakespearean passage, if I know it, I would be happy to recite it," he said.

Several people spontaneously raised their hands. One man asked for the soliloquy from *Macbeth*. Another asked for the balcony scene from *Romeo and Juliet*. And then a young woman asked for *Sonnet 14*. One after the other, the actor brought these passages to life—boldly, brilliantly, tenderly, thought-fully, each excerpt matched perfectly with its corresponding emotion.

Now an elderly gentleman toward the back of the banquet hall raised his hand and the actor called on him. As it turned out, the old man was a priest. "Sir," he said, standing in his place to be heard, "I realize it's not Shakespeare, but I was wondering if you would recite for us the twenty-third Psalm."

The actor paused and looked down as if he were remembering some event far in the past, perhaps a moment in his childhood. Then he smiled and spoke up. "Father, I would be happy to recite the Psalm on just one condition, and that is, when I am finished, you too will recite the Psalm for us here tonight."

The priest was taken aback. He hesitated. He was a little embarrassed now and, looking down, he fidgeted with the tablecloth. But he really wanted to hear the actor recite the Psalm. So finally, he smiled and agreed. "Very well."

The crowd hushed in anticipation and the actor began in his pow-erful and eloquent voice. "The Lord is my shepherd, there is nothing I shall want . . ."

When the actor finished reciting the Psalm the audience rose to their feet in ovation. They clapped and cheered as if they would never stop, and their adulation again echoed through the castle and out into the midsum-mer's evening.

After what seemed like several minutes, the guests finally settled and returned to their seats. Then the actor looked down the banquet hall to where the old priest was sitting and said, "Father, it's your turn now."

As the priest stood up at his table a whirl of whispers raced around the room. Shifting in his place, the old priest looked down, placed one hand on the table to steady himself, and took a deep breath.

A look of vivid recollection came across his face. He seemed to slip away to some other place. Then in a voice that was gentle and deeply reflective, he began.

"The Lord is my shepherd,

there is nothing I shall want.

He lets me lie down in green pastures.

He leads me beside peaceful waters.

He restores my soul.

He guides me along the way of righteousness as befits his name.

Even though I walk through

the valley of the shadow of death,

I will not be afraid. For the Lord is at my side. His rod and his staff

comfort and protect me.

He prepares a table for me in the presence of my enemies.

He anoints my head with oil.

My cup overflows.

Surely goodness and mercy will follow me all the days of my life.

And I will live in the house of the Lord, forever."

When the priest was finished not a sound could be heard in the banquet hall. Nobody clapped, nobody moved, and nobody spoke. A profound silence had descended upon the castle. Women wiped tears from their eyes. Men sat staring openmouthed. A tear slipped from the eye of the host. And as the humble old priest gently sat down, every set of eyes in the banquet hall was fixed upon him.

The faces of the guests radiated awestruck amazement. The actor was perplexed. He wondered why the priest's gentle words had touched the people so deeply. Then like a shaft of light passing across his face, it dawned on him.

Seizing the moment, the actor stood up and said, "My friends, do you realize what you have witnessed here tonight?" They gazed back at him with a communal stare of wonderment. They knew they had witnessed something profound, but were uncertain of its meaning. The actor continued, "Why was the old priest's recital of the Psalm so much more powerful than my own? As I see it, the difference is this: I know the Psalm, but Father, he knows the Shepherd."

Get to know the Shepherd. Stop trying to put together a master plan for your life and for your happiness. Instead, seek out the Master's plan for your life and for your happiness. Allow him to lead you, to guide you, to be your companion, your friend, your coach, and your mentor. He will lead you to green pastures. He will restore your soul. And your cup will overflow.

Chapter Fourteen

THE MASS

The Mass is at the center of Catholic tradition, and yet, the general consensus today seems to be that the Mass is boring. We have become used to hearing children say, "I don't want to go to Church. Mass is boring!" Children have been saying this for generations. The disturbing reality is that more and more adults are saying, "Mass is boring!" "It's not relevant to my modern life!" "I don't get anything out of it!" This is now a multi-generational problem, and one that deserves our urgent attention.

On any given Sunday if I look around church I see a large number of men, women, and children who are disengaged. Not distracted at moments, but massively disengaged throughout the whole Mass. We have been talking about this problem for longer than I have been alive. Some people say the problem with the Mass is the way the altar servers behave, others say the problem is that the music is too modern or too old-fashioned, while still others say that the problem with the Mass is the readers, the Eucharistic ministers, the parking lot, the coffee they serve after Mass, or their priest's homilies. We have tried to make Mass more engaging by changing things, adding things, and involving more and more people, but despite all of this, an increasing number of people have stopped attending Mass on a regular basis and profess to be bored or actively disengaged during Mass.

In truth, there is no problem with the Mass. People of all places and times have found it to be the life-transforming centerpiece of their spiritual lives. It has nothing to do with age. Many people, young and old, still find the Mass to be an experience that provides incredible spiritual comfort and clarity. I am one of them. So I am simply unable to accept that the Mass is boring. I am not willing to accept that it is irrelevant to our lives, though

I do think we need to consider if our lives are irrelevant to the Mass. I am, however, willing to accept that many, many people are bored at Mass. They have no reason to lie. If they were not bored, I am convinced that they would not say that they were. The question is: How do we move them beyond their boredom to a richer experience of the Mass?

The Mass is not boring, but many people are bored when they go to Mass. This is the essential dilemma we face as a Church. What is the answer? How do we demonstrate the powerful relevance of the Mass? I have studied it for years and have come to the conclusion that two things are necessary if we are to demonstrate the powerful relevance of the Mass to Catholics today.

First, there needs to be a change in the way we approach Mass each Sunday. Every day God is speaking in our lives. The Sunday liturgy is an opportunity for us to take time to listen. We need to teach and learn real and practical ways of listening to God's voice.

Second, we need a renewed understanding of the workings of the Mass and how they relate to our daily lives. Most people know so little about the Mass that it might as well be in a foreign language. Very few Catholics have a working knowledge of what is actually happening at each moment during the Mass. We need to bring the Eucharistic experience to life for people.

In this chapter I will seek to give you some practical insight on both of these points. There are more than a billion Catholics on the planet. The central experience of Catholicism is the Mass, and I believe that we have an obligation together as a Church to engage people. I hope this chapter can be a powerful first step.

• Prepare Yourself •

You wouldn't show up to play in a football game and expect to win if you had not been training. You wouldn't show up unprepared to give a big presentation at work and expect to get the project. We don't expect to excel in exams if we have not studied. Consider the preparation that goes into hosting a BBQ, a dinner party, or a wedding. We prepare for everything we consider important in life. In every case preparation makes a wonderful experience possible. When was the last time you prepared for Mass?

The first step is preparation. It is necessary for a high-level experience. It is unreasonable to walk through the church doors as the music is beginning on Sunday and expect to have a powerful and personal spiritual experience without some preparation.

When does Mass begin for you? For my wife, Meggie, and me, Sunday Mass begins on Wednesday evening. I would like to say we do it every Wednesday, but sometimes we forget and other times we are too lazy. I can tell you that our best experiences of Sunday liturgy come when we have diligently taken a few minutes on Wednesday night to prepare.

Our process is very simple. We read through the Mass readings for the following Sunday, we talk about what strikes us from each of the readings and why, and then we each close with a spontaneous personal prayer. It takes about fifteen minutes, but it places the readings of the coming Sunday in our minds several days before we attend Mass. It's simple, it's powerful, and I encourage you to try it. Do it with your spouse, with your whole family, with some friends, or do it alone. But find a way to prepare for Mass.

Every Sunday we get to experience the Word of God at Mass. I believe the Word of God has the power to transform our lives. I have experienced this power in my own life and witnessed it in the lives of countless others. I believe the Word of God can have a powerful impact in your life right now, beginning today. But I am equally convinced that the Word of God will not transform your life, or mine, with one quick reading on a Sunday morning in a church full of people, where we are surrounded by a thousand distractions. In order to deliver its soothing waters to our souls, the Word of God needs an opportunity to linger in our minds and to sink its roots deep into our hearts. This simply cannot take place in the context of Sunday Mass.

The priest stands up to read the Gospel and everyone in church rises to their feet. At that moment, you get distracted by who is at church or who is not at church, by what someone is wearing or what someone is not wearing, by a child running up and down the aisle throwing his crayons and eating a snack, or throwing his snack and eating his crayons. The point is, you get distracted. The next thing you know, the priest is beginning his homily. You have no idea what the Gospel was about and you go home spiritually undernourished.

Allow me a question to make my point. What was last Sunday's Gospel reading? Do you know? Do you have to think about it? Is it coming to you? Maybe you know and maybe you don't. My experience has been that more than ninety percent of Catholics can't tell you what last Sunday's Gospel was about.

For many people, their only experience of the Scriptures is during Sunday Mass. If we don't know what last Sunday's Gospel reading was, only a few days later, then I have to believe that it didn't significantly impact our lives.

Let me offer you the first practical resolution that will radically improve your experience of Mass on Sunday and your relationship with God. Preparation may be the most powerful tool at your disposal to improve your experience of the Mass. We have spoken about the value of preparation in business, at school, and in sports, so why wouldn't the same truth apply when it comes to Mass? Preparation elevates every worthwhile human endeavor.

I would like to suggest that once a week, perhaps on Tuesday or Wednesday, you take time to read and reflect upon the coming Sunday's Gospel. Just start with the Gospel. Perhaps in time you will move on to reflect on all of the readings, but for now, just start with the Gospel. If you are married, you may wish to share this experience with your spouse. Don't just rush through it. Read next Sunday's Gospel slowly and pick out a word or a phrase that strikes you or jumps out at you. Take turns reading and then explaining which word jumped out at you. Then read through it again. Again, be attentive for a word or phrase that strikes you. Maybe it will be the same word; maybe it will be a different word. It doesn't matter. Read the passage three times. If the Word of God is to transform us we need to allow it to sink its roots deep into our lives through repetition and reflection.

Each time, think about why that particular word or phrase is prodding you. Is there something happening in your life that this word or phrase speaks to? Is there something you should be doing that makes this word or phrase prick your conscience? Perhaps there is something you shouldn't be doing, and this word convicts you. That can be uncomfortable. Or maybe a word comforts you. Inspires you. Let the Holy Spirit work in you.

When you familiarize yourself with next Sunday's Gospel, the Mass will no longer be just part of your routine. It will become a spiritual experience and part of your own personal adventure of salvation.

We love what we know. When you get into the car, what songs do you want to hear on the radio? Songs you know. When you go to the theater, what language do you want the play to be in? The language you know.

If you apply this one resolution to your life, and practice it with an open, honest, and humble heart, your whole experience of Mass on Sunday will improve tremendously. And little by little, you will begin to draw closer to the man whose footprints have left an indelible mark in the dusty paths of human history.

The Word of God needs opportunities to linger in our hearts and minds. If we give it these opportunities it will move like running water toward the cracks in our lives. These cracks are our questions and heartaches, and God wants to speak directly to them. Only then will the powerful and personal modern relevance of God's ageless wisdom become unquestionably apparent in our modern lives.

Taking a few minutes during the week to prepare is the first step toward a more engaging experience of Mass each Sunday. Beyond that, turning the radio off as we drive to Church and arriving a few minutes early to consciously place ourselves in the presence of God are simple, practical ways to prepare for Mass. Find what works for you and make it a habit.

• Get Yourself a Mass Journal •

Having prepared ourselves for Mass, the next step is to approach Mass with an open heart and open mind—expecting God to communicate with us.

While many people complain about being bored at Mass, I have to believe that most Catholics would like to have a richer experience of it each Sunday. With that in mind I would like to propose a simple approach that I think could change the whole way we experience the Mass, and at the same time transform our relationships and parishes.

When you walk into Mass next Sunday, simply ask God in the quiet of your heart, *God, show me one way in this Mass that I can become a-better-version-of-myself this week!* Then listen. A critical component of successful relationships that is missing from our spiritual lives is listening. Listen to what God is saying to you in the music, through the readings, in the homily. Listen to the prayers of the Mass, and listen to the quiet of your heart. The one thing will strike you. Once it is revealed to you, spend the rest of the Mass praying about how you can live that one thing in the coming week.

Better than that, sometime this week, go out and get yourself a small journal. Bring it home and write down inside the front cover, "God, show me one way in this Mass that I can become a-better-version-of-myself this week!" Not "God, show me one way in this Mass my spouse can become a-better-version-of-him/herself this week!" Not "God, show me one way in this Mass my children can become better-versions-of-themselves this week!" No, God will speak to your spouse and your children in his own time and in a way that is specific to them. For now, the request you are laying before God is, "God, show me one way in this Mass that I can become a-better-version-of-myself this week!"

Then bring that journal to Church with you on Sunday. Try to arrive a few minutes early for Mass. Place this request before God: *Show me one way in this Mass that I can become a-better-version-of-myself this week!* Then listen to the music, the readings, the prayers of the Mass, the homily, the quiet of your heart. When that one thing strikes you, write it in your Mass Journal. Now spend the rest of the Mass praying about how you can become a-better-version-of-yourself in that way during the coming week.

If you do that every Sunday for a year your Mass Journal will become an incredibly powerful spiritual tool. You will be able to take it to your daily prayer and pass from page to page. Each page will inspire a deeply personal dialogue between you and God.

For many years now I have been doing just this at Mass each Sunday. It is usually fairly simple things that God says to me in these pages: "Avoid using negative humor." "Cherish your wife." "Take time each day to be grateful." "What are you holding back from God?" Each entry provides a unique and personal opportunity for prayer and for growth.

But perhaps the most powerful aspect of this Mass Journal has been the way it subtly tracks our progress. Consider this question: Are you a-better-version-of-yourself today than you were a year ago? Most people cannot answer, or they really have to think about it. But once you have kept your Mass Journal for a year or many years, you will be able to look back and see what you were struggling with a year ago or five years ago, and recognize that you have grown. This is of critical importance, because as human beings we need to know that we are making progress. We need to be able to look in the mirror each night and say, "I'm not perfect, but I am better today than I was yesterday." Even if our progress is only tiny in one area of our lives, it is important that we acknowledge it.

Visit DynamicCatholic.com/massjournal and request a free Mass Journal.

I have said it over and over again, and I will say it some more: Our lives change when our habits change. Get yourself a Mass Journal and bring it to church with you each Sunday. Write down that one thing that God whispers into your soul. This one habit will change your whole experience of the Mass, your relationship with God, and your appreciation of the Church. This one habit will help you become a-better-version-of-yourself, will make you a more engaged and contributing member of your parish community, and will invigorate your relationships.

Now take it a step further. Imagine if every person in your parish came to church each Sunday with a Mass Journal looking for one way they could become a-better-version-of-themselves in the coming week. Imagine the conversations you could have with your spouse, your children, your pastor, your friends.

And finally, take it one more step. There are more than sixty-five million Catholics in the United States. Imagine if every one of them came to church each Sunday with a Mass Journal looking for one way they could become a-better-version-of-themselves in the coming week. This one habit alone is powerful and practical enough to awaken a hunger for continuous learning, a desire for best practices, and a willingness to listen to the voice of God in our lives. This single habit is practical and powerful enough to transform the entire Church.

Our lives change when our habits change. Our relationships change when our habits within those relationships change. Our families change when our habits as families change. And our Church will change and become the invigorated life-giving community God intends it to be when our habits as members of the Church support that mission.

I believe that God is constantly speaking to us, through people and events, through the Scriptures and the Church. But each Sunday we have an intimate encounter with God in the Mass. Perhaps here more than anywhere else, God wants to speak to you. If you believed God was going to speak to you at Mass, I suspect you would bring pen and paper. Get yourself a Mass Journal.

• Rediscovering the Mass •

I offer the concept of a Mass Journal as a starting point. This single habit is enough to completely alter the way we approach Mass because it opens us up to listening to the voice of God in our lives. It is also a great place to begin because you can activate it now. You already know enough to practice this habit, you don't need years of study to understand it, and it is not dependent on good music, an outstanding homily, or any other variable factor surrounding the Mass. It depends only upon you opening yourself to listen to the voice of God in your life. So it provides a wonderful starting point, but as I said earlier, two things are necessary if we are going to invigorate our experience of the Mass: a change in the way we approach Mass each Sunday, and a renewed understanding of the workings of the Mass and how they relate to our daily lives. These new habits of preparing for Mass and keeping a Mass Journal will radically alter the way most people approach Mass each Sunday, but we also need to move toward a deeper understanding of what we are actually witnessing, experiencing, and participating in at Mass.

Recall in Chapter Eight that during the life and times of Francis of Assisi religion had become more of a habit and empty tradition than a genuine conviction. Just as in the time of Francis of Assisi, for many modern Catholics Mass (and the practice of religion) has become more of a habit and a social gathering than an expression of any genuine spiritual conviction.

On my way to Mass this morning, it occurred to me that if Muslims believed that God was truly present in their mosques, and that by some mystical power they could receive and consume him in the form of bread and wine, they would crawl over red-hot broken glass for the chance. But as Catholics, we are so unaware of the mystery and the privilege that most of us cannot be bothered to show up to church on Sunday and many of those who do can hardly wait to get out.

Modern Catholics complain about the Mass in a constant litany: "Mass is boring." "The music is too old-fashioned." "I couldn't understand what the priest was trying to say." "The sound system is no good." "It went for too long." "I cannot relate to the priest." "The people at Mass are not my age." Maybe, just maybe, we are missing the point.

It seems we have lost our sense of wonder. This is true in almost every area of our lives, but particularly when it comes to matters of faith and spirituality. We have lost the quintessential quality of childhood—wonder.

Do you experience the wonder? Are you able to look beyond what appear to be routine actions of the Mass to the timeless meaning? Do you sense the mystery and power of receiving and consuming Christ in the Eucharist? Do you marvel at the fact? If we believe that Christ is truly present in the Eucharist, then the power unleashed within us by the consumption of the Eucharist is immeasurable.

I often wonder as I watch great athletes compete, knowing that they are not Catholic, how much better they would perform if they believed Christ was present in the Eucharist and they could receive him right before a race. What is true for these athletes is also true for our lives. There is incredible power in the Eucharist.

We don't go to Mass to socialize. We don't go to be entertained. We go to give ourselves to God, and in return to receive God. Open your heart, open your mind, and open your soul to the miracles God wants to work in and through you.

Life is not about what sort of shoes you wear. It's not about what street you live on. It is not about how much money you have in the bank or what sort of car you drive. It's not about whether or not you get that promotion, or where you and your family vacation each year. Life is not about whom you have dated, whom you are dating, or whom you married. It is not about whether or not you made the football team. Life is not about what college you went to, what college may or may not accept you, or what college your children are going to. Life isn't about these things.

Life is about whom you love and whom you hurt. Life is about how you love yourself and how you hurt yourself. It's about how you love and hurt the people in your life. You can't see these things, but they are powerful and real.

Mass is not about whom you sit next to. It's not about which priest says Mass. It is not about what you wear or who is there. Mass is not about the music. It's not even about the preaching. It about gathering as a community to give thanks to God for all the blessings he fills our lives with. It is about receiving the body and blood of Christ, not just physically, but spiritually. Perhaps you have been receiving the Eucharist physically every Sunday for your whole life. Next Sunday, prepare yourself, be conscious of the marvel, the wonder, the mystery, and receive spiritually.

Rediscover the wonder.

• A Quick Journey Through the Mass •

As I work my way through these seven chapters covering the Seven Pillars of Catholic Spirituality I have paused time and time again and thought, *I really need a whole book to explain each pillar.* Each time I fall into this pattern of thought I have to remind myself that my intent here is to give you an overall perspective of Catholicism and what it could mean to your life, while at the same time whetting your appetite and inspiring you to take the next step in your journey. I hope spiritual reading will become a daily part of your life after you read this book, and that this is the first of many spiritual books you will read.

With this in mind, I would now like to take you on a quick journey through the various parts of the Mass. In doing so, I hope to unveil some of the meanings that too often remain unknown and hidden, and instruct you about ways you can become more actively engaged throughout the Mass.

Introductory Rites. These essentially consist of the entrance procession and song, a greeting, the Sign of the Cross, the penitential act, the Gloria, and an opening prayer.

Entrance. After the people are assembled the entrance song begins. Like every single part of the Mass, the opening song and procession have intended meaning. This song opens the celebration. It is designed to bind us together as a community, to intensify our unity. The song should also be carefully selected to lead our thoughts to the mystery of the particular feast or season.

Engage: Make an effort to sing. You may not enjoy singing, or you may be unable to sing. In that case, follow the words of the song in your hymnal, reflecting on how they challenge or comfort you.

Penitential Act. This is the moment when we acknowledge that some of our thoughts, words, and actions have not helped us become the-best-version-of-ourselves, have prevented other people from being all God created them to be, and ultimately have created an obstacle between us and the infinite love of God.

Engage: Identify a specific thought, word, or action that created an obstacle between you and God this week and ask forgiveness.

Gloria. *Glory to God in the highest and on earth peace to people of good will . . .* The Gloria is an ancient hymn that praises God. Our earthly relationships have become very transactional. We tend to speak to people only when we want something or if they have done something wrong. This transactional mentality has overflowed into our spiritual lives, and as a result the practice of praising God has fallen largely into disuse.

Engage: Set yourself and your life aside for a moment, and praise God for something specific. Praise God for his goodness. Praise God for creation. Praise God for his wisdom.

Opening Prayer. This is one of my favorite parts of the Mass. I find the opening prayers to be ever fresh and phenomenally profound. They also provide a prelude to what we are about to hear and experience. The opening prayer is designed to place us in the presence of God and focus our hearts and minds. This is the opening prayer from the twenty-first week of Ordinary Time: *Father, help us to seek the values that will bring us lasting joy in this changing world. In our desire for what you promise, make us one in mind and heart.* The opening prayers of the Mass guide us to focus on the themes that will emerge in the readings that day. This is the opening prayer for Friday during the fourth week of Lent: *Father, our source of life, you know our weakness. May we reach out with joy to grasp your hand and walk more readily in your ways.*

Engage: Get yourself a missal and begin to follow the prayers of the Mass.

Liturgy of the Word. This essentially consists of the Scripture readings, homily, profession of faith, and the general intercessions.

Scripture Readings. The readings that make up the Liturgy of the Word for Sunday Mass include an Old Testament reading, a responsorial Psalm, a New Testament reading, and a Gospel reading. The readings are not randomly selected; they are related to each other in some way, and belong to a flow that moves us from the readings last week to the readings next week.

Engage: Take time during the week to read over and reflect upon next Sunday's readings. Find the readings in your Bible and underline them. Over time this will give you a sense of the parts of the Bible you have experienced.

Homily. The average homily lasts approximately seven minutes and for many people this is the only exposure they have to religious education all week. This is the priest's moment to speak to the community—and a singular opportunity to nurture Christian life. The challenge the priest faces is to develop some point from the readings and transform it into a powerful teaching moment. Jesus always met people where they were, and from there he led them to a better life. The homily is the priest's opportunity to convince people that Jesus has answers to the issues and questions they are struggling with, and that the life Jesus invites us to is simply the best way to live.

Engage: As a lay participant in the Mass the homily is largely outside of your control. But more often than not God uses a single phrase to speak to us. Listen. Stay open to what God might be trying to say to you. On many occasions I have attended Mass in foreign countries where I had no knowledge of the language, and yet God has spoken to me powerfully.

Our Profession of Faith. This is where we proclaim our faith as individuals and as a community. If you really reflect on the Creed I suspect you will have questions or doubts almost every time you say it. Those doubts and questions are invitations to explore and study our faith more, but also to place our trust in God and his Church. I used to find it comforting when we pray together, "We believe . . ." (before they changed it to "I believe") because whatever was lacking in what I believed on any given Sunday (because of doubts and questions that I may have) was made up for by the faith of someone in the pew in front of me or behind me, on the other side of town or the other side of the world. Together we have a complete faith.

Engage: Whatever you have questions or doubts about in the Creed, begin to explore them vigorously, one at a time. Examine why the Church teaches what she teaches in each instance and allow your questions and doubts to strengthen your faith rather than diminish it.

General Intercessions. The Mass is the most powerful prayer in human history. At every moment of every day, a Mass is taking place somewhere, and we (the Catholic Church) are praying for the entire human family. This is really quite beautiful if you stop and think about it. At this point of the Mass we offer specific intentions to God as a community. These usually include a prayer for the Church, a prayer for world leaders, prayers for those who are oppressed and those in need, prayer for the local community, and others.

Engage: Consider whom and what you are praying for. Immerse yourself for a moment in that person's need, responsibilities, or pain.

The Collection. At this time a basket is passed so that we can contribute financially to the mission of the Church. What we place in the basket we are giving to God and to the needy. It is a real and practical expression of loving God and neighbor. These funds are used to cover the expenses of the Church and the various ministries that the community is involved in.

Engage: Give generously—not because your parish needs the money, not because the priest gave a good homily, and not because others might know what you gave. Give generously because we have a real and present spiritual need to give. We also need to guard against the allure of money. It is easier to trust money than it is to trust God. "In God we trust," it says on our money. But do we? This regular Sunday giving is a sign of letting go, a sign of surrender. Too often in our society we give with lots of strings attached. Often I hear people say, "I don't give to the Church because I don't like how they spend the money." Whether this is true or not in any particular situation, this statement is filled with judgment and generalization, the pride that we know better, and a desire to control. These are all the behaviors that spiritual giving is designed to liberate us from. Give generously. It is hard, I know. You will feel torn; such is the pull of money in our lives.

Liturgy of the Eucharist. This is the "center and the summit of the entire celebration" and consists of the Eucharistic prayer, Consecration, the Our Father and sign of peace, and Communion.

The Offertory. Representatives from the community bring forward the bread and wine, along with our offerings for the Church and the poor. At the same time, the priest and servers are preparing the altar for our offering.

Engage: As the gifts are being brought forward and as the priest is preparing the gifts, in your heart bring the different aspects of your life forward and offer them to God. Offer God your marriage, your family, your career, your business, your friendships. In a special way offer him your successes and failures. Hold up to God a friend who is suffering in some way. Offer him a particular struggle that you are enduring. Offer God everything. Mentally and spiritually place them all on the altar so that God can transform them.

Eucharistic Prayer. The word *Eucharist* means "thanksgiving." During this sequence of prayers the priest invites us to lift up our hearts to the Lord. In this way, we are offering ourselves with Jesus to God the Father. This prayer also reminds us of God's goodness and his friendship with humanity throughout history.

Engage: Bring the words to life. Live them out. With your spiritual senses, lift up your heart and offer it to the Lord. Place your heart on the altar and allow God to transform it as he will transform the bread and wine.

The Consecration. Leading up to the consecration, the priest recites the narrative of the Last Supper connecting what we experience in every Mass with Jesus' institution of the Eucharist. The actual consecration is the moment when the bread and wine become the body and blood of Jesus Christ. This happens when the priest recites the words of Jesus over them: "This is my body which is given up for you; this is the blood of the new and everlasting covenant, do this in memory of me."

Engage: Simply allow yourself to be in the presence of God. Quiet your mind. Imagine yourself close to Jesus at the Last Supper or at the Crucifixion. Then as the priest elevates the host and the chalice, say with Thomas in your heart, "My Lord and my God." These mysteries are mysteries, but if we approach them humbly, often, and with reverence, God will give us an ever-increasing love and understanding of them.

The Lord's Prayer. Now we join together as a community to pray in the way that Jesus taught us.

Engage: You have prayed these words a thousand times before, but allow them to be new and fresh. Focus on a particular word or phrase and allow it to permeate your whole being. If you are struggling to cooperate with God's will perhaps you will focus on *thy will be done.* Or maybe you have real and human needs that are not being met, so your focus may fall on the words *give us this day our daily bread.* Perhaps you feel the need to be forgiven for something you have said or done: *forgive us our trespasses.* Maybe you need the grace to forgive someone who has wronged you: *as we forgive those who trespass against us.* Or perhaps you are struggling with a particular temptation at this time in your life: *lead us not into temptation, but deliver us from evil.*

Sign of Peace. The priest has asked God to grant us peace and unity. Nobody needs to be reminded of how fractured our world and Church have become, which makes this an especially powerful moment in the liturgy. Here we embrace the whole world. Jesus has loved us in this Eucharist by sharing his peace with us, and now we share the peace and love of Christ with those around us. This is symbolic of the way we are called to take the peace and love of Jesus out into the world.

Engage: Everybody has had their heart broken by something or someone. Jesus wants to soothe and heal our broken heart. He offers his peace to you to heal your broken heart and invites you to pass that peace on to others. As you offer the sign of peace to those around you at Mass be mindful that while they may look happy and seem like they have it all together, we all have a broken heart that needs healing.

Communion. This is the moment when we receive the body and blood of Jesus Christ in the form of bread and wine. It is almost beyond belief, and many have left the Church, just as many left Jesus in his own time, because of this single teaching: "This teaching is just too difficult." (John 6:60)

Engage: As you approach the altar to receive Communion be mindful of what is about to take place. I pray this short prayer over and over to allow me to focus on what is happening: *I wish, my Lord, to receive you as generously as your holy mother Mary did.*

Thanksgiving. These moments of reflection after receiving the Eucharist can be extremely powerful if we make ourselves present to them. The fruits of Holy Communion include unity with Jesus, nourishment for the spiritual life, a hunger for virtue, a desire to do the will of God, cleansing from past sins, a fanning of the flames of Christian love, grace to avoid sin in the future, sensitivity to the promptings of the Holy Spirit, and a desire to know God more intimately.

Engage: For these precious moments when Christ is so mysteriously present in you, kneel or sit, close your eyes, and just thank God in your own words for all the blessings in your life. Name them specifically—people, places, things, and opportunities that you are grateful for. Allow your heart to fill and overflow with gratitude.

Concluding Rites. The concluding rites are made up of the final blessing and the dismissal.

Final Blessing. On the way into church we blessed ourselves with the Sign of the Cross. Before the Gospel we blessed our mind, our lips, and our heart. Now we receive a blessing.

Engage: Bow your head, close your eyes, and allow the words of the final blessing to penetrate the very depths of your being.

The Dismissal. The Mass takes its name from this final statement: "Go in peace, glorifying the Lord by your life." *Ite, missa est* is a Latin phrase that means "Go, you are sent."

Engage: In this final moment of the Mass we are being sent on a mission to light up the ways of this world with the love of Christ, a love that is willing to sacrifice for others, a love that knows no limits. As you leave Church and return to the world, consider how you might live out your Christian mission this week.

There is incredible genius and beauty in the Mass, but to discover it we need to be constantly delving into it a little deeper. At every moment of the Mass there are rich opportunities to engage personally in the experience, thus transforming it from a monotonous ritual into a deeply relevant and ever-changing experience of God.

I have taken just a few minutes to give you a glimpse of the depth, the beauty, and the relevance of what we knowingly or unknowingly witness at church every Sunday. Now let us make the journey from being mere witnesses and become actively engaged participants.

• Spiritual Game Changer •

Working as business consultants, my partners and I are often asked by clients to help them identify what would be a "game changer" for their business. As I was engaged in this process with a client a few weeks ago I started to wonder, *What would be a game changer for my spiritual life?* This led me to reflect on what had been the game changers in the past. The first was definitely when I started spending ten minutes a day at church on the way to school. The second was the first time I really read the Gospels. The third was my first regular experience of daily Mass.

I didn't go every day, but a couple of months after I started spending ten minutes at church each morning, I began attending Mass on Tuesday evenings at my parish in Sydney. It was at Mass during the week that I discovered the genius of it. It was at these quiet and intimate daily Mass experiences that this sacred ritual really began to ignite my love for Catholicism. I would follow the opening prayer, the readings, and the closing prayer in my missal, and the words began to probe my heart and ignite the fire in my soul.

I would walk down to church and it would be just me, the priest, and about ten other men and women much older than I was. It was quiet, peaceful, and intimate. It was there in that daily Mass experience that I fell in love with the Mass, and the Church. By some grace, I started to listen to the prayers of the Mass, really listen . . . and it was like the pieces of a puzzle coming together to form an incredible vision.

The Mass reveals God's vision for us as individuals, his vision for marriage and family, for community and society, and for the Church and the world.

There is genius and beauty in the prayers of the Mass, and yet, most people tune out the prayers. It seems to me that keeping God's dream for us to become the-best-version-of-ourselves in the forefront of our mind unlocks the language of the many prayers that make up the Mass.

The prayers of the Mass remind us that we are pilgrims on a journey, that we are not on this journey alone, and that we are called to be responsible stewards of our own lives while at the same time living in a way that is mindful of the needs of others and mindful of the needs of all of creation. Over and over again, the prayers of the Mass orient us toward God and remind us of his desire to have a relationship with us.

There is great beauty in these prayers, but too often we don't hear them because we are distracted by our thoughts or by those around us. Some of the prayers are the same for every Mass. Others change with the seasons of the Church calendar. And still others change every day. If you take time to listen and truly pray these prayers as the priest says them, you will discover the intimate knowledge the Church has of our spiritual needs.

I will be the first to admit that at times it is difficult to concentrate on these prayers during the Mass. For that reason, I would encourage you to get yourself a missal. It may seem a little old-fashioned to some people, but owning a missal took my understanding and appreciation of the Mass to a whole new level. If you don't want to carry around a large missal, get yourself a subscription to *Word Among Us* or *Magnificat*. These are small monthly prayer companions that have morning prayer, the readings and prayers for Mass each day, evening prayer, and a variety of inspirational spiritual readings. They are very powerful spiritual tools in our busy times.

Visit DynamicCatholic.com/missal to order your subscription.

The prayers of the Mass are beautifully integrated and carefully designed to keep us focused on God's dream for us to become the-best-version-of-ourselves. For example, the opening prayer on the second week of Ordinary Time is: *Almighty and ever-present Father, your watchful care reaches to the ends of the earth and orders all things in such power that even the tension and tragedies of sin cannot frustrate your loving plans. Help us to embrace your will, give us the strength to follow your call, so that your truth may live in our hearts and reflect peace to those who believe in your love.* The opening prayers of the Mass guide us to focus on the themes that will emerge in the readings that day. This is the opening prayer for the Thursday after Ash Wednesday: *Lord, may everything we do begin with your inspiration, continue with your help, and reach perfection under your guidance.*

Get yourself a missal and just begin to follow the opening prayer, the readings, and the closing prayer, and your experience of the Mass will increase exponentially. Then during the week, begin a habit of going to Mass once or twice. This more intimate experience of the sacrament will truly fan the fire of your soul. On the days when you don't attend Mass, use the prayers and the readings from Mass that day during your time of prayer. And once in your life you should try to go to Mass every day for a whole week. Try it; you will be amazed.

Our lives change when our habits change. The only way for the Church to become more spiritual is for the people who make up the Church to become more spiritual. We become more spiritual when we seek the will of God by establishing spiritual habits. This is one real and practical way to unearth the riches of Catholicism in our day-to-day lives.

• My Favorite Prayer •

Do you have a favorite prayer in the Mass? My favorite is right before the sign of peace, when the priest prays, *Deliver us, Lord, from every evil and grant us peace in our days. In your mercy keep us free from sin, and protect us from all anxiety as we wait in joyful hope for the coming of our Savior, Jesus Christ.*

These words mean so much to me. To live a life free from sin is a humble and simple ambition, but a noble one. There is an Australian song I remember from my childhood titled *Tenterfield Saddler*. It's about a man named George who lived in a small country town. All day long he would sit on his verandah making horse saddles, and over the years he became a sage-like figure for the locals. The song begins:

> *The late George Woolnough*
> *Worked on High Street*
> *Lived on manners*
> *For fifty-two years he sat on his verandah*
> *And made his saddles.*

> *And if you had questions*
> *About sheep or flowers or dogs*
> *You just asked the saddler*
> *He lived without sin*
> *They're building a library for him.*

The line that arrests me is *He lived without sin.* I have seen how sin complicates our lives, confuses our minds, and hardens our hearts. I have seen the devastating effects of sin in my own life, in the lives of the people I love, and in the lives of complete strangers. I want to live a life free from sin, and the prayer *keep us free from sin* resonates with the deepest desires of my heart. I love the peace that is the fruit of a clear conscience. The truth is, the happiest times of my life have been when I was actively trying to live free from sin.

Protect us from all anxiety—all anxiety, not some anxiety. How much of our lives do we waste worrying? A friend of mine has a quote by Corrie ten Boom on her answering machine that says, "Worry doesn't empty tomorrow of its suffering; it empties today of its strength."

I know it is the sin in my life that causes my pain, anguish, impatience, anxiety, irritableness, restlessness, and discontentment. We waste so much time and energy on sin. Imagine how much you and I could accomplish if we didn't waste so much time and energy on sin!

It is also during the Mass that we are reminded of the good, kind, and gentle love of God as Father, as we join together before Communion to pray the Our Father.

A good friend of mine volunteers in Chicago prisons, visiting the inmates and leading Bible studies. Not too long ago, he invited me to visit a maximum-security facility and speak to the prisoners. I accepted the invitation, and a couple of weeks before the event was scheduled to take place, I asked to speak with the three chaplains from the prison to get a sense of the group. They told me many things about the group, but the most alarming fact they shared was in relation to the entire male prison population in America. In fact, ninety percent of male prisoners in America today between the ages of sixteen and thirty grew up separated from their biological fathers. Ninety percent!

I believe the present fatherless generation is the result of the evil forces that tempt our hearts. You may not be separated from your biological father, but these same evil forces want to sow in you the seeds of doubt, skepticism, and cynicism. And in doing so, they separate you from your heavenly Father.

I don't speak of them often, but I believe evil spirits exist, and that they are at work in the world and in our lives. Like C. S. Lewis, I believe that it is a mistake to give the devil too much attention while it is also a mistake to give the devil too little attention.

The devil wants to orphan you. He wants to drag you away from your Father. He wants to crush the Spirit in you that leads you to cry out to God, *Abba Father*. He wants to kidnap you from your spiritual Father. He wants to distract you from the gentle and persistent call of your heavenly Father. Don't let him. Ponder just those first two words of this ancient prayer: *Our Father*. If we could really understand this single truth of God as Father, we would weep for joy every time this prayer crossed our lips.

I also believe that the liberty and equality that men and women have struggled with and searched for throughout history have been revealed through this simple prayer. If only we could understand and grasp the fact that we are all children of God. Only then can we relate to each other as we should.

The prayers of the Mass are profound and powerful. Rediscover them.

• Beyond You and Me •

The Catholic Church is a family of prayer. At every moment of every day the Mass is being celebrated all over the world and we are praying as Catholics not only for ourselves and our own needs, but for the whole human family.

Beyond our own personal experience of the Mass, it is important to be aware of the much greater scope of it. It is in the Mass that the 1.2 billion Catholics around the world come together to share a common experience. But the wisdom of regular worship has a much deeper meaning than bringing us all together once a week; it is a profound reflection of God's blueprint for all of creation.

I wrote *The Rhythm of Life* not only for a Catholic audience, nor alone for a Christian audience, but for the whole cross section of society. And yet, I learned the premise upon which I based the book from the way the Church structures our practice of Christianity. Everything in creation has rhythm.

Rhythm is at the core of God's genius for creation. As we turn to God, we are invited to use this same blueprint for our life. In Genesis, we read that God created the world in six days and rested on the seventh. He didn't rest because he was tired. God rested on the seventh day because he foresaw our need for rest.

The seasons change to a rhythm. The tides come in and go out to a rhythm. The sun rises and sets to a rhythm. Your heart pumps blood through your body to a rhythm. Plants grow according to the process of photosynthesis, which is based on a rhythm. And ultimately, the workings of a woman's body are based on a rhythm—and that rhythm gives forth new life. The rhythm gives birth to harmony, efficiency, effectiveness, health, happiness, peace, and prosperity. Destroy the rhythm and you invite chaos, confusion, destruction, and disorder.

This is the wisdom upon which the Church bases our worship as Catholics. The Church bases the calendar on the rhythm that God has placed at the center of creation. In turn, the Church hopes this will help us to place this essential rhythm at the center of our own lives.

It is within this context that we can begin to understand Sunday as a day of rest and renewal, and more specifically, the role of the Mass in the Catholic lifestyle.

• Embrace the Gift •

God doesn't call us to church on Sunday because he has some egotistical need for us all to fall down before him and worship him at ten o'clock each Sunday morning. It isn't designed to help him; it's designed to help us. It isn't intended to make him happy; it's intended to allow us to share in his happiness.

There is a beautiful song titled "Come to the Feast Divine," written by Liam Lawton, from his album *In the Quiet*. Everything about this piece of music invites us to an incredible celebration. It begins with a simple question, "Will you come to the Feast Divine?" I hope you will. I will be there with you in spirit with all the angels and the saints. Pray for me as I pray for you. The Mass is filled with riches. It is an unfathomable gift. Embrace the gift.

Chapter Fifteen

THE BIBLE

The young man's name was Michael. It was a little more than a week before his eighteenth birthday when he stopped by his father's office one day after school. He had been disagreeing with his father about most things lately, and as he walked into the office, Michael said, "Dad, it's going to be my birthday next Tuesday, and if you love me you'll get me a new car for my birthday." His father just looked at him and Michael continued, "And if you really love me, you'll get me the car I've always wanted." Then, without giving his father a chance to reply, he left.

The next morning at breakfast his father said jokingly, "Michael, yesterday when you stopped by the office, you didn't mention what sort of car you've always wanted."

Michael replied, "You know, Dad, a red Porsche."

The boy's father smiled and asked, "And how much do they cost?"

"Ninety-two thousand dollars, and if you really love me, Dad, that's what you'll get me for my birthday. Don't let me down," Michael replied and left for school.

Tuesday came, and as was the family's custom, they celebrated Michael's birthday with dinner and the cutting of the cake. And as they enjoyed their cake, one by one Michael's brothers and sisters handed him a gift. He opened the gifts and thanked them each graciously, but his mind was elsewhere. Finally, the moment he had been waiting for arrived.

Even as Michael's father handed him a small rectangular parcel, he hoped he would find the keys to his new car. Michael ripped at the wrapping paper and discovered that it was a book, a Bible. He didn't even finish unwrapping it. Disgusted, he stood up, pushed his chair away from the table and against the wall behind him, and rushed from the dining room. Racing upstairs to his bedroom, he slammed the door and threw the still-unopened gift against the wall. It hit the wall, then the floor, and bounced into the corner.

Michael went to bed without talking to anyone. The next morning he got up early and went to school, again without speaking to anyone.

Just before lunch that day, Michael's father suffered a massive heart attack. He was rushed to the hospital, and arrangements were made to bring Michael from school to the hospital to be with his father. For seven hours, Michael sat at his unconscious father's bedside, playing the events of the night before over and over in his head. Exhausted and hungry, he got up and went to get some coffee and a sandwich, and while he was gone his father died.

Michael was devastated. He went home, lay on his bed, and cried. He wept inconsolably for hours, and then out of the corner of his eye he saw the gift, still unopened, sitting in the corner.

Getting up off the bed, he went over and picked it up and finished unwrapping it. For some time he just sat there holding the leather Bible and staring at it. Then, opening the Bible, he discovered an inscription on the inside front cover.

Dear Michael,
Within these pages, you will find the answers to all of life's questions,
and the secrets to all of life's success. With love on your eighteenth
birthday,
Dad

Michael wept some more. The tears streamed down his face, falling to the page and smudging his father's handwriting. To console himself, Michael opened the Bible and flicked through the pages, hoping to find some words to comfort him. What he discovered was that his father had placed a bookmark in the Bible. He removed the bookmark and stared at it with openmouthed amazement.

It was a check for ninety-two thousand dollars.

This father was able to give his son everything from a material standpoint, it seems. But more important, he wanted his son to place the Word of God at the center of his life. His son was surprised to find the check in the Bible, but I hope it was just one of many wonderful surprises he found in its pages.

In the same way, God wants us to discover the many surprises he has tucked away in the pages of the Bible. And, as it was with Michael, we often value the wrong things and set our hearts on our own selfish plans. But God has a better plan for each of our lives than we could even imagine for ourselves, and he always wants to give us more.

• Where Did the Bible Come From? •

Of all the books ever written or published, the Bible is the most widely read, studied, translated, printed, sold, gifted, distributed, and quoted. It is the best-selling book of all time. When it comes to teaching about the nature of God and his desires for us, no other book comes close. In the Bible, we discover the depth and generosity of God's love, as well as his desire to soothe humanity's yearning for truth and happiness. Where did the Bible come from? How did we come to be blessed with such a rare treasure?

I begin our discussion of the Scriptures with these questions because in recent Christian history the Bible has been kidnapped by Protestant and Evangelical Christians.

At one time or another, most Catholics have been cornered by an over-zealous Christian in the workplace or supermarket. They immediately start quoting Scripture, and oftentimes their well-argued ideas leave their Catholic targets tired, confused, filled with doubts, and feeling spiritually inadequate. Chances are, if the conversation proceeds to any length, they will approach the idea that the Bible is the one and only source of inspiration, direction, and Revelation. This of course, is a direct attack upon the Catholic Church. It may be carefully masked or subtly presented. Those presenting the idea may not even be aware that it is an attack on Catholicism. But as Catholics, we believe that both the "Sacred Scriptures and sacred tradition form one sacred deposit of the word of God" (*Dei Verbum*). God reveals himself in nature, he reveals himself in the Scriptures, and he reveals himself in the life of the Church.

It is this dynamic interaction between the Scriptures and tradition that keeps the Word alive. If you separate the Scriptures from the living, breathing institution they were entrusted to, they lose their life. This is a major point of contention between Catholics and other non-Catholic Christians. But with this background and as an attempt to shed a little light on this point of contention, let us return to the original question. Where did the Bible come from?

Well, it didn't just drop down from Heaven one fine day, nor did it appear suddenly on the earth, delivered by an angel of God. The Bible was written with some form of primitive inks and pens by people just like you and me. They were divinely inspired in a way that none of us will fully understand in this life, but they were ordinary people with strengths and weaknesses.

The Bible isn't a book. It is a collection of books—seventy-three in all: forty-six in the Old Testament and twenty-seven in the New Testament. Hence the name *Biblia* in Greek, which means "the books" or "library." It is important to note that most Protestant and Evangelical Bibles contain only sixty-six books. It was during the Reformation that non-Catholic Christians removed the following books: Tobit, Judith, Maccabees 1 and 2, Wisdom, Sirach, and Baruch.

It is important to note that for more than fifteen hundred years all Christians were Catholic, and they all accepted these books as part of the Bible. It is also interesting to note that the great majority of non-Catholic Christians have no idea that there are books missing from their Bible, just as all non-Catholic Christians are Protestants, whether they are aware of it or not. Though the great majority could probably not tell you what they are protesting.

The Bible wasn't written all at once, nor was it all written by one person. In fact, one thousand years elapsed between the writing of the book of Genesis and the writing of the book of Revelation.

If you had lived in the court of King David (1000–962 BC), the only parts of what is today the Bible that you would have read are some of the stories from Genesis, the stories of the Exodus, the journey from Egypt to the Holy Land, and the stories of the Israelites settling in the Holy Land that we find in the book of Judges.

The Old Testament was written and compiled between the twelfth century and the second century BC. It is made up of forty-six books, and is divided into three categories: the Pentateuch, the Prophets, and the Writings.

The Pentateuch, which is also known as the Law, Torah, or the Five Books of Moses, consists of the first five books of the Old Testament: Genesis, Exodus, Leviticus, Numbers, and Deuteronomy. This was the embryo of the Bible. The section known as the Prophets includes all the major and minor prophets of the Old Testament. And finally, the Writings section includes the historical documents.

The New Testament was written between AD 45 and AD 150 and includes twenty-seven books. It is made up of four narratives of the life, death, and resurrection of Jesus: the Gospels, a narrative of the apostles' ministries in the early Church; Acts of the Apostles, twenty-one early letters consisting of Christian counsel, instruction, and encouragement; the Epistles; and Revelation, a book of prophecy.

It is perhaps needless to say that the Bible was not originally written in English (though the way some people represent it you might sometimes wonder). The prominent original language of the Old Testament was Hebrew; Greek was the language of the New Testament. What we have today is a translation into English from the original languages of the prophets, apostles, and evangelists.

In every case, it is important for us to realize that the cultures, countries, and times were very different than what we experience today. Some things can mean one thing in one culture and something quite different in another culture. I learned this very quickly as I began to travel from country to country in the earliest years speaking. In our own lives, we experience this in misunderstandings between generations as close as parents and children.

It is also critically important that we remember that the Bible, as we have it now, was not printed at all until almost fifteen hundred years after the birth of Jesus Christ. It is easy to forget in our modern world, where we can print and publish works from home computers and download them to digital devices, that not all eras have enjoyed the luxury and convenience of the printing press. For almost one and a half millennia after the life, death, and Resurrection of Jesus, the only books that existed were handwritten. This certainly places the modern Protestant-Evangelical idea that every person must carry around a Bible in perspective, along with their criticism that Catholics didn't read the Bible before the Reformation.

If you had lived prior to the invention of the printing press, like the men and women of the first fifteen hundred years of Christianity, you would have had no access whatsoever to a physical Bible. This is not because the Church wanted to keep people ignorant, nor was it because Church leaders did not want people reading the Scriptures. It was simply because every single copy of the Bible was an original manuscript that a Catholic monk or friar had laboriously copied onto pages of parchment or vellum. For a millennium and a half Christians learned about the stories that fill the Scriptures from sermons at Mass, by seeing them in stained glass windows, or by watching them performed in mystery plays.

Today, our non-Catholic Christian brothers and sisters place an enormous emphasis on reading and studying the Bible. And while I am in favor of both, it is critical that we do not lose sight of the fact that hundreds of millions of people came to know Christ without ever owning or studying the Bible. Many modern Christians make it sound like it is impossible to receive salvation without a Bible. If that were the case, what happened to the people who lived before the Bible was printed? What happened to the people who lived before it was even written in its present form? How were men and women introduced to Jesus before the sixteenth century? How were the people of foreign lands inspired to live the Christian life before the Bible was available in mass production? It is here, in the gap of most Protestants' understanding of Christian history, that you find the beauty of Catholicism.

Does God have favorites? Did he favor those born after the fifteenth century more than those before? Surely God desired that the countless millions of people who lived before the fifteenth century would know and follow the life and teachings of Jesus. But how could they if they had no Bibles, or had no money to buy Bibles, or could not read the Bible even if they could buy one, or could not understand the Bible even if they could read it?

From the Catholic perspective, salvation is available to the men and women of every age and every culture. Through the teachings of the Church, the people of every land for two thousand years have learned about the life and teachings of Jesus Christ. The people of every place and time have been encouraged to believe and do all that Jesus taught. And in many cases, this great work has been achieved in all corners of the globe without a written or printed Bible.

With this clear and concise understanding of the history of the Scriptures, the Protestant theory of *sola scriptura,* or "the Bible and the Bible alone," self-destructs into the most monumental case of well-argued nonsense in the history of humanity.

Christians of all denominations around the world owe an enormous debt to the Catholic Church. The Catholic Church, inspired and guided by the Holy Spirit, is responsible for the formulation, preservation, and integrity of the Sacred Scriptures. For fifteen hundred years, when there were no Baptists, Lutherans, Pentecostals, Methodists, Anglicans, Evangelicals, Non-denominationals, or any other Christian Church of any type, the Catholic Church preserved the Scriptures from error, saved them from destruction and extinction, multiplied them in every language under the sun, and conveyed the truths they contained to people everywhere. Time and time again, people have tried to manipulate and corrupt these writings—and in some cases have succeeded—but the Catholic Church has preserved a version that is complete and free from human tampering.

It seems strangely paradoxical that so many who claim to love Jesus Christ would be so hostile toward the Church, which has single-handedly protected the records of his life and teachings for so long.

The Bible is the most profound and sublime collection of writings in human history. It therefore goes without saying that these writings are difficult to understand. Individual interpretation of the Bible is a very slippery path that leads people to great confusion, heartache, and distress. The history of Christianity in the past five hundred years is proof enough of this point. This type of approach doesn't promote unity, and always leads to division among Christians. What sadness Christ must feel as he stands witness to the bickering and division of Christian history. After all, in his final prayer he prayed "that all may be one." (John 17:22)

This is why the Catholic Church has, in her wisdom, so vigorously defended her sole right to interpret the meaning of the Scriptures throughout history. The living voice of the Catholic Church stands as a beacon for all men and women of good will, and announces the life and teachings of Jesus Christ with tradition in one hand and the Scriptures in the other.

Ultimately, interpreting the Scriptures comes down to a question of authority. It perhaps is no surprise that the greatest obstacle to Christian unity is also the question of authority. The greatest challenge that faces us, as Christians, in our quest for unity is to free so many from the blind subservience to a book and deliver them to a loving obedience to God alive and present in the one, holy, catholic, and apostolic Church.

• Jesus: The Turning Point in Human History •

Throughout human history, every civilization has reached out to God. Different societies have reached out to God in different ways, and many of them seem strange to us today, but they all point to a single truth: Deep in the heart of every person, there is a desire to know God and a yearning to draw nearer to him. Similarly, at every moment of human history, God has reached out to man. God desires to be with his people.

God's ultimate expression of this reaching out was the coming of Jesus Christ. Born two thousand years ago, Jesus of Nazareth is not a myth or a legend, but a well-documented figure in history. But more than that, he is the Messiah who had been prophesied in the Jewish Scriptures—our Old Testament—and long awaited by the Jewish people. There is evidence to support this claim in his miracles, but ultimately we must each decide for ourselves: Was Jesus a liar, a lunatic, or the Messiah, as he claimed to be? I suppose it is only by that mysterious and wonderful gift of faith that we are able to conclude that Jesus was who he claimed to be.

Every noble human endeavor in history has been a preparation for the coming of Jesus or a response to his life and teachings.

Jesus lived a life on this earth. He ate, he drank, and he walked down the street. Do you know him as a person? Or is he just a historical figure to you? It is crucial that we move beyond the facade of the story of Jesus Christ. We must delve deep into his life and teachings. We must allow his Spirit to flood the thoughts, words, and actions of our daily lives. In order to do all this it is necessary that we come to know the Gospels intimately.

Saint Jerome once wrote, "Ignorance of the Scriptures is ignorance of Christ." The great tragedy in the modern environment is that people know more about their favorite music group or sports players than they do about Jesus Christ. Get to know Jesus. Read the Gospels. Never let a day pass without pondering a few of the precious words in those four books. Don't just race through them. Choose a small section and read it slowly. Reflect on the meaning. Then reread it and ponder those words. Allow the words to penetrate the hardness of your heart. Allow the words of the Gospels to erode your personal prejudices, to wash away your narrow-mindedness, to banish your judgmental tendencies. You don't have to read five chapters a day—just a small passage. But allow the life and teachings of Jesus Christ, alive and present in the Gospels, to sink their roots deep into your life.

Imagine yourself there with dusty sandals, on those hot days, edging just to get a little closer to him, the crowd pressing in on every side. Only then will we form an intimate relationship with this man we call Jesus.

Only then will we discover that he is God and Savior, but also coach, companion, mentor, guide, brother, teacher, healer, and friend.

• Where Should You Start? •

There are many ways to approach reading the Bible. You could, of course, start at Genesis and read your way through to Revelation. It is one way to do it and millions of people do it this way every year. They start the year with a resolution to read the Bible, and they do, from start to finish. The primary problem with this approach is that the books are not even placed in chronological order, and so the bigger picture can be lost. The Bible was not assembled to be read from beginning to end.

Start with the Gospels—Matthew, Mark, Luke, and John. Don't just read them once. Read them over and over, fifteen or twenty minutes a day, for a whole year. Allow the life and teachings of Jesus Christ to sink their roots deep into your heart, mind, soul, and life.

You may have read them before, or feel that you have been adequately exposed to them at church. But this passing familiarity with Jesus and the Gospels can actually be a disadvantage. It can lead us to overlook the radical nature of Jesus' teachings. The teachings of Jesus Christ were radical two thousand years ago, and they are just as radical today. If you doubt that, consider Matthew 5:44: "Love your enemies and pray for those who persecute you." Before this, what had been the teaching? An "eye for an eye, tooth for a tooth." (Exodus 21:24) It is easy to read this teaching and accept it intellectually, but living it requires a constant vigilance.

Unless we are willing to constantly examine the way we live, love, work, think, and speak under the piercing light of the Gospels, we will almost certainly find ourselves gradually adopting a Gospel of convenience. A Gospel of convenience consists of, taking what we find easy and comfortable from the teachings of Jesus and ignoring the rest.

For example, let us consider the teaching, "Love your enemies and pray for those who persecute you." Each year I visit more than one hundred cities in the regular course of my work, and so I have the opportunity to attend many different parishes for Mass throughout the year. In the course of the Mass we pray for many people. We pray for the sick, the addicted, the hungry, the lonely, the depressed, the marginalized, the dead, and many others. But since September 11, 2001, I have not heard a single prayer in any of our Churches for Osama bin Laden, or for Al Qaeda, or for terrorists. And not only that, if your priest stood up at the beginning of Mass next Sunday and announced that he was offering Mass for Osama bin Laden, what sort of reaction do you think he would get?

The teachings of Jesus are as radical today as they were when they were first announced. They call us to a way of life that is both more challenging and more rewarding. Catholicism is not easy. It is an advanced way of life that requires all of our being; the Gospels are a constant reminder to us all of what we are created for and called to.

• Beyond the Gospels •

Once you have familiarized yourself with the Gospels, I would suggest that you then read the narrative books. Of the seventy-three books in the Bible, fourteen are narrative books:

Genesis

Exodus

Numbers

Joshua

Judges

1 Samuel

2 Samuel

1 Kings

2 Kings

Ezra

Nehemiah

1 Maccabees

Luke

Acts

By reading these narrative books in order you begin to see the big picture—the chronological story of God's relationship with humanity.

Begin by familiarizing yourself with the Gospels. Then read the fourteen narrative books in order to get a sense of the whole story. Finally, explore the other books of the Bible, keeping in mind the Gospels and the big picture revealed by the narrative books.

The Bible is the most influential book in history. Certainly, the Old Testament has special value for those of Jewish belief and both the Old and New Testaments have special significance to those of Christian belief. But even outside of the religious significance it is impossible to ignore the relevance and influence the Bible has had on human history. From historic and sociological perspectives it would seem to me impossible to ignore its value. Even from a purely secular point of view the Bible has enormous relevance, even when viewed solely from an academic perspective. But our modern secular culture seems intent on ignoring the most influential writings of all time. I am continually astounded at how many so-called educated people have not read the Bible.

• Stories, Questions, and Prayers •

Whether you are beginning your first quest to read the Bible or your next quest, as you do I would encourage you to pay attention to stories, questions, and prayers.

Stories. The Bible is the single story that has shaped and is shaping human history. At the same time, it is a collection of stories. We find that the greatest stories ever told are in the Bible, and every other story is only a variation of one of the biblical tales that echo throughout history. The reason they echo throughout history is because they are the stories of men and women as they struggle to know themselves, to know God, and to work out their salvation. In this way they are the stories of all men and women, and thus are ever fresh.

People are often shocked by the human weakness of key characters in biblical stories. Many are surprised, even scandalized, that God would use people with such monumental vices and shortcomings to reach out to humanity and give us hope for the future.

The danger is to read the Bible as an observer. It is easy to read these stories from the cold distance of an objective observer and not allow them to penetrate our lives. People have been doing just this ever since these stories were written. The challenge is to get involved.

It is all too easy to read the story of Moses leading the Israelites out of slavery and into the desert and think that we have nothing to learn, or that we would never complain like the Israelites did when food was scarce. The temptation is to read the Gospels and believe that we would never be cruel, calculating, vindictive, and hard-hearted, like some of the Pharisees were. We are tempted to presume that we would be the one leper who returns. But the ultimate temptation is to read the Bible and see ourselves only in Jesus.

Every single person in the Bible is put there to serve you. This procession of people, with their strengths and weaknesses, their faults, failings, flaws, talents, and abilities, their virtues and their vices, are your servants. Hidden between the lines of these ancient texts, they wait, wanting to teach you the great truths of the journey.

They provide this invaluable service by acting as mirrors. What do you see when you look into a mirror? Yes, yourself. These men and women afford you the opportunity to look deep into your divided heart and see your *self*— the good and the bad, that which is worthy and that which is in need of redemption. Until you have learned to see yourself in every person in the Scriptures, you have not read the Bible.

The stories that fill the Bible are the stories of hundreds of men and women and their struggles to walk with God, to make the journey of the soul, to surrender and allow God to save them. These are the stories of men and women who have tried and succeeded, or struggled and failed in their quest to become the-best-version-of-themselves. In some of these characters we find great success in this journey. In others we find great failure. But in most we find an intriguing mixture of both failure and success, the humanity that resonates with us deeply because it reminds us of our own struggles.

Most draw near to God only to abandon his ways; then from the anguish of the brokenness and emptiness of their sin, they once again draw near to God and return to his ways.

There is perhaps no better example than Peter. One of the first to be gathered into Jesus' inner circle, Peter leaves everything behind to follow Jesus. Later, he turns his back on Jesus, denying he even knows him. But after Jesus' Resurrection, Peter becomes the unifying voice for the early Church.

Can you relate to Peter? Have you ever ignored what you knew in good conscience was the right thing to do because you were afraid what people might think of you?

As we discussed earlier, stories have a very powerful impact on our lives. They can transform civilizations. A story can win or lose a war. Stories can conquer the hearts of millions and transform enemies into friends. They can help heal the sick. The proud despise them because they are simple, but stories are one of the most powerful agents in history. They can reform the political or spiritual temperament of an age. Stories can be either light or darkness.

What stories are you allowing to direct your life?

Questions. We all have questions, and how we respond to them often determines the direction of our lives. In fact, the questions we ask of ourselves and of life are often more important than the answers we find. The reason is because if you ask the wrong questions you always get the wrong answers.

Our modern culture is asking all the wrong questions, and that is why so many are living lives of quiet desperation. These are the questions we are encouraged to ask by this so-called advanced culture: What do I want to do? What's in it for me? Will it feel good? How can I get people to serve me? How can I do less and get more? How can I get more power? What do I need to do to feel safe and secure? All of these questions lead us along the lonely path of self-centeredness. In this scenario, we place ourselves at the center of the universe. Do we really expect to find happiness by building our lives on such a distorted view of life and reality? We place ourselves at the center of human history, and by doing so isolate ourselves from any chance of lasting happiness.

As we read the Bible, we come across many people who fled from God's designs, but they never found happiness in their own plans. It was not until they turned back to God and said, "Here I am Lord, I come to do your will," (1 Samuel 3:4) that they experienced the wholeness and fulfillment they had been yearning for all along. Humanity's greatest foolishness is the discredited fantasy that we can find lasting happiness separate from the will of God.

The questions we ask are important—those we ask of ourselves, of our spouses, our children, our employees and employer, our friends, and the occasional pilgrim stranger who crosses our path.

Questions are an integral part of the spiritual journey. The temptation is to despise questions and the uncertainty they represent. But uncertainty is a spiritual gift designed to help us to grow. From time to time, great questions arise in our hearts and our minds. When that happens to you, don't let your heart be troubled. Learn to enjoy uncertainty. Learn to love the questions. The questions are life.

Three or four years ago, my brother Andrew gave me a copy of a book titled *Letters to a Young Poet*. It is a small book that contains a collection of letters written by the great German lyric poet Rainer Maria Rilke to Franz Kappus, who at the time was a young aspiring poet. In one of the letters, Rilke penned some words that have remained ingrained on my heart since I read and underlined them in that small volume: "Be patient toward all that is unresolved in your heart and try to love the questions themselves like locked rooms and like books that are written in a foreign tongue. Do not now seek the answers, which cannot be given you because you would not be able to live them. And the point is, to live everything. Live the questions now. Perhaps you will then gradually, without noticing it, live along some distant day into the answer."

Try to enjoy the wonder of the questions in your life. Allow your soul to breathe deeply, as the body must do sometimes to live among certain circumstances. Stand amid the uncertainty of the great questions life proposes, take a deep breath, and enjoy them.

The Bible is full of questions. Every person we experience in the Scriptures is asking a question, explicitly or implicitly, of life, of God, of themselves. As you pass from book to book, and story to story, be mindful of the questions each person is asking.

And if you happen upon God asking a question, pay close attention. God has no need to ask questions; he already has all the answers. So when he does ask a question, he asks not for his sake, but for ours. He asks questions like a great teacher: God asks questions to educate.

The perfect example of this divine questioning is in the third chapter of Genesis. God arrives in the garden at the time of the afternoon breeze as he does each day. Only on this particular day, Adam and Eve have hidden themselves. God calls out to them, "Where are you?" (Genesis 3:9) He doesn't ask because he doesn't know where they are. He asks because he wants them to realize where they are. God wants Adam and Eve to realize the absurdity of trying to hide from him. He wants them to be aware that they have turned their backs on him, gone against his life-giving designs, and rejected his friendship. By calling out to them, "Where are you?" he causes them to realize where they are and where they should be.

I often hear his call in the moments of the day in the very same way: I find myself wandering from the path, and he calls out to me, "Where are you?" I pray we can all learn to hear his gentle voice in the circumstances of our daily lives.

Prayers. Woven into these ageless stories and the great questions the Bible raises we also find some of the most beautiful prayers ever written.

The prayer of Jabez is just one example: "Oh, that you would truly bless me and enlarge my territory, that your hand might be with me, that you would keep me from evil, that I may cause no pain." (1 Chronicles 4:10) But this is just one example of the hundreds of prayers that emerge as we read the Bible.

When you are confused or troubled, weary or distracted, and finding it difficult to concentrate during prayer, use these prayers. I often use a Psalm as my last prayer of the day. I kneel beside my bed and just pray the words of the Psalm slowly. Sometimes I go through them one after another, day by day. At other times, at the end of a long day I just turn to one of my favorites in search of guidance or comfort.

The Bible is the richest treasury of prayers. Some of the prayers are obvious, like the Psalms, but others are treasures hidden among the stories, waiting to be discovered.

Amid the hustle and bustle of a busy day, I like to use what I call the First Christian Prayers to keep me in tune with my spiritual priorities. The First Christian Prayers is the name I have given to the words people spoke to Christ during his lifetime. When we pray, we speak and listen to God. These words were spoken directly to Jesus—true God and true man—so I believe they have a special power.

When I sense that God is calling me to something, but I'm not sure what, or when I have a decision to make and don't know which option to favor, I pray the words of the blind man: "Lord, open my eyes so that I may see." (Matthew 20:33) I pray them over and over in the moments of the day, using them as a mantra in the gaps between activities—at a stoplight, in line at the supermarket, when I am on hold on the telephone.

During times of doubt, questioning, or confusion, I use the prayer of the father of the possessed boy: "Lord I believe, help my unbelief." (Mark 9:24)

At other times I use the words of the criminal next to Jesus on the cross: "Jesus, remember me when you come into your Kingdom." (Luke 23:42)

And one of my very favorite prayers is the words of Peter when Jesus asks him three times, "Do you love me?" and Peter replies, "Lord, you know all things, you know that I love you." (John 21:17) Sometimes I use this prayer when I have offended God with my words or actions. At other times I use them when I feel hopeless or inadequate in my attempts to express my love for God.

When my sinfulness overwhelms me, I pray, "If you wish you can make me clean." (Matthew 8:2)

I pray these simple prayers over and over again throughout the day. They allow me to stay connected to God even among the many activities that can make my days very busy.

• 77 Years •

If you were born in 1900 your life expectancy was forty-seven years. Today the average American lives for seventy-seven years. This is my question for you: How are you going to tell God that you didn't have time to read his book?

The Bible is not just another book or collection of books. Words have value according to who writes them or speaks them. If a liar tells you something, you don't give his words any attention. But if an honest and honorable man tells you something, even if what he says challenges your deepest personal beliefs you will consider his words carefully, because you respect him as a man of integrity.

The Word of God deserves to be approached with reverence and awe. It is all too easy to think that we know a certain story, and to tune out as a result. But to do so would be a mistake. The Word of God is constantly new and fresh, even for those who have spent a lifetime exploring it. The reason is because our lives are constantly changing, we are constantly changing, and our relationships with God and others are constantly changing.

If you have not yet had a life-changing experience with the Bible, I am so excited for the opportunity that is before you at this time. My hope is that this chapter has intrigued you, and made you comfortable enough to pick up the Bible and begin a fabulous new adventure in your spiritual life.

Chapter Sixteen

FASTING

In a world obsessed with pleasure the fifth pillar may demonstrate the relevance of our spirituality more than any of the other spiritual disciplines. You and I were created to love and be loved, and as such we yearn to love and be loved. As long as men and women have this yearning, the practices and traditions of our faith will be relevant. Let me explain.

It is often said that in our present age there is a poverty of love. Divorce rates are usually cited to support this claim. But I would like to suggest that our culture is not experiencing a poverty of love, but rather a poverty of self-possession. Our ability to love is directly linked to the level of self-possession that we have. In order to love, in order to put another before ourselves, we need self-possession. The person who has little self-possession thinks only of himself and constantly places his desires before the needs of others. The very act of loving is an act of self-donation, of giving ourselves to another. But in order to give ourselves, we must first possess ourselves. It is this self-possession that has been massively diminished by the hedonistic ideas of our culture. Broken relationships, soaring divorce rates, relationships that stay together only for convenience, and dysfunction within even the healthiest relationships are just the symptoms. The disease is our lack of self-possession.

All the spiritual disciplines that make up the incredible landscape of Catholic spirituality are designed in one way or another to restore our lost self-possession so that we can once again love God and neighbor, and be loved the way we were created to be loved.

• In Search of a Vision •

Our age is in search of an authentic vision of the human person. Are we just animals? Are we intelligent animals? Or are we children of God? Are we the result of evolution, a big bang, the loving hand of a creator—or some combination of these? Are we here to grasp as much pleasure as possible in our brief time or is there a higher calling and purpose to our lives? The way we live, love, work, vote, and participate in society is a direct result of the vision of the human person that we subscribe to.

Here in America we spent more than thirty billion dollars last year on diet products. That is more than we spent on books, and more than the gross domestic product (GDP) of at least fifty nations in the world. Now, it would seem to me that the only diet most of us need is a little bit of discipline. But we don't want any discipline. We want someone to get on the infomercial and tell us that if we take this little pill twice a day, every day, we can eat whatever we want, whenever we want. We want someone to tell us that if we buy this piece of exercise equipment and work out for twenty minutes twice a week we will look like a supermodel. We want someone to tell us, "You can be healthy and happy without discipline."

The truth is, you cannot be healthy and happy without discipline. In fact, if you want to measure the level of happiness in your life, just measure the level of discipline in your life. You will never have more happiness than you have discipline. The two are directly related to one another.

And this, of course, is where the great gulf appears between the Church and the culture. The message delivered with unrelenting enthusiasm by our culture is, "You can be happy without discipline. Do whatever you feel like doing and you will be happy!" While the Church says, "You cannot be happy without discipline. In fact, discipline is the path to happiness!" Both messages promise happiness and yet they could not be more diametrically opposed. So which is it that will actually lead to the happiness we yearn for and were created for?

The message the Church conveys is a tough one to deliver. At one time or another, we have all had the difficulty of delivering a message about the importance of discipline. And yet, the Church consistently delivers this message, because the Church is deeply rooted in an understanding of what is required for the human person to thrive and flourish. Don't miss this: The

Church has a vision of wholeness and holiness for the human person, and everything the Church does should help her members to become more perfectly who God created them to be.

This vision of the human person is critical in our development as individuals, communities, nations, and an entire human family. The reason is because our position on everything else flows from this vision of the human person. Our position on health care, social security, education, human sexuality, the role of work, business and economics, and so many other things all flow from this primary vision we have about the purpose of man. The Church's message stands so counter to that of the present culture because the Church is driven by this incredible vision for the human person.

But when you ask, "What is the culture's vision for the human person?" the silence is deafening. The culture doesn't have a vision for the human person. So what drives today's culture? Consumption.

And if the culture doesn't have a vision for the human person, it certainly doesn't have a vision for the family. In fact, the culture would prefer that every family be broken, because a broken family needs two dishwashers, two lawn mowers, and two of almost everything else. And if the culture could break families up two, three, or four ways, it would prefer that.

The absence of any desire to help people become the-best-version-of-themselves and explore the potential of the human person in our culture is alarming on a level so profound that it is more than likely that most people will not realize it until it is too late.

But it doesn't have to be that way. Imagine a culture in which music and the arts celebrated the beauty of the human person and inspired people to explore all of their God-given potential. Imagine a culture in which lawmakers were less concerned with special interests and more concerned with creating a society that encouraged and actively helped people to become the-best-version-of-themselves. Imagine a culture in which all men, women, and children were educated not simply to perpetuate commerce, but in such a way as they came to understand who and what they are, who and what they are capable of becoming, and how they could use their talents and abilities to make a unique contribution.

It may seem far from where we are, but such a culture is possible.

• Body and Soul •

You are a delicate composition of body and soul. This is the essential makeup of the human person. Your body and soul are carefully linked by your will and intellect. In its present form, your body is temporal. One day it will die, be buried, and decay. Your soul, however, is eternal. The body and the soul are constantly vying for dominance—so which should steer the ship? Does it make sense for something that is temporal to lead something that is eternal? No. That which is eternal should lead and guide that which is temporal. But as much as that makes sense in the context of an intellectual discussion, you and I both know how easy it is to allow ourselves to be seduced by the things of this world.

There are many voices in our lives: the voices of family and friends, the voices of teachers and culture, and the voices of art and history. Of course, in the midst of all these voices, deep within you is the voice of conscience. All of these voices influence us at different times and to varying extents. But there is another voice that plays a powerful role in our lives—the voice of the body.

Your body has a voice, and it talks to you constantly. You wake up, and the body cries out, "feed me," so you eat. A couple of hours later the body cries out, "I'm thirsty," so you drink. Later the body cries out, "I'm tired," so you rest. Again the body cries out, "feed me," and you do. When it's time to exercise your body cries out, "I don't feel like it," so you don't. And at the end of the day, the body calls out, "I'm ready for bed," so you sleep. Whether we are aware of it or not, our body is ordering us around most of the day. The body is always crying out, feed me, sleep me, please me, pamper me, nourish me, wash me, relieve me, water me. . . .

But where is this voice leading us?

In the modern climate, most people's bodies are winning the battle for dominance between body and soul. In a sense, the body is like money—a great servant, but a horrible master. Fasting is one of the ingenious practices that the Church teaches us to ensure that the body does not become our master.

• The Death of Discipline •

We seem to want to avoid discipline at almost any cost. Far from seeing discipline as a friend in our quest to love and be loved, we treat discipline as a disease. The notion of freedom proclaimed by the modern world is anti-discipline. But true freedom cannot be separated from discipline.

The most obvious example of this paradox is in our cultural approach to dieting, mentioned earlier. For more than two decades the diet industry has been among the fastest-growing industries in any sector of the economy. Every day, more and more products stock the shelves, while infomercials cram the airwaves. These programs claim their products perform wonders, and yet, if you've been to the beach lately, you can see that for the billions of dollars we spend on such products, we are still growing more and more overweight as a culture with every passing year. But now it has gone from the bizarre to the absurd!

What is it that people are looking for in these diets and diet products? And why do so many people fail in their approach to dieting?

As I have observed it, people want a diet that will allow them to eat whatever they want, whenever they want, yet still allow them to look great, feel great, and lose that undesired extra weight. Basically what we are looking for is a miracle product that will remove the need for any discipline in our eating and exercise habits so that we can continue to indulge in the hedonistic ways that violate the-best-version-of-ourselves at every turn.

Diets don't fail because the program wasn't any good. They don't fail because the product wasn't any good. Diets fail because we lack the discipline to adopt a program of eating and exercise that nurtures and promotes our maximum physical potential as a human being.

Moderation is the only diet most people need, but we seem to lack the inner strength to choose what is good, true, and right for us. We want what is good for us, but we lack the strength of will to choose it. This problem is not new or unique to the modern world. Men and women of every age have experienced this same difficulty. And this is one of the reasons that for thousands of years men and women have been practicing a variety of spiritual exercises. One of the many benefits of these spiritual exercises is that they strengthen our will.

Fasting is a primary example of these spiritual exercises. Open your heart and your mind. Set aside your prejudices and rediscover the genius of fasting and how it can change your life.

• Fasting in the Scriptures •

For the Hebrew people, fasting was infrequent and was usually employed as a sign of repentance. The Torah requires only one day of fasting each year: Yom Kippur, the Day of Atonement. Four extra days of fasting were added to the Jewish tradition much later, to commemorate the events leading to the destruction of Jerusalem.

The Israelites fasted at Samuel's urging, as they put away the false gods Baal and Ashtoreth and returned to Yahweh (cf. 1 Samuel 7:2-6). The entire Israelite army employed fasting as part of its preparation for battle (cf. Judges 20:26 and 2 Chronicles 20:3–4). Daniel fasted as he prayed, asking God to grant him the ability to understand the Scriptures (cf. Daniel 9:3). At the urging of Jonah and to save the city of Nineveh, the King proclaimed a fast, calling on the people to abandon wrongdoing and violence (cf. Jonah 3:7–9).

In each of these cases, fasting was used to humbly seek out God's will. Over and over again, the Old Testament makes it abundantly clear that genuine fasting involves turning away from evil and turning back to God. Fasting that involves no such conversion of the heart is useless. Isaiah speaks out against fasting detached from conversion, announcing the worthlessness of fasting in the wrong spirit (cf. Isaiah 58:3–7). The Scriptures continually remind us that external actions are insufficient; they must be joined to some internal conversion of the heart.

The New Testament also highlights the ancient spiritual practice of fasting, and the life and teachings of Jesus provide particular insight into its roles and meaning.

Before Jesus began his public life, he was "led by the Spirit into the desert," where he fasted for forty days (Matthew 4:1). Jesus didn't fast in atonement for his sins; he was sinless. He fasted in preparation for his mission. And the fact that Jesus was led by the Spirit out into the desert to fast is perhaps the greatest evidence we have that fasting is not merely a physical practice or another personal accomplishment; rather, it is a spiritual exercise.

In the desert, Jesus was tempted by the devil to abandon his fasting and have his fill. Jesus rebuked him, saying, "Man does not live on bread alone, but on every word that comes from the mouth of God." (Matthew 4:4) Fasting is a sharp reminder that there are more important things in life than food. Authentic Christian fasting helps to release us from our attachments to the things of this world. It is often these worldly attachments that prevent us from becoming the-best-version-of-ourselves. Fasting also serves as a reminder that everything in this world is passing and thus encourages us to consider life beyond death.

Go without food for several hours and you quickly realize how truly weak, fragile, and dependent we are. This knowledge of self strips away arrogance and fosters a loving acknowledgment of our utter dependence on God.

Later during his public life, Jesus was challenged and questioned as to why his disciples didn't fast like the disciples of John the Baptist and the Pharisees. In his response, he revealed one of the prime purposes of fasting: "Can the wedding guests fast while the bridegroom is with them? As long as they have the bridegroom with them, they cannot fast. But the days will come when the bridegroom is taken away from them, and then they will fast on that day." (Mark 2:19–20)

One of the prime purposes of fasting is to help us become aware of God's presence in our lives and in the world around us. Fasting also makes us aware of God's absence in different areas of our lives. Since Jesus—God and man—was already in their presence, the disciples did not need to fast as we do while Jesus was with them.

Jesus instructed his disciples only once specifically concerning fasting. During the Sermon on the Mount in Matthew's Gospel, Jesus speaks of fasting in the same way he spoke of almsgiving and prayer. "When you fast, do not look gloomy like the hypocrites. They neglect their appearance, so that they may appear to others to be fasting. Amen, I say to you, they have received their reward. But when you fast, anoint your head and wash your face, so that you may not appear to be fasting, except to your Father who is hidden. And your Father who sees what is hidden will reward you." (Matthew 6:16–18)

As with prayer and almsgiving, Jesus calls us to remember that fasting is a spiritual exercise, and as such is primarily an action of the inner life. We do not fast to impress other people. We fast to cultivate the inner life. Fasting should be an occasion of joy, not a cause of sadness. Authentic fasting draws us nearer to God and opens our hearts to receive his many gifts.

There is one other occasion when Jesus mentions fasting. In my own life, this has been the most important passage relating to the great spiritual exercise of fasting. I believe this passage holds one of the greatest practical spiritual lessons, and yet, most modern Bibles have removed this passage or altered it.

In Mark's Gospel, we are told of a man who brings his possessed boy to Jesus for healing. The father of the boy explains that he brought the boy to Jesus' disciples, but they were unable to heal him even though they were able to heal many others with similar afflictions. When Jesus arrives at this scene, he rebukes the unclean spirit, ordering it to come out of the boy, and the child is cured. The disciples were confused about why they were not able to cast out the demon. So, when the crowd had dispersed and they were alone with Jesus, "his disciples asked him in private, 'Why was it that we could not cast it out?' And he told them, 'This kind of spirit can only be cast out through prayer and fasting.'" (Mark 9:28–29)

You may believe that people do not suffer from possession by demons in our modern age. Don't be so sure. The demons of our modern age are in some cases subtler than the demons of Jesus' time. I assure you that many drunks take on the qualities of a person possessed by a demon, and there are many other types of possession that have become frighteningly common today. Next time someone loses his temper, ask yourself if he resembles someone possessed. Look around and I think you will discover that you quite often cross paths with people who are possessed in one way or another by "evil spirits."

In my own life, I have known the demon of habitual sin. When I first turned to God in my late teen years, I was possessed by such a demon. I tried with all my might to wrestle with it, but nothing worked. I prayed, begging God to free me from this sin, but he didn't. I employed all the power of my will, but that didn't work either. Then one day I noticed the previous passage in Mark's Gospel and at that moment I felt the hand of God upon my shoulder. Encouraged by the example of a friend, several weeks later I began to fast each Friday, eating only bread and drinking only water. I offered this fasting to God, asking him to liberate me, and it was then that God cast the demon of habitual sin from my life. I believe with my whole being that some demons in our lives "can only be cast out through prayer and fasting." (Mark 9:29) If you are suffering under the slavery of ingrained bad habits, turn to God through prayer and fasting. If you are being tormented by the demons of habitual sin, turn to God through prayer and fasting.

It is important to note how different the reasons for fasting are from the reasons for dieting. Fasting is by its very nature a statement of humility, while dieting is usually linked to ego, vanity, and pride. It is also interesting to realize that the secular culture takes all things sacred and waters them down, ridicules them by adopting the opposite extreme, or separates them from their true meaning and purpose. Dieting is the secularization of the great spiritual exercise of fasting. But dieting is devoid of the strongest motives and reasons: repentance, self-denial, humility, self-mastery, and the spiritual power that comes from these dispositions.

You are a delicate composition of body and soul. Fasting is to the body what prayer is to the soul. Indeed, fasting is the prayer of the body, and bodily fasting leads to spiritual feasting.

• The History of Christian Fasting •

After the death, Resurrection, and ascension of Jesus, fasting quickly became an integral part of early Christian practice. At that time, several Jewish groups were fasting on Tuesdays and Thursdays. To distinguish their own practice, the first Christians fasted on Wednesdays and Fridays. In the Judeo-Christian world, a fast day generally implied abstaining from food until the evening meal, which would be served after sundown.

While some people argue that fasting was not introduced into the Christian way of life for centuries, there is considerable evidence that this is not the case. In fact, fasting was a part of the earliest Christians' way of life. A very early manuscript known as *The Didache,* which outlines Christian practice and belief, recommends to Christians, "fast for those who persecute you."

Fasting was also common among these early Christian communities in preparation for the sacraments, including the Eucharistic meal and baptism. In the case of adult baptism, both the baptizer and the one to be baptized would observe a fast in preparation.

In the fourth century, the Church began to regulate the practice of fasting, and since then, the practice has changed considerably at different junctures. In the Middle Ages, distinctions began to emerge regarding the amount and kind of food to be taken on a fast day. It was at this time that it became a rule to abstain from meat, eggs, and dairy products on fast days.

The number of fast days gradually increased over the years, as the eves of major feast days and the ember days were designated as fast days. And while the number of fast days was increasing, dispensations were being granted for a growing number of reasons. All this conspired to make the whole practice of fasting more and more complex. These growing complexities tended to transform the practice into more of a legal matter than a spiritual practice, and moved the focus from inner transformation to outward display. The motive for fasting began to shift toward obligation and away from conversion and penance.

While there have been many changes in the practice of fasting over the centuries, the Church's understanding of it has remained consistent. The great thirteenth-century scholar, saint, and doctor of the Church, Thomas Aquinas, wrote of these three values of fasting: for the repression of one's concupiscence (strong desires) of the flesh, for the atonement for one's sins, and to better dispose oneself to higher things.

It was perhaps in the monasteries that the purpose and goals of fasting were preserved throughout the ages. Here it remained clear that that primary goal and purpose was union with God. It is this point that has been grossly underemphasized. This was largely due to the erroneous view that union with God was a reward reserved only for a few saints and mystics.

In the modern age, we have also seen many changes in the practice of fasting. Prior to 1917, Catholics were required to fast throughout Lent except on Sundays, taking only one meal per day. We were also expected to abstain from meat, eggs, and dairy products on all prescribed fast days, as well as every Friday and Saturday. By the early 1950s, fast days for Catholics in the United States consisted of one main meal and two small meatless meals.

In 1966, Pope Paul VI warned of the dangers of a legalistic approach to fasting and offered some new direction for the practice of fasting in the modern era in his Apostolic Constitution on Penance. He reminded Catholics that the outward expression of fasting should always be accompanied by the inner attitude of conversion. In this document, Paul VI not only stressed the value of fasting and other forms of penitence but also reminded Catholics everywhere of the importance the early Christians placed on linking the external act of fasting with inner conversion, prayer, and works of charity. In doing so, Paul VI echoed Saint Augustine's idea: "Do you wish your prayer to fly toward God? Give it two wings: fasting and almsgiving." Having reasserted the value of fasting among prayer and charity as the "fundamental means of complying with the divine precepts of penitence," Paul VI then simplified the regulations for fasting and abstinence and handed authority over to local bishops' conferences to establish guidelines according to their culture.

Here in the America, the United States Conference of Catholic Bishops issued a pastoral statement later that same year announcing, "Catholics in the United States are obliged to abstain from the eating of meat on Ash Wednesday and on all Fridays during the season of Lent. They are also obliged to fast on Ash Wednesday and Good Friday." The pastoral statement encouraged the faithful to continue the traditional practice of Friday abstinence and also urged Catholics to perform works of charity in the spirit of penance, including visiting the sick and imprisoned, caring for the indigent, and giving alms to those in need. At the time, this was a radical shift that eliminated many of the old rules and regulations regarding fasting, abstinence, and penance. As a result, many Catholics felt they were no longer obliged to follow any specific penitential practices. Only a few were able to see the wisdom of the changes and realize that they were being called to a deeper spirit of penitential conversion.

Despite the fact that many modern Catholics have abandoned penance and particularly fasting, at every level the Church continues to affirm the great value of these practices as means for authentic spiritual growth. Throughout this modern era, popes and bishops have invited Catholics to fast and abstain, to pray and perform charitable works as time-tested ways of turning our attention toward God and the needs of our brothers and sisters. But amid the abundance and great wealth of advanced modern nations such as the United States, it is all too easy to be seduced into the self-absorbed lifestyles promoted by today's popular culture.

Today, fasting is more popular in secular circles than it is among Catholics. Health enthusiasts are turning to periodic fasting for cures to everything from insomnia to cancer. Others are adopting this ancient spiritual practice to "cleanse" the body of impurities such as oxidants and the excess chemicals used to fertilize our foods. Fasting has even found a place in many diet programs as a tool to achieve dramatic weight loss and proper weight maintenance.

I pray we can rediscover the value of this ancient spiritual practice as modern Catholics—not for God's sake, but for our own. I am utterly convinced that if we are to develop the inner freedom to resist the temptations that face us in the modern world, we must learn to assert the dominance of the spirit over the body, of the eternal over the temporal. If the spirit within each of us is to reign, then the body must first be tamed. Prayer won't achieve this, works of charity won't achieve this, and power of the will won't achieve it. This is a task for fasting, abstinence, and other acts of penance.

• Lenten Fasting •

There is great wisdom in the Christian practice of fasting. Though Christian fasting has been largely abandoned, the one expression of fasting (and penitential practice) that seems to have survived the turmoil of this modern era is that of Lenten penance. Although I suspect it is hanging on by a very thin cultural thread, which will break unless we can make people aware of the great beauty and spiritual significance of these acts.

As I have said over and over again in my books and talks, our lives change when our habits change. The Lenten experience is a perfect example of the Church's intimate understanding of the nature of the human person. The forty days of Lent are an ideal period for renewal. Lent is the perfect span of time to form new life-giving habits and abandon old self-destructive habits. But most of us just give up chocolate and when Easter arrives we are not much further advanced spiritually than we were at the beginning of Lent.

• Fasting and You •

Our faith seeks to integrate the relationship between body and soul. There is a war taking place within you. It is the constant battle between your body and your soul. At every moment of the day, both are vying for dominance.

If you wish to have a rich and abundant experience of life, you must allow your soul to soar. But in order to do that, you first need to tame and train the body. You cannot win this war once a week, once a year, or even once a day. From moment to moment, our desires need be harnessed.

Fasting should be a part of our everyday spirituality. For example, suppose you have a craving for a Coke, but you have cranberry juice or a glass of water instead. It is the smallest thing. Nobody notices. And yet, by this simple action you say no to the cravings of the body that seek to control you and assert the dominance of the soul. The will is strengthened and the soul is a little freer. In that one action you create an ounce of self-possession.

Or, say your soup tastes a little dull. You could add salt and pepper, but you don't. It's a little thing. It's nothing. But if it's done for the right reasons, with the correct inner attitude, it is a spiritual exercise. You say no to the body. In doing so, you assert the dominance of the spirit. The will is strengthened and the soul is a little freer. Again, you create an ounce of self-possession.

Never leave a meal table without practicing some form of fasting. It is these tiny acts that harness the body as a worthy servant and strengthen the will for the great moments of decision that are a part of each of our lives.

Beyond these small moments of fasting, we should each seek more intense encounters with fasting and abstinence if we are serious about the spiritual life—not because it is in the catechism, but because it will help us to turn away from sin and turn back to God, which is why it is in the catechism. Fasting helps us to turn our backs on the-lesser-version-of-ourselves and embrace the-best-version-of-ourselves.

Perhaps you can fast one day a week—two small meals, one full meal, and nothing to eat between meals. Perhaps you can fast one day a week on bread and water. Or maybe all you can manage at this time is to give up coffee for a day. Maybe you can't even give up coffee for the whole day, maybe just for two hours. Personalize your fasting. You know what it is that has a grip on you. Friday has always been a traditional day of fasting, and I would encourage you to employ this tradition in your own way. Only you can decide what the right fast is for you.

Try not to be prideful about it. Come humbly to God in prayer, and there in the classroom of silence, decide upon some regular practice of fasting and abstinence. Then, from time to time, review this practice. If you feel called to add to it, add to it.

It is also important to recognize that not all forms of fasting involve food. You can fast from judging others, criticizing, cursing, or complaining, to name but a few.

Two powerful forms of fasting that helped me to grow tremendously were the practice of silence and of stillness. From time to time, fast from noise and movement. Sit perfectly still in silence for twenty minutes. It isn't easy. This is perhaps why so many people never seriously adopt the habit of prayer. After you have become comfortable in the silence, be still for twenty minutes. Be completely still. It is difficult. Yet I am convinced that silence and stillness are two of the greatest spiritual tools.

Fasting is a simple yet powerful way to turn toward God. If there is a question in your life, fast and ask God to lead you. He will. If you have a persistent sin that you just cannot seem to overcome, then fast. Some demons can only be cast out by prayer and fasting together.

Fasting is radically countercultural, but so is Christianity.

• The Universe and You •

Until this point, I have avoided discussing the idea of fasting as a form of penance to reverse the effect of sin. I have done this because there is such a negative stigma that goes with this idea in our modern world. But I would be remiss not to discuss it and try to shed some positive light on this idea.

Even before kindergarten, we are taught the governing laws of the universe. One of these is the law of cause and effect: Every cause has an effect; every action has a reaction.

In a sense, the universe has a perfect accounting system. This is just one tiny aspect of the wonder and perfection of God's creation. These laws are designed to help keep everything in balance and harmony. As a result, no debt in the universe goes unpaid. All debts must be settled.

This is where the link between penance and fasting emerges. I repeat, sooner or later, all debts must be repaid.

We practice fasting as a form of penance not because we want to punish ourselves or destroy ourselves, but rather to express sorrow for our moral failings and to be restored to wholeness. The Church invites us to the spiritual practice of fasting not because she wants us to feel guilty or have a poor self-image, but rather so we can be liberated. In the process we are given grace to strive with ever more determination to become the-best-version-of-ourselves.

It goes without saying that if you sit on the couch every day for ten years eating potato chips and drinking beer, the effects of those actions will be increased weight and poor health. In order to erase the weight gained and return to optimum health, you would need to exercise and focus on eating foods that fuel the body with nourishment and energy. Neither of these is enjoyable at first, but they erase the effects of poor past actions that led you to become less than the-best-version-of-yourself.

The same is true spiritually. Every time we sin, it has an impact on our souls. Every word, thought, or action that betrays the-best-version-of-yourself also damages your relationship with God and neighbor. You can't see it, but it's there. When you sin, you not only damage your soul but you also increase your *tendency toward sin* and your *appetite for sin* in the future.

It is true that God forgives our sins through the Sacrament of Reconciliation, but if the effects these sins have on our character and soul are to be reversed, some form of penance will be required. Fasting is one spiritual practice that can help restore the soul to its intended beauty, reduce our tendency toward those actions that are self-destructive and sinful, and reduce our appetite for sin in the future.

• Always a Means, Never an End •

Fasting is a means, but never an end. The purpose of fasting is to assist the soul in turning back to God. The benefits of fasting are innumerable, but all these benefits are secondary to the desire to embrace God more fully in our lives.

Whatever form of fasting you decide to employ in your life, you will have good days and bad days. You will have successes and failures. Stick to it. Don't give up. If you fail, try again.

I was back in Australia at the beginning of Lent several years ago. On Ash Wednesday evening, the phone rang as I was walking past it, so I answered it. "Is that you, Uncle Matt?" a little voice said. It was my niece Zoe.

"How are you, Zoe?" I asked.

"I'm good, Uncle Matt."

"What did you do today?" I inquired.

"Oh . . . it was a busy day. I went to school, then I went to volleyball practice, then I came home and did my homework, and then we went to church and I got ashes."

"What did Father talk about at church?" I asked.

"He talked about giving up things for Lent. Guess what I'm giving up, Uncle Matt," she said.

"I don't know, what are you giving up this year, Zoe?"

"I'm giving up Coca-Cola."

"But Zoe, you really like Coca-Cola."

"I know, but Father talked about giving up something that will be really hard. So I'm giving up Coke."

Two days later, on Friday evening, I was at a basketball game with my two nieces, Emma and her sister, Zoe. Emma is the elder and she was about fourteen at the time; Zoe was twelve. Emma was playing in the basketball game, and Zoe was sitting next to me with five or six of her giggling little friends from school.

About half way through of the game, I looked over and Zoe was guzzling down a large bottle of Coke. I didn't say anything. I just smiled to myself and turned back to the game. But about five minutes later, I felt a tug on my shirt and a tap on my shoulder.

"Uncle Matt, I forgot."

"You forgot what, Zoe?" I asked.

"Oh, Uncle Matt, I forgot I gave up Coke for Lent and I just drank a bottle of Coke." I didn't say anything. I just looked at her and smiled. She sighed and said, "Oh well. It's all over now. I'll have to wait till next year."

Our lives change when our habits change. Our habits change when we make resolutions, remind ourselves of those resolutions, hold ourselves accountable for them, and perform them. Sometimes we fail, but there is no success that isn't checkered with failure. Don't give up. Press on, little by little.

The spiritual journey is not made a mile at a time. More often than not, the advances in the journey are too small even to measure. But they all add up to a lifetime of joy-filled challenges and an eternity in union with God and everything that is good, true, beautiful, and noble.

Our bodies are vehicles that God has given our souls to experience life in the material realm. Until we get a grip on our bodies, we will never get a grip on life. Until we learn to reign over our bodies we never really experience all that life can be.

Chapter Seventeen

SPIRITUAL READING

Books change our lives. Most people can identify a book that has marked a life-changing period for them. It was probably a book that said just the right thing at just the right time. They may have been just words on a page, but they came to life for you and in you, and because of them you will never again be the same. Books really do change our lives, because what we read today walks and talks with us tomorrow.

Earlier, in our discussion of prayer and contemplation, we spoke of the cause-and-effect relationship between thought and action. Thought determines action, and one of the most powerful influences on thought is the material we choose to read.

Reading is to the mind what exercise is to the body and prayer is to the soul.

• An Ancient Tradition •

Spiritual reading is an ancient tradition. It existed in the Church long before we had books to read, when every manuscript had to be copied by hand because the printing press had not yet been invented. In those days, this spiritual tradition was mostly confined to the monasteries, where the monks had access to manuscripts of the Scriptures and other great spiritual writings.

The goal of spiritual reading is to ignite the soul with a desire to grow in virtue and thus become the-best-version-of-oneself. Like all other spiritual exercises and activities, spiritual reading seeks to encourage us to live a life of holiness.

• What Should We Read? •

Reading of the Scriptures, especially the New Testament and in particular the four Gospels, obviously holds first place on our spiritual reading list. It has been my experience that all men and women of good will take delight in the Gospels as they become familiar with them. They are the best education of the life and teachings of Jesus Christ. Nothing ignites the soul to imitate the Divine Master more than an intimate familiarity with the story of his life, work, and teachings.

The Old Testament can also be very valuable as a source of spiritual reading, though in this case some books are harder to draw nourishment from than others. In books such as Psalms and Proverbs, our hearts are easily stirred to live a better life and to strive for virtue through our relationships with God, neighbor, and self. On the other hand, many of the historical and prophetic books require some rather serious preparation if we are to understand the culture and context in which they were written and their intended message.

Beyond the Scriptures, there are also a great many spiritual writers who can be of assistance to us in our adventure of salvation. These masters and mentors of the spiritual life are always available for consultation.

The great masters of spiritual writing are able to set aside the issues of the day and their own personal agendas, and place at the center of their writing God's dream for us to grow each day in virtue and holiness. In their writings, you will always hear a call to become a better person. As you read their words, you will constantly feel inspired and challenged to change, grow, and to become the-best-version-of-yourself.

They are also very worthy mentors, and if you allow them into your life, they will reveal your defects for you with great discretion and kindness. They point out your weaknesses not to belittle you, but so that you might grow and become all you are capable of being. They do this by holding a spiritual mirror before you and calling you to self-examination. They then encourage you to make generous resolutions. They lead you into divine cooperation with the Holy Spirit. They will also teach you how to maximize the impact and influence of your strengths.

It is within these bounds that the classical definition of spiritual reading has been confined until now. But for the sake of the modern Catholic who finds him- or herself in the midst of the information age, I would like to stretch those boundaries a little, while at the same time keeping our sight firmly fixed on the goal of this ancient practice.

I believe there is also a place within the context of spiritual reading for us to study certain issues, and that most former Catholics, non-practicing Catholics, and many disengaged Catholics are separated from the Church over one issue. It may be a different issue for each person, but there is usually one issue that sparks the separation and leads people to turn their backs on the Church. For some the issue is contraception, for others it is abortion, and for many modern Catholics it is divorce. I suspect that the great majority of non-practicing Catholics are not joining us each Sunday because of a very limited number of issues, perhaps five or six at the most. With that in mind, we have a duty to study and know those issues so we can build the necessary bridges of truth and knowledge that will allow them to return to the fullness of our ancient and beautiful faith.

If you want to grow in faith, identify the teaching of the Catholic Church that you find most difficult to understand and accept, then read about it. Study that issue. Get yourself a catechism and read what it says, but then look up the source texts, find other books that explain why the Church teaches what it teaches about that issue, and get to the heart of the matter. Don't read books by bitter authors who seek to tear the Church down. Read books by men and women of prayer who seek by their writing to reveal the truth and depth of the Church's teachings. If you approach that issue humbly the wisdom and beauty of Catholicism will be unveiled before your very eyes. The issues are so few; let's begin to study them.

• When, Where, and for How Long? •

When I first began to take the spiritual life seriously, I was very fortunate that my path crossed with that of a very holy priest. He was a man of prayer who was striving to grow in virtue and clearly focused on trying to live a holy life. His only concern in any of my conversations with him was my spiritual growth. He would say to me, over and over again, "God is calling you to a life of holiness." In the context of Confession, he would remind me that God calls us all to holiness. In our conversations about my struggles with prayer, he reminded me that I was called to holiness. When I asked his advice on situations in my personal life, and later in my business or ministry, he always reminded me that our number one concern must be to honor God's call to holiness in our lives and the lives of the people who cross our paths.

I say all this because he also used to suggest books for me to read. In each of them, I found worthy guides, spiritual masters, and grace-filled mentors who reinforced this teaching that God calls us all to become the-best-version-of-ourselves. God invites us to holiness.

Perhaps we find the litmus test of a good book right there: Is this book inviting me to live a life of holiness?

"Fifteen minutes a day," this old priest would say to me. "It's amazing how powerfully fifteen minutes with the right book can stir your soul." In the morning, in the evening, at lunchtime, whenever you can, find fifteen minutes each day to nourish yourself spiritually and intellectually with a good book. Try to do it at the same time every day. Perhaps it is before you go to work. Maybe it is in bed late at night. Then again, perhaps it is while you are eating your lunch. Find a quiet corner at work or at home and read. If you're not sure what to read, visit DynamicCatholic.com and send me an e-mail, and I'll send you a list of ten books that changed my life.

You don't need two hours of reading every day, just fifteen minutes. But do it every day. Embrace spiritual reading as a daily discipline. Make it a part of your lifestyle. Remember, Catholicism is not a set of lifeless rules and regulations; Catholicism is a lifestyle. Start to build that lifestyle. Read for fifteen minutes every day, and it will become a habit—and our lives change when our habits change.

• Adult Education •

One of the challenges that is staring the Church in the face is the great need for adult education. Several generations have now managed to pass through the Catholic education system with little more than an elementary understanding of Catholicism. Over this time, more and more Catholics have decided not to send their children to Catholic schools or religious education programs. All this is having a devastating effect on future generations.

We could dream up all types of elaborate adult education programs, but my proposal is that we encourage Catholic adults to read good spiritual books. We cannot make up for lost ground overnight, but fifteen minutes a day is as good as any place to start.

My proposal will no doubt be overlooked by most, and frowned upon by others, because of its sheer simplicity. Nonetheless, let me assure you the simplest solution is usually the best, and hidden in our ancient traditions we will find the solutions to most of our modern problems.

Spiritual reading is a perfect example of an ancient solution to a modern problem. If every Catholic were to read a good Catholic book for fifteen minutes a day this habit alone could be a game changer for the Church in our times.

What percentage of Catholics do you think have read a Catholic book in the past twelve months? This is a question I have been posing to audiences of late. The consensus seems to be about one percent.

Now imagine for a moment what would happen if every Catholic in your parish read a good spiritual book for fifteen minutes a day. How would your parish change? If every Catholic spent fifteen minutes a day, every day, learning about his or her faith, how different would our Church be in a year? Five years? Ten years?

Rome wasn't built in a day. Most great things are achieved little by little.

• Keeping the Star in Sight •

Spiritual reading is a great tool to help us keep the great spiritual North Star in sight. When we view everything in relation to our call to become the-best-version-of-ourselves, everything finds meaning. Even the smallest and most menial tasks take on new life, for we come to understand that every action is a character-building action, for better or for worse.

Direct all your thoughts and actions toward the great spiritual North Star. What I mean is, find ways of spending time with your friends that help you all become the-best-version-of-yourselves. Similarly, find activities you can do as a family that draw the best out of each of you and challenge you to grow. In the same way, read books that make you want to become a better person, books that show you how to become the-best-version-of-yourself. Cast off the whimsical modern reading materials. What is in those magazines that will help you live a richer, fuller life? When was the last time you read a newspaper and said to yourself, "I'm a better person for having read that newspaper?" We have bought into the modern myth that we have to be up on everyone else's business.

Books change our lives. If you really want your life to change, read some good spiritual books. If you approach these books with a spirit of faith, a desire to grow in holiness, and a sincere intention to practice what you read, spiritual reading will become a powerful tool in your life.

Chapter Eighteen

THE ROSARY

Jim Castle was tired when he boarded his flight one night in Cincinnati. The forty-five-year-old management consultant had put on a weeklong series of business meetings and seminars, and now he sank gratefully into his seat, ready for the flight home to Kansas City.

As more passengers boarded, the plane hummed with conversation, mixed with the sound of bags being stowed. Then, suddenly, people fell silent. The quiet moved slowly up the aisle like an invisible wake behind a boat. Jim craned his neck to see what was happening and his mouth dropped open.

Walking up the aisle were two nuns clad in simple white habits with blue borders. He immediately recognized the familiar face, wrinkled skin, and warm eyes of one of the nuns. This was the face he'd seen so often on television and on the cover of *Time*. The two nuns halted, and Jim realized that his seat companion was going to be Mother Teresa.

As the last few passengers settled in, Mother Teresa and her companion pulled out rosaries. Jim noticed that each decade of the beads was a different color. The decades represented various areas of the world, Mother Teresa told him later, adding, "I pray for the poor and dying on each continent."

The airplane taxied to the runway, and the two women began to pray, their voices in a low murmur. Though Jim considered himself a not very engaged Catholic who went to church mostly out of habit, inexplicably he found himself joining in. By the time they whispered the final prayer, the plane had reached cruising altitude.

Mother Teresa turned toward him. For the first time in his life, Jim understood what people meant when they spoke of a person possessing an aura. As she gazed at him, a sense of peace filled him; he could see it no more than he could see the wind, but he felt it, just as surely as he felt a warm summer breeze. "Young man," she inquired, "do you pray the rosary often?"

"No, not really," he admitted.

She took his hand, and her eyes probed his. Then she smiled. "Well, you will now," and she dropped her rosary into his palm.

An hour later, Jim entered the Kansas City Airport, where he was met by his wife, Ruth. "What in the world?" Ruth asked when she noticed the rosary in his hand.

They kissed and Jim described the encounter. Driving home, he said, "I feel as if I met God's daughter."

Nine months later, Jim and Ruth visited Connie, a longtime friend of theirs. Connie told them she had ovarian cancer. "The doctor says it's a tough case," said Connie, "but I'm going to fight it. I won't give up."

Jim clasped her hand. Then, after reaching into his pocket, he gently twined Mother Teresa's rosary around her fingers. He told her the story and said, "Keep it with you, Connie. It may help."

Although Connie wasn't Catholic, her hand closed willingly around the small plastic beads. "Thank you," she whispered. "I hope I can return it."

More than a year passed before Jim saw Connie again. This time, face glowing, she hurried toward him and handed him the rosary. "I carried it all year," she said. "I've had surgery and have been having chemotherapy, too. Last month, the doctors did a second-look surgery, and the tumor's gone. Completely!" Her eyes met Jim's. "I knew it was time to give the rosary back."

The following fall, Ruth's sister Liz fell into a deep depression after her divorce. She asked Jim if she could borrow the rosary, and when he sent it, she hung it over her bedpost in a small velvet bag.

"At night I held on to it, just physically held on. I was so lonely and afraid," she said, "yet when I gripped that rosary, I felt as if I held a loving hand." Gradually, Liz pulled out of her depression and found a new perspective on life, and mailed the rosary back. "Someone else may need it," read the note that accompanied it.

Then one night a year or so later, a stranger telephoned Ruth. She'd heard about the rosary from a neighbor and asked if she could borrow it to take to the hospital where her mother lay in a coma. The family hoped the rosary might help their mother die peacefully.

A few days later, the woman returned the beads. "The nurses told me a coma patient can still hear," she said, "so I explained to my mother that I had Mother Teresa's rosary and that when I gave it to her she could let go; it would be all right. Then I put the rosary in her hand. Within minutes, we saw her face relax! The lines smoothed out until she looked so peaceful, so young." The woman's voice caught. "A few minutes later, she was gone." She gripped Ruth's hands, looked deep into her eyes, and said, "Thank you."

Is there special power in those humble beads? Or is the power of the human spirit simply renewed in each person who borrows the rosary? Jim only knows that requests continue to come, often unexpectedly. He always responds, though whenever he lends the rosary, he says, "When you're through needing it, send it back. Someone else may need it."

Jim's life has also changed since his unexpected meeting on the airplane. When he realized Mother Teresa carries everything she owns in a small bag, he made an effort to simplify his own life. He says, "I try to remember what really counts—not money, or titles, or possessions, but the way we love others."

• Why Have We Abandoned the Rosary? •

There are perhaps many reasons why modern Catholics have abandoned the rosary. One reason, no doubt, is the overemphasis some people have placed on the role of Mary and the rosary. But I very much doubt that this is the whole reason that Catholics en masse have stopped praying the rosary and teaching their children to pray the rosary in their homes and schools. And as I pointed out in our discussion of the saints, the solution to the distortion or overemphasis of a good is never to abolish the good in question.

I suspect one of the reasons the rosary has become so unpopular during this modern era is because it is stereotypically considered the prayer of an overly pious old woman with little education and too much time on her hands. In a world where we bow to knowledge and academic degrees, piety is considered to border on superstition. But in truth, piety is reverence for God and devotion to God. Isn't part of the goal of every Christian life to devote oneself to God?

Catholics have abandoned the rosary today because we have been seduced by complexity. We give our allegiance and respect to complexity, but simplicity is the key to perfection. Peace in our hearts is born from simplicity in our lives. All the great leaders throughout history have agreed that usually the simplest solution is the best solution. The genius of God is simplicity. If you wish to tap into the wonder and glory of God, apply simplicity to your life and to your prayer.

Our lives are suffering under the intolerable weight of ever-increasing complexities. We complicate everything. And as this diseased fascination with complexity has swept across modern culture, it has also affected the way we approach prayer. Subsequently, as modern Catholics, we have deemed the rosary worthless. Don't despise simplicity. There is real power in it.

The rosary is not a prayer just for gray-headed old ladies with too much time on their hands. It is a rich practice of prayer that we can all benefit from.

Perhaps your objection is that you were forced to pray the rosary as a child. If this is the case, move beyond that experience and discover this beautiful prayer anew for yourself. Don't let your past rob you of your future.

• Benefits •

Contrary to what most people think, the first book I ever published was titled *Prayer & the Rosary*. Now, the fact that someone publishes a book about the rosary at the age of nineteen probably leads most people to assume that I grew up in one of those homes where the rosary was prayed together every night. I didn't. In fact, I have never prayed the rosary with my family—not even once.

So how did I come to have such a high regard for this simple prayer, which has been so ardently rejected by our sophisticated modern world? Let me tell you.

When I was in fourth grade, Mrs. Rutter taught us how to pray the rosary and gave us each a pair of rosary beads. I didn't pay much attention and I wasn't very interested, but for some reason I kept the beads in a place with my childhood treasures.

In fifth grade, Mr. Greck spoke a lot about Lourdes. His son had been miraculously cured there and every Friday he would lead the rosary in the chapel at lunchtime. If you got detention, you had to go to the rosary. I got detention occasionally, but the compulsory rosary didn't do much for my love of this prayerful devotion.

At sixteen, I met a man who was to become very instrumental in my spiritual journey. He was teaching a study-skills course that I was attending after school, and invited me one Saturday to visit a local nursing home. We walked to the nursing home and spoke about a lot of things, mostly about me, my sports, my part-time job, my aspirations in life, and my girl-friend. The experience that afternoon was the first of many encounters at nursing homes in my area that would begin to awaken my moral senses. As we walked home that day, he asked me if I would like to pray the rosary. I agreed. I mean, what else can you do in a situation like that? But for some reason, the prayers soothed me, and I began to pray the rosary on my own in the days and weeks ahead. Not long after that, I began to pray the rosary regularly with my good friend Luke.

I began praying the rosary because it is a form of prayer that I find very soothing, both mentally and spiritually. Today, I pray the rosary because I believe it is the simplest way to reflect upon the life and teachings of Jesus Christ. To place this in the context of our spiritual journey, I believe that as Christians we are called to imitate Jesus. It is impossible to imitate someone you do not know. We come to know him in the Scriptures, in the Sacraments, and through so many different people and places. The rosary is one other way. By praying the rosary, we can ponder many aspects of Jesus and his life in a relatively brief period of time. And, as we discussed earlier, the actions of our lives are determined by our most dominant thoughts. If our actions are to be like those of Christ then it helps to ponder his life and teachings regularly.

We spoke earlier about the power of stories. There is no more powerful story than that of Jesus Christ. This is the story that has formed and focused human history, and it is essential to our mission as Christians that we are intimately familiar with it. The rosary helps us to know his story and teaches us to integrate it into our own lives.

• Growth in Virtue •

One of the practical spiritual benefits of the rosary is its ability to help us grow in virtue. As I have studied the great spiritual masters of our Catholic tradition, I have discovered how essential virtue is to our journeys. When we connect the good and noble external acts of our lives with positive internal attitudes and intentions, we grow in virtue. As we begin to practice a virtue intentionally, it develops into a habitual virtue. But I have also learned that when you intentionally focus your energies toward growing in a particular virtue, you automatically grow in every other virtue. Virtue begets virtue. Eventually, the habitual effort to practice a virtue blossoms into spontaneous right action. I have found the rosary particularly helpful in my attempts to increase the practice of various virtues in my life.

The fruit of all spiritual exercises is an increase in the supernatural virtues: faith, hope, and love. Saint Paul speaks of them in his first letter to the Corinthians: "So faith, hope, and love remain, these three; but the greatest of these is love." (1 Corinthians 13:13) At a time when the world is so filled with doubt and skepticism, the beauty of faith shines forth. With so many people's hearts and minds suffering with depression, despair, and hopelessness, the splendor of hope is radiant. In a culture that exults the selfish attainment of pleasure and possessions, one eternal truth remains clear to all: Love is the only way.

Beyond the supernatural virtues, each decade of the rosary introduces practical examples of human virtues, and teaches us to practice these virtues in our own lives. Let's explore those human virtues now, one decade at a time.

• Twenty Lessons •

The actions of your life are determined by your most dominant thoughts. So turn your mind to those things that are good, true, beautiful, and noble, and your life will be a reflection of these things.

A calm mind is the fruit of wisdom. Calmness of mind is the result of the patient practice of self-control. I know few practices that will help you acquire this calmness of mind, heart, and spirit like the rosary will. And by learning to direct your thoughts toward God, you will learn to direct your life toward God.

In the rosary, we have twenty mysteries that beget twenty lessons in life, love, the attainment of virtue, and the genius of God's plan for humanity.

The Joyful Mysteries

The Annunciation: In the First Joyful Mystery we learn about the power of saying yes to God's will in our lives, as we witness Mary surrendering with her whole heart to God's designs for her life (cf. Luke 1:28–38). Fruit of the Mystery: Desire to do God's will.

The Visitation: In the Second Joyful Mystery we learn the value of service as Mary leaves her home to attend to her cousin Elizabeth (cf. Luke 1:39–42). Fruit of the Mystery: Humility.

The Birth of Jesus: In the Third Joyful Mystery we encounter the humility of Jesus, the Son of God, born in a stable (cf. Luke 2:1–7). Fruit of the Mystery: Detachment from the things of this world.

The Presentation: In the Fourth Joyful Mystery we witness a powerful example of obedience as Mary submits her child, the Son of God, to the Law of Moses (cf. Luke 2:23–32). Fruit of the Mystery: Obedience.

The Finding of Jesus in the Temple: In the Fifth Joyful Mystery we learn that true wisdom does not come from the mere attainment of knowledge; rather, it is a gift from God (cf. Luke 2:45–49). Fruit of the Mystery: Vocation & Evangelization

The Luminous Mysteries

The Baptism of Jesus: In the First Luminous Mystery we hear the voice of the Father saying, "This is my beloved Son in whom I am well pleased," (Matthew 3:16–17) and we learn to stay close to the Father. Fruit of the Mystery: Openness to the Holy Spirit.

The Miracle at Cana: In the Second Luminous Mystery Jesus transforms water into wine (John 2:12) and we are reminded of his ability to transform our lives and the world. Fruit of the Mystery: Trust in God's Providence.

The Proclamation of the Kingdom: In the Third Luminous Mystery Jesus invites all people of all times to conversion—"Repent, for the Kingdom of God is at hand" (Mark 1:15)—and we ask to be filled with a desire for holiness. Fruit of the Mystery: Repentance.

The Transfiguration: In the Fourth Luminous Mystery we witness Jesus as he really is, the light of the world, and we ask for the spiritual courage to seek truth and light wherever it leads us (Luke 9:28–31). Fruit of the Mystery: Desire for Holiness.

The Institution of the Eucharist: The Fifth Luminous Mystery, in which Jesus teaches us how to love by holding nothing back, surrendering himself completely (John 6:51). Fruit of the Mystery: Love for the Eucharist.

The Sorrowful Mysteries

The Agony in the Garden: In the First Sorrowful Mystery we learn the importance of perseverance in prayer (cf. Luke 22:41–45). Fruit of the Mystery: Patience.

The Scourging at the Pillar: In the Second Sorrowful Mystery our spirits are renewed for the sacrifices of each day, and we learn never to despise the little things and the value of attention to detail (cf. John 19:1). Fruit of the Mystery: Self-Control.

The Crowning with Thorns: In the Third Sorrowful Mystery we learn compassion for those who are mocked and rejected, and we ask forgiveness for the times we have added to the insults of others (cf. Matthew 27:27–30). Fruit of the Mystery: Moral Courage.

The Carrying of the Cross: In the Fourth Sorrowful Mystery we are moved to help Jesus carry his cross by standing up to injustice and influencing our environment in a positive way (cf. John 19:17–18). Fruit of the Mystery: Desire to lay down our lives for others.

The Crucifixion: In the Fifth Sorrowful Mystery we experience the pain evil causes and feel the weight of our own sins (cf. Luke 23:42–46). Fruit of the Mystery: Surrender.

The Glorious Mysteries

The Resurrection: In the First Glorious Mystery we are reminded of the reality of life after death, and we learn to live with that in mind (cf. Mark 16:1–7). Fruit of the Mystery: Faith.

The Ascension: In the Second Glorious Mystery we are reminded of the great commission to continue the work of Jesus on earth by spreading the Gospel (cf. Mark 16:15–20). Fruit of the Mystery: Hope.

The Descent of the Holy Spirit: In the Third Glorious Mystery we are reminded that we are assisted in our efforts to do good by the unfathomable power of the Holy Spirit alive within us (cf. Acts 2:1–4). Fruit of the Mystery: Wisdom.

The Assumption: In the Fourth Glorious Mystery we are reminded of the beauty of purity of mind, body, spirit, and intention (cf. Revelation 12:1, 12:17). Fruit of the Mystery: Purity.

The Crowning of Mary Queen of Heaven: In the Fifth Glorious Mystery we learn to honor and seek the counsel of those who attain virtue in their lives (cf. Song of Songs 4:7–12). Fruit of the Mystery: Friendship with Mary.

These are twenty lessons worthy of constant reflection; twenty lessons that never cease to challenge us. I hope you will consider making this ancient spiritual exercise a part of your spiritual routines.

• More Than One Way •

There is more to praying the rosary than just saying the rosary. Anyone can say the rosary—just teach them the words and they can rattle them off. But to genuinely pray the rosary, we must have a clear objective in our minds. The rosary is not magic. There is no deal-making to be done with God. So many rosaries don't equal a prayer answered by God.

Prayer doesn't change God; prayer changes us. It is more rewarding to approach prayer seeking to understand God more, rather than seeing an opportunity to give God his instructions for the day. If we approach prayer with the hope of growing in virtue we will never be disappointed.

There are many different practical approaches to the rosary. The first is to focus on the words, which are deeply rooted in the Scriptures and Christian tradition. The Our Father was, of course, given to us by Jesus himself (cf. Matthew 6:9–13). The Creed represents the first expression of Christian conviction. The first part of the Hail Mary comes from the message delivered by the angel to Mary in Nazareth: "Hail, full of grace. The Lord is with thee." (Luke 1:28) This greeting is then followed by the words Elizabeth used to greet Mary during the Visitation: "Blessed art thou among women, and blessed is the fruit of thy womb." (Luke 1:42) The Glory Be is the simplest expression of Christian praise and belief in the triune God. And from the times of antiquity, Christians have placed themselves under the name of God and the sign of redemption, thus giving us the Sign of the Cross.

The words of the rosary are powerful and filled with meaning, but so are the mysteries that we use as a backdrop to each decade.

One thing is certain: Your mind cannot do two things at once. This is where many people become discouraged with praying the rosary. They try to pray the words and meditate on the mystery at the same time. Impossible! We must decide between the two.

On those occasions when you choose to meditate on the mysteries, allow the words to float by. Get lost in the scene. Imagine yourself there. When you choose to focus on the words, it may help to meditate on the mystery for a few moments before each decade.

I also find it very fruitful to identify an intention with each decade. Offering each decade for a person or a situation helps me to stay focused, and avails me the opportunity to pray for many people in my life.

There are some people who think that we should pray the rosary every day. In my own life, there have been months, even years, when I have prayed the rosary every day. At other times, I have gone weeks and months without praying the rosary. Generally, I have discovered that when I make time for this simple but profound practice of prayer I am a better person. When I have the discipline to pray the rosary regularly I seem to have a certain calmness and awareness, which makes me more readily disposed to living a life of virtue.

I don't think we need to enter the debate of whether or not every Catholic should pray the rosary every day. I do, however, think that all Catholics should be able to bring forth the rosary from their spiritual storehouse from time to time as the Spirit prompts them.

Our prayer lives should be dynamic, like love. Our love should be constant, but it may express itself in many different ways at different times. So it is with prayer. Learn to allow the Spirit to guide you to the type of prayer that will most benefit you on a particular day—not the type of prayer you "feel like" doing, but the type of prayer that will most benefit you on that day, depending on the disposition of your soul.

• The Real Objection •

I suspect the real reason modern Catholics don't have a more passionate relationship with the rosary is because, in general, I don't think we are comfortable with the role Mary plays in our spirituality. For hundreds of years, our non-Catholic Christian brothers and sisters have been accusing us of worshipping Mary and the saints, and I don't think we have done a good job of settling this question.

Do Catholics worship Mary and the saints? No. We pray to them but not to worship them, and not in the same way we pray to God. Think of it in this way: If you got sick and asked me to pray for you, I would. This does not make me uniquely Catholic, or even uniquely Christian. There are many non-Christians who believe in the power of prayer. If I ask my non-Catholic Christian friends whether they pray for their spouse or their children, they will say yes. If I ask them to pray for me, they will say yes. This is the same principle. We believe that Mary and the saints are dead to this world, but we also believe they live on in the next world. And we believe that their prayers are just as powerful—even more powerful. We are essentially saying to them, "We have problems down here. You know what it is like because you have been here; pray for us!"

Our non-Catholic Christian friends don't believe people can still pray in the afterlife. We do. Our spiritual universe is just bigger. In fact, one of the most incredible things about our Catholic faith is the vastness of our spiritual universe.

• Mary •

Mary is the most famous woman in history. She leads all prominent women who have earned their fame by living a life of virtue. She has inspired more art and music than any other woman in history, and even in the modern age, she fascinates the imaginations of men and women of all faiths. In our own age, Mary has appeared on the cover of *Time* magazine more often than any other person.

I suspect that if we are to reconcile the great disharmony that exists between the role of men and the role of women in modern society we will need the insight of this great feminine role model. Is it possible for us to understand the dignity, value, mystery, and wonder of women, without first understanding this woman?

But beyond her fame and her historical importance is her centrality to Christian life. The first Christians gathered around her for comfort and guidance, yet some modern Catholics treat her like she has some contagious disease. One of the great challenges that we face as modern Catholics is to find a genuine place for Mary in our spirituality.

My wife recently gave birth to our first child, a son. Being a father has filled me with many new spiritual insights. I love this little boy so much and if I can love him so much in all my brokenness and with all my limitations, how much more God must love me. Through my son I have experienced the love of God in a whole new way. I also just yearn to be with him. When I am on the road, or even at the office for the day, I yearn to get home and hold him, play with him, be with him. It strikes me that perhaps above everything else God just yearns to be with us.

The birth of our son has also renewed my relationship with Mary. It has occurred to me that no matter how much I love my son, my wife will always have a unique perspective on his life. It doesn't mean that she loves him more or that I love him less. It just means that a mother sees her child's life in a way that nobody else can. If I don't take time occasionally to ask her about this motherly perspective I unnecessarily miss a part of my son's life.

A mother has a unique perspective. Nobody sees the life of a child the way the child's mother does—not even the father. This is Mary's perspective of Jesus' life. It seems to me that every genuine Christian, not just Catholics, should be interested in that perspective—and not just interested, but fascinated. In the rosary we ponder the life of Jesus through the eyes of his mother. This is an incredibly powerful experience if we enter into it fully.

Part Four

NOW IS OUR TIME

• • •

The mission entrusted to the Catholics of every era is to transform the world they live, work, and play in. Transforming these various arenas of life is a constant challenge. Every environment you and I touch should be better because we were there. It is all too easy for us to say that our time is more difficult than some other time. All periods of history have unique challenges. Ours is no different. The people of every age think that their time and place is special, and that their circumstances are extraordinary. They are not. Humanity faces the same challenges in every age. They may come wearing different masks, but they are essentially the same.

There is genius in Catholicism. The human heart yearns for happiness, and God wants us to be happy. But we only experience this happiness, and the fulfillment that accompanies it, when we are changing, growing, becoming more like Jesus Christ and through him becoming the-best-version-of-ourselves. Catholicism is the dynamic lifestyle and learning system divinely designed to assist us in this transformation.

The benefits of this transformation are not confined to the individual. When Catholicism is lived as it is intended to be, it elevates every human activity, every human person, and every human environment that it touches.

In 1517, when Martin Luther began the Reformation, there was no doubt that the Catholic Church was in need of reform. Today the Church is in need of reform again. I pray that this reform will be the result of the flourishing caused when you and I embrace the ancient tradition we call Catholicism in a dynamic way, becoming the-best-version-of-ourselves, helping others to do the same, and bringing unity to all Christians.

• • •

Chapter Nineteen

TIME FOR A CHANGE

I have spent the past two decades traveling the world and speaking to men, women, and children of all ages and cultures. During this time, I have been blessed with the opportunity to see more of the world than most presidents, and more of the Church than most bishops. I suspect these rare experiences have produced in me a unique perspective, but I hope that the ideas that make up this perspective resonate also in your heart.

I love the Church. To me, Catholicism is a gift that can never be fully appreciated, described, or understood. But in order to even begin to appreciate Catholicism in all its beauty we must experience it. My travels have affirmed that people love the Church. The press may attack the Church, fallen-away Catholics may ridicule it, and even practicing Catholics may criticize it, but I firmly believe these are curious expressions of love. At the very least, they are expressions of a desire for the Church to be the beacon of light it should be in the world. Sometimes love goes sour, as it has for many modern Catholics in their relationship with the Church. When love goes sour, it is usually for one of four reasons: misunderstanding, indifference, selfishness, or the pride that makes a person unwilling to apologize or forgive. Sometimes it is a combination, and usually both parties are at fault to some extent.

It is true that the Church has many problems at this moment in history. These problems fill my heart with a great sadness, but they do not lead me to despair. I see them as opportunities for us to change, grow, and become more effective at meeting people where they are and leading them to where God calls them to be. I see the challenges of our age as a chance for us to envision once again what it truly means to be Catholic, and what role the Church should play in the modern world from local communities to the national stage. And so, as members of the one, holy, catholic, and apostolic Church, we also need to ask: Is the Church the-best-version-of-itself?

• Are We Willing to Change? •

The circumstances of this moment in history have conspired to present this question to the Church: Change or more of the same?

Change is one of the laws of the natural universe. Nature teaches us that everything of this world is constantly changing. Everything God created is constantly in the process of either growing or dying. History also teaches us that those who try to prevent or avoid change always fail.

While these laws of change are true of the natural realm, we also experience supernatural realities. Faith, hope, and love are perfect and personal examples—and they are unchanging. Amid this dynamic and ever-changing natural environment, we also experience truth—and truth is unchanging. The environment changes, the culture changes, people change, but truth does not change; the supernatural realities of faith, hope, and love do not change; and God does not change.

Interestingly the yearnings of the human heart do not change either. It is for this reason that the unchanging truth of the Gospel resonates with the people of all eras.

The question, therefore, is not *"Will* the Church change?" For it certainly will, just as it has in every century for two thousand years. The question is not *"Should* the Church change?" The problems and dilemmas we face are proof enough of that. The question is *"How* should the Church change in the twenty-first century?"

To answer this question, it is important to understand that the Church is the connection between two worlds. The first is the supernatural world. The second is the natural world, as we know it. In one hand, the Church holds truth, eternal and unchanging. In the other hand, she holds the practices that encourage and enable us to apply the unchanging truth of the Gospel to the ever-changing circumstances of our daily lives.

So before we get overexcited about the changes that we think the Church needs to make, or the changes that we think need to be made to the Church, it is important that we understand what constitutes authentic change. Most of all, we need to develop an intimate understanding of the relationship between any particular issue and the eternal and unchanging truth that guides the Church's position on that issue.

What the Church most certainly does not need is change for the sake of change. And we do not need change that is driven by philosophies such as individualism, hedonism, minimalism, relativism, and materialism. We are where we are today because we have allowed these self-centered philosophies of compromise to direct change in society, the Church, and our lives over the past several decades.

Some believe the answer is to go back to the 1950s model of the Church. Others would like to drag us all the way back to the Middle Ages. I promise you, the answer is never to go back. Throughout salvation history, God himself teaches us this lesson. Adam and Eve were blessed to experience Eden, but were banished from the garden after they disobeyed the guidelines God had given them for their own good (cf. Genesis 3:23). God always acts for the good of humanity. In the fullness of time, God sent his only Son to redeem us (cf. Galatians 4:4 and John 19:30). After this reconciliation, God didn't send us all back to the Garden of Eden. No, he imagined something new and greater. God never goes back; he always moves forward, and God always wants our future to be bigger than our past.

The story of salvation never goes backward; it is always marching forward. There is no question that we will need to draw on the wisdom of the past in moving forward, but drawing from the past is not the same as going backward. The answer is never to go back; the answer is always to move forward. What new place is God calling the Church to now?

Whatever that new place looks like, it will require change to get us there, and the transition will likely not be easy. How should the Church change in the twenty-first century? Will we learn to bring forth from both the old and the new (cf. Matthew 13:51) as we press forward?

Dynamic renewal in the Church comes when we consider the future with respect for the past. A simple reorganization is not going to do it. We need some radical change, but not in the way that most people might think. When change and the Catholic Church find themselves together in a conversation these days, more often than not people are talking about the most controversial issues. All of these issues are peripheral to the real challenges that we face.

It is true that we need change, but we need life-giving change that will bring forth genuine fruit, season after season. We need to start educating Catholics about their yearning for happiness and the role discipline plays in the fulfillment of that yearning. We need to show people in practical ways how we are happiest when we allow the timeless insights of the Gospel to direct our actions. We need to rediscover the abundant riches of Catholic spirituality. We need to provide answers to the pressing questions of our age and the common objections to Catholicism, answers that resonate deeply with the people of our times. We need to articulate the relevance of Catholicism in the modern world in ways that are bold, brilliant, coherent, and inspiring. We need to encourage lay Catholics to actively participate in the mission of the Church. And above all, we need to become prayerful people, and thus a people of prayer.

But first and foremost, we need to inspire people. There is no point having all the knowledge, insight, and wisdom of the ages if you cannot inspire anyone to activate these in their lives. Nobody does anything worthwhile until they are inspired. The Spirit at work always stirs our emotions to the heights of inspiration. We need to inspire people to live life to the fullest (cf. John 10:10). We need to inspire people to follow Christ. We need to inspire people to get involved. We need to *inspire* people.

Change is necessary and inevitable. Rather than allowing the spirit of the world to direct us, I pray we allow the life-giving Spirit of God to direct this change in the Church and our own lives.

If you don't think something needs to change, go to Church next Sunday and look around. Then ask yourself, "Where are the young people?" Not the very young, but the twentysomethings and thirtysomethings. I find myself right in the middle of what is now statistically the largest age segment of Catholics in America, and yet, it is also the least practicing segment of Catholics in America.

For the most part, they went to Catholic schools and were raised in Catholic families, but we didn't teach them to pray or lead them to an effective relationship with God. Somewhere along the way, something went drastically wrong. Somehow we have failed to communicate the value of living a life of virtue and faith. In some way we have failed to convince young people today that walking with God is the best way to live. We have failed to demonstrate the relevance of Jesus and the Church in the modern climate. And unless we can do this, and do it convincingly, these young people will not be back anytime soon.

There are now more than thirty million former Catholics in the United States alone. That is one in every ten Americans, making former Catholics the second-largest Christian denomination in America.

Are we willing to change? I hope so. Almost every person I speak to about the future of Catholicism says, "The Church really needs to change," or something to that effect. What we perhaps forget in making this statement is that we are the Church, and so the real question becomes: Are *you* willing to change? Am I willing to change? Are you and I willing to become the change the Church needs? It has been my experience that most people are not. We appoint ourselves experts, criticize from afar, and use the Church's shortcomings as excuses not to get involved.

We call for change, but we forget how difficult it is to change. We call for change, but often refuse to get involved. Think about how hard it is for you to change a bad habit, especially one that is deeply ingrained in your personality and lifestyle. Take just one tiny aspect of your own life as an example. Pick one of your bad habits and try to replace it with a good habit. How long does it take? How many times do you fail before you finally succeed?

It is the same for the Church. So I urge you, be patient with the Church, which is two thousand years old and made up of 1.2 billion wonderfully flawed human beings like you. Change will come slowly, because the Church will change for the better only as quickly as you and I respond to God's call to grow in virtue and become better-versions-of-ourselves. When you become a-better-version-of-yourself the Church becomes a-better-version-of-itself.

• What Should We Focus On? •

If the Catholic Church is to change, grow, thrive, and fulfill its mission in this modern climate, it will be for one reason: because we become a more spiritual people. Only then will this renewed spiritual health burst forth into authentic action.

It would seem to me that education and evangelization are the keys to helping the whole Church to blossom. They are the pillars of renewal. It is impossible to know God and not love him. Those who do not love God simply do not know God. It is equally impossible to experience God and not want others to experience him as a result. Those who do not evangelize simply have not had an intimate experience of God.

The first step is to acknowledge that the systems and processes surrounding education and evangelization in the Church today are significantly flawed, or at the very least woefully inadequate. From there we can begin to build whatever is necessary to engage the people of our time.

• Education •

Sooner or later, someone is going to start suing Catholic high schools and colleges for false advertising. How is it possible that so many can pass through the Catholic education system and know so little about the Church, Catholicism, and even Christ? How is it possible that so many graduate from Catholic school without an understanding of how to build an affective relationship with God?

The Catholic education system as a structure is one of the marvels of world history. It is the cause of envy among countless other groups and organizations. Those with an agenda dream of getting access to a system as powerful as the Catholic education system. Why? Because they realize how powerful it could be if it was actually employed. That's why it is under attack, and why so many people have forced their agendas upon the Catholic education system. All the while, we have failed to use it for the good it was created to produce in students, families, the Church, and society.

Do we want to teach our children about Jesus, the value of virtue and character, and the beauty of the Church? Or do we just want privileged educational environments to teach them what they need to get into the best colleges? Do we want to prepare them for life? Or do we just want to prepare them to become cogs in the global economic wheel? Do we believe that by teaching them about Jesus and the role the Church can play in their lives we are better preparing them for college and for life? Or have we resigned ourselves to the spirit of the world?

Catholic education is one of the great miracles of modern civilization. It is unprecedented and it is genius. That is why it has been imitated by every other religious organization on the planet. They know the power of the Catholic education system. But this ingenious system is misemployed, underemployed, ineffective, failing to fulfill its mission, and in desperate need of renewal.

At the same time, Catholic schools are under tremendous pressure with growing regulation and compliance requirements, shrinking enrollment, and never-ending financial challenges. All these circumstances inevitably lead to a focus on maintenance rather than mission. We are too concerned about surviving to really explore what it will take for Catholic education to thrive again.

Education in any context is best directed with questions. Many educators throughout the ages have tried to impose their views on others. Such teachers, if they can be called that, tend to lecture. That is to say, their style is a monologue. But true teachers don't try to impose their views on their students; rather, they try to lead them through the forest of reason, doubt, reflection, and questioning to the beauty of truth. In the process they draw out the-best-version of each student. Great teachers propose questions. That is to say, their style resembles more of a dialogue than a monologue.

The questions we ask are as important as or even more important than the answers we find. If we ask the wrong questions, we will always find the wrong answers. If Catholic education is to change in a way that is authentic and life giving, it will do so only because we choose the right questions to base Catholic education upon.

In modern society, the Church's position on any matter is now habitually questioned, doubted, and belittled as being out of touch and unreasonable. The teachings of the Church are ridiculed by self-appointed "experts," who know little or nothing about the Church and the wisdom that forms her teachings. This cultural mood is a real and formidable enemy when it comes to Catholic education.

The only response to this cultural environment that will hold our students in good stead for a lifetime is to ignite in them a love of learning and a hunger for the truth.

If you want to win a war, there are three things you need to know: First, you need to know you are at war. Second, you need to know who or what your enemy is. And third, you need to know what weapons and strategies can defeat your enemy.

Our enemies are ignorance and indifference. It is amazing how many academic degrees you can award in a culture and still have the masses almost completely ignorant of any life-giving truth. Ignorance of and indifference toward the truth are the enemy of the Church, Catholic education, and indeed Christ.

Are you hungry for truth? Do you seek it out in all areas of your life?

If we take the time to study the teachings of the Church, we will discover in them a rare beauty and a profound wisdom. Some may argue that the teachings of the Church are too difficult to understand. Truth was never designed for the twenty-second sound bite. We have that against us in a sound-bite-driven culture. But in the context of a Catholic school, we are not confined by twenty-second time limitations. Instead, we have years to explore the wonders of the essential questions regarding life and faith.

Instead of questioning the Church's teachings with no effort to understand her point of view, or simply dismissing the Church's view as outdated and old-fashioned, perhaps we should try to understand her position.

Do we actually believe that we know better than the collective towering genius of Catholic philosophers and theologians of the past two thousand years? How did we become so proud and arrogant that we question these extraordinary men and women without hesitation or investigation? What bias and personal prejudice might be clouding our position? Do our objections have any real basis, or is it simply that we find the teachings of the Church inconvenient?

It is true that our times face unique challenges and questions that the great Catholic minds of the past did not, but surely at the very least they provide an elevated starting point. If we had keen minds and keen spirits, if we were truth-seekers, in every instance we would humbly ask, "Why does the Church teach what she teaches about . . . ?"

This is the question that should shape Catholic education and our personal exploration of the faith. Perhaps we should allow high school students to raise all the questions about Catholicism and all the objections they have heard against the Church. Perhaps we should assign students the task of defending certain issues or answering the big questions of our times. Then, in each case, together we could explore the question "Why does the Church teach what she teaches about that?"

We should not ask this question with the sarcastic, cynical, and even dismissive tone that many in academic circles ask it with today. They ask it as if the question itself were an answer. We should ask this question with the greatest confidence. We should ask it knowing that before too long, the fruits of thousands of years of great practical, intellectual, and spiritual wisdom will be eclipsed before our eyes. This kind of spiritual and intellectual eclipse is a life-forming experience, a life-changing moment, and a life-directing influence. If we could expose each Catholic high school student to just one such experience, they would have a newfound respect for the great wisdom of the Church. If we could show them the truth, and the beauty of that truth, in relation to just one of their questions or objections, we would infinitely elevate their love and understanding of the Church. They may still wander away from the Church, and they may still act contrary to its teachings, but deep in their hearts they will know that the Church is not merely another earthly human institution, but rather a divinely appointed custodian of truth and wisdom.

Let's face it, there are probably only a dozen issues that are being used by this modern secular culture to rob today's Catholics of their faith. Would it be that hard to put together a learning system that clearly answers the objections, eloquently outlines the Church's position, explains the modern relevance of each of these issues, and inspires people to live the truths they discover?

We may not be able to explain everything about Catholicism, but we shouldn't let what we can't do interfere with what we can do. If we can develop a love of learning and a hunger for truth in young Catholics, and then empower them to seek truth, we will have served them rightly. To do this, we must stimulate within them a positive form of curiosity, the ultimate curiosity: curiosity for truth. This quality of the philosopher will guide them morally and ethically through life. Truth seekers always end up with God. It is much harder for those who are indifferent to truth, or who deny the existence of objective and unchanging truth, to come to know God.

Truth is beautiful. If only we could harness the energies of the Catholic education system to show young people how this truth of the Gospel can *set them free* (cf. John 8:32). Only then will we be able to show young people the beauty within themselves. Only then will they believe us. Authentic love of self and genuine self-esteem are born from the right relationship with God and the truth he has revealed.

Educators, parents, politicians, and psychologists all seem to agree that quite possibly the largest problem among young people today is poor self-esteem. You cannot correct this problem by simply showering a child with compliments. Self-esteem has three sources: right action; right relationship with God, others, and self; and service. Right action is as simple and difficult as listening to the gentle voice of conscience and allowing it to guide us. Right relationship with God, and everyone and everything in the universe, is developed by an ever-increasing awareness of all that is good, true, beautiful, and right. And nothing will foster a healthy sense of self like the experience of being of value to others through service.

It is impossible to have a healthy sense of self unless we are proactively seeking to live out the truth that God has revealed to us. I hope we can learn to value truth again, even amidst this culture of appearance, deception, and compromise. There is great beauty in the truth. When we hear it, read it, or experience it, our souls soar. As John Paul II put it so poetically and powerfully in his encyclical letter, *Veritatis Splendor,* "THE SPLENDOR OF THE TRUTH shines forth in the works of the Creator, and in a special way, in man, created in the image and likeness of God (cf. Genesis 1:26). Truth enlightens man's intelligence and shapes his freedom, leading him to know and love God."

The Catholic education system is perfectly positioned to ignite within the hearts and minds of young Catholics a sense of passion, awe, and hunger for truth. It is critical that we reassess at this juncture what we wish to bestow upon those who attend Catholic schools. If it is simply an elite education for a privileged few, then surely we are in direct conflict with the very Gospel that we claim to be guided by. But if we wish to bestow upon our children the values and beliefs that emerge from the life and teachings of Jesus Christ, then clearly it is time for a change.

The ironic thing is that most young people are looking for someone who has the courage to look them in the eye and tell them the truth. Young people want above all to be their own person, but not just any version. They yearn deeply to be the-best-version-of-themselves. Sometimes they are aware of that yearning and sometimes they are not. To discover and realize their highest potential they need and want guidance.

Teaching young people to recognize and celebrate the-best-version-of-themselves is also the best way to teach them to participate in society, to find work that is uniquely suited to them, and to engage their social responsibilities.

The Catholic education system has the potential to play an unfathomable role in the renewal of the Church. More than any other activity in the Church, education has a rare opportunity to reorient modern men and women toward God. It seems to me—and I may be wrong—that the Catholic education system will actualize its potential not by shying away from all things Catholic, but by doing what it claims to do and offering a Catholic education.

I appreciate that there are enormous challenges involved in running a school, I realize that our teachers' compensation is dangerously close to an unjust wage, and I know that all too often teachers have no voice when it comes to important issues regarding the future and welfare of their schools. Nonetheless, with so many of our Catholic high school students rejecting the faith in high school or shortly after they graduate—and I assure you the percentage is enormous—it is impossible not to question our current approach. At the very least we should be asking ourselves constantly how we can engage Catholic school students in their faith so that it becomes a touchstone for the rest of their lives.

It is also critical to note that most Catholics now receive their Catholic education outside Catholic schools. More than two-thirds of Catholic students do not attend Catholic schools. This means their primary faith education outside the home takes place in CCD classes. This number is increasing with every passing year as more parents decide not to send their children to Catholic schools and more and more Catholic schools close. The bottom line is, we get one hour a week to captivate the imaginations of these young men and women, demonstrate the genius of Catholicism, and convince them that following Jesus is the best way to live. I think we can all agree that this is no small task.

If we cannot afford to lose another generation of Catholics, and I think we all know we can't, isn't it time to start allocating serious resources to developing world-class CCD programs? Shouldn't we be allocating more of our parish and diocesan budgets to genuinely engaging young people with the Catholic faith?

• Evangelization •

My experience has been that most Catholics today are uncomfortable with the word *evangelization*. It may be because the term has been kidnapped by Protestant-Evangelical churches, and their methods of evangelization are often quite argumentative, intimidating, and forceful. In addition, a number of self-promoting and self-serving television evangelists seem to have been linked with every imaginable scandal over the past twenty years.

Not only have they abducted the term *evangelization*, but they have also snatched the term *Christian*. Amazingly, many modern Christian churches don't even consider Catholics to be Christian. That's like saying Coca-Cola isn't cola. Nonetheless, the issue before us is evangelization, which in essence means "sharing the Gospel with the whole world."

Organizations have a tendency to become preoccupied with day-to-day pressures, problems, and programs. The danger in this is that we lose track of what we are trying to accomplish. It is for this reason that most institutions, from colleges to multinational corporations, are constantly reviewing and revisiting mission statements, core values, long-term and short-term goals, and overall strategic plans. Otherwise it is all too easy for us to get caught up in maintenance and lose sight of our mission.

If you went into an ice cream parlor and there was no ice cream, you'd say, "There's a problem!" If you went to a chocolate shop and there was no chocolate, you'd say, "There's a problem!" The mission of the Church is to share the Gospel, and to teach, encourage, and challenge people to become more like Jesus Christ. So how is it that we can belong to a local church community that goes on year after year with almost no outreach to the unchurched and underchurched in the area, with very few people becoming markedly more Christ-like, and not think there is a problem? Let me tell you, if this describes your church community, *there's a problem!*

I suppose what it really comes down to is whether or not we sincerely believe that knowing and following Christ is the best way to live. I suspect that, on some level, most Catholics don't. If we did we would be more excited to share it.

The nature and purpose of the Church is to influence people and communities by bringing the life and teachings of Jesus Christ to life in every place and time. A local church community should be contagious. Everyone who belongs to that community should be reaching out both actively, with efforts to evangelize, and passively, with the example of their lives.

One thing seems more than apparent: We need a strategy. Today's Catholics are not just going to drift into a more Christ-centered lifestyle on their own. Our church communities are not going to become contagious overnight. We need a strategy, because these types of things only ever happen on purpose.

Allow me to suggest a simple four-step plan for evangelization:

Step One: We must begin to nurture friendships. Friendship was the original model of evangelization. The first Christians did not seek to spread the faith by means of political power, and they didn't have the use of the mass media. They simply engaged the oldest and most reliable method of influence—friendship.

Every year, advertisers spend millions of dollars to create a positive perception of their products. But every advertising executive on Madison Avenue knows that the word-of-mouth endorsement of a friend, someone you know and trust, will influence your decision more than any advertisement ever will.

We live in a culture in which spiritual authorities and religious institutions are increasingly questioned, distrusted, and ignored. But fortunately, friends still listen to and trust each other. Visit any culture on any continent and you will discover this universal human dynamic.

Step Two: The next step in our evangelization strategy is to pray for the people we are trying to reach with the life-giving values, principles, and ideas of the Gospel.

Prayer is powerful. Prayer is essential. It cuts through and clarifies. It gives us vision, courage, strength, and endurance. Prayer dissolves our prejudices, banishes our narrow-mindedness, and melts away our judgmental tendencies. It erodes our impure motives. Prayer opens our hearts to God and his ways.

Our work to share the Gospel with others should never be separated from our prayer for those people. For if this separation occurs, we run the great risk of falling into personal agendas.

Step Three: The third step in our strategy of evangelization is to tell your story.

Stories change people's lives. The stories of Francis of Assisi, Mother Teresa, John Vianney, Thomas More, and John Paul II have had tremendous influence on my life. Theirs have changed my life, but the stories of hundreds of ordinary people that I have met along the way have also greatly impacted me.

We have already discussed the great power of stories in Chapter Eleven. Now you need to discover yours. We all have a story—the sequence of events that led us through trials and troubles, doubts and questions, to a time and place where we came to believe that right living is the only way to be happy. That doesn't mean we don't still sometimes have trials and doubts and questions. Nor does it mean that we are not attracted to actions and things that are self-destructive from time to time.

Tell your story. Despite how ordinary you may think it is, you will be amazed how easily people will relate to your journey and be inspired by it. Despite all your faults and failings, there is real power in your story.

Step Four: The final component of this evangelization strategy is to invite your friends and neighbors to outreach events at your church.

This poses a problem in most Catholic communities, because we don't have outreach events. Some may argue that we have the RCIA program for those interested in exploring Catholicism. But this program runs for months and only those with a high level of interest will attend. What we need are some monthly or quarterly programs that parishioners can invite their family, friends, and neighbors to attend—programs that inspire, that ignite a little passion in people for right living, that speak to the very real human needs and struggles people are facing. We need outreach programs, and they need to be relevant and innovative.

These outreach events don't need to have anything to do with the faith directly. Your church could host an event about how to deal with credit card debt, or a seminar for the unemployed, or a gathering for those who are grieving the loss of a loved one.

This was Jesus' model. He never preached to anybody before he met their temporal needs. He healed them, comforted them, fed them, and then he shared the message with them. He met them where they were and led them to where God was calling them to be.

Our lack of outreach events is one of the major barriers to Catholic evangelization. Protestants and Evangelicals can just easily invite their friends to church on Sunday. But Catholics won't. Why? Because it becomes awkward around Communion time, when everyone is going to receive and you have to tell your friends that they can't. Result: The invited guest doesn't feel welcome, she feels left out, and she never comes back.

When was the last time you showed up to a party you were not invited to? People are not comfortable coming to events where they don't feel welcome. And the truth is, there are a lot of *Catholics* who don't feel welcome in the Catholic Church. So it is not surprising that a non-Catholic would feel a little left out. As Catholics, we need to engage the power of invitation. We need to invite people, and we need something to invite them to.

And once they are there, we need to make them feel welcome, whether we are the ones who invited them or not. We need to go out of our way to help people feel welcome in our Church, to make them feel that they belong. This sense of belonging is important to all of us. If people don't find it in their local Catholic church, they will go to another church, one where they feel they belong.

Perhaps this strategy is too simple, and I am sure that it is not perfect. But I am convinced that we need a step-by-step plan that is specifically geared toward reaching the people we live, work, and socialize with.

The early Church was unstoppable, and as far as I can tell, it was because they followed this simple strategy. They believed that the values and principles of the Gospel were the best way to live. They nurtured friendships. They were deeply committed to a life of prayer. They were courageous in telling their story. They were generous and welcoming.

The people of today desire happiness just as the first Christians did. So, we come back to the question: "Do you believe that knowing and following Jesus is the best way to live?" You and I are not spectators in the great mission of the Church. We are participants.

Now, let's be practical for a moment. How can you help others to discover the beauty of the life and teachings of Jesus Christ? We can fulfill our call to share the Gospel by teaching our children and by living the values and principles of the Gospel in our own life. But we also have a unique opportunity to share the life-giving teachings of Christianity with our friends. No one is better positioned to touch your friends with the beauty and goodness of our faith than you are. We learn more from our friends than we ever will from books. Each of us influences the lives of our friends more than we could ever imagine. Whether we are aware of it or not, we are all exerting a tremendous influence upon the people that we spend time with. Let me ask you, are your friends better people because they know you? Are you helping them to become the-best-version-of-themselves? Are you living your life in such a way that those who know you but don't know God will come to know

God because they know you?

The primary vehicle that God wants to use to share the truth, beauty, and wisdom of his ways with the modern world is not the mass media or the Internet. The vehicle God wants to use is friendship.

Friendship is the original model of evangelization, and it is the model that will triumph in the modern context. Friendship establishes trust and mutual respect, which together bring about the openness and acceptance that give birth to vulnerable dialogue. Only then can we begin addressing the questions that every human heart longs to answer: Who am I? Where did I come from? What am I here for? How do I do it? Where am I going? Friendship is the key to evangelization.

How can you practically apply these ideas to your life? Sometime today, take a few moments in the classroom of silence and ask God to point out five people in your life who would benefit from a greater knowledge and appreciation of God and the Church. Write down the names of those five people. Mentally attach one of their names to each finger on your right hand.

Pray for those people every day for the next month. Pray for each of them by name, every day. Make yourself available to God. Tell God that you would like to help them discover the benefits of living a life of virtue and the adventure of walking with him.

After you have prayed for these five people each day for a month, call them and arrange to spend an hour or two with each of them individually. Take them to lunch, go for a walk, play golf, or meet for coffee. When you have this time with them, one-on-one, talk to them about what is going on in their lives.

Do this once a month with each of the five people individually. For three to six months, don't talk about God, religion, or the Church, unless they introduce the topic into the conversation. After these months have passed, during one of your monthly visits, invite them to join you on a visit to a local homeless shelter, soup kitchen, or nursing home. Go to these places and help out, or just visit with the people there. Nothing awakens the moral, ethical, and spiritual senses like encounters with the underprivileged.

Then, and only then, having formed the friendship and developed some level of mutual respect, begin the dialogue about the place God has in our lives. This mutual respect is essential to the process of evangelization. Without it, you will speak but people will not listen. But once you have won their respect people will listen to what you have to say, even if they vehemently disagree with your point of view. If someone we don't respect says something that we disagree with, we simply dismiss it. But if a good person, someone we know has our best interests at heart, says something that we disagree with it is much more difficult to dismiss. We will consider this opinion and weigh it more carefully. In this way, the truth will have a chance to settle on the good soil in their hearts (cf. Mark 4:8).

Over time and as the dialogue continues, give them a good book about the spiritual life, a book that will challenge them to think, to change, to grow, and to become the-best-version-of-themselves. Be sure it is a book that connects with them where they are in their journey, and not one that is too far beyond them. Then when you get together each month, talk to them about the ideas in the book. Ask them: What do you like about the book? What don't you like about it? Which parts challenge you? Which ideas comfort you? How does it make you want to live differently?

When the time is right, invite them to join you for an outreach program at your church. Afterward, invite them for brunch or coffee and talk about the program.

Continue to foster these five friendships and God will use you powerfully. I will never forget the people who did this for me. Without their time and effort, without their passion for the life-giving ways of Christ, I don't know where I would be today. I am eternally grateful to them. And one day your friends will be eternally grateful to you.

It is impossible to live a Christ-centered life and not want to share the wisdom of right living with others. I pray we will embrace virtue more and more in our own lives. And I pray we will begin to share the infinite treasures of the Church with others more enthusiastically.

The great evangelization that is needed will not take place via the mass media, though we certainly should harness the media and the Internet to further the Kingdom of God. It will take place through the simple and timeless treasure of friendship. This is the original model of evangelization, and it is still the most effective.

• Vocations •

We all have a vocation, and it is in finding and following that vocation that our restless hearts find rest. Your vocation is God's intimate response to your individual desire for happiness. He places within you the desire for happiness, and he calls you to that happiness with a specific vocation. Such is the genius of God.

Life is vocational.

In many modern nations, we are experiencing a great shortage of priests. The crisis is much greater than most are aware of. The situation is so dire that statistics suggest that if something does not change, fifteen years from now half the parishes in America will not have a resident priest.

What is the solution to this problem? Why is there such a great shortage of priests? I believe the primary reason is because we have stopped preaching the Gospel. Maybe one out of ten times do I come out of church on a Sunday and think to myself, *That homily really challenged me, inspired me, convicted me, showed me the changes I need to make, and taught me how to practically apply today's Gospel to my life.*

We have stopped preaching the Gospel. We are preaching for the lukewarm. Paralyzed by fear, we have watered down the message so much that most Catholics struggle to find the relevance. It is true in our schools, it is true in our colleges, and it is true in our churches on Sundays. I may be accused of being critical, but unless we are willing to admit we are failing, we will never succeed. Until we are willing to admit we have big problems, we will not turn our efforts to finding big solutions.

Young people want to give their lives to something worthy. They may not be consciously aware of this desire. Nonetheless, they are moved by it.

Young people don't want to be shown the path of compromise and least resistance. They want to be challenged to explore their incredible potential. They want to be guided in the paths of truth, virtue, and happiness. They want to be coached to become the-best-version-of-themselves. In short, they want to know the Gospel.

If we preach the Gospel, we will have vocations. If we live the Gospel, our seminaries will begin to overflow. Nothing is surer.

Chapter Twenty

LEADERSHIP

People need leadership, and in the absence of genuine leadership they will listen to anyone who steps up to the microphone. People want leadership, but when they perceive that leaders lack courage and are self-serving, they reject them and assume the role themselves. They realize they are not qualified, but they would rather go to their peril under their own leadership than under the leadership of an inauthentic leader.

As Catholics, we are desperate for some bold leadership. Fifty years ago, people gave their allegiance and support to those in leadership positions merely because they had a position of prominence or authority. Not anymore. People don't respect authority today. In fact, they question it, they are skeptical of it, and they are cynical toward it.

Does it not strike you as a great poverty of leadership that here in America we cannot put one person on the evening news who can be acknowledged by Americans from coast to coast as a Catholic leader? Where is the "someone" who speaks for us? It is true that occasionally a bishop or cardinal effectively harnesses the media in his diocese and establishes a vibrant identity as a Catholic leader in his geographic area. It is also true that some lay Catholics who occupy positions of prominence in the business world, the entertainment world, or the political realm have successfully established a Catholic identity in different ways. But we have no national figures, not within the clergy and not among the laity. Does that not strike you as a massive poverty of leadership? Where is the Catholic leader who can speak to the people of our time in ways that are bold, brilliant, logical, articulate, and inspiring? Where is the Catholic we can put on the evening news who resonates with all Catholics and intrigues non-Catholics? All this has become self-evident in the midst of the recent controversies that have enveloped the Church. Why are we unable to put forth even a single national Catholic figure who can speak to the issues of the day clearly and articulately, in a way that is bold, brilliant, and inspiring?

Perhaps we are doing it the wrong way. It is possible that the whole system of organization that has helped us in the past is now hurting us. Perhaps the provincial model of administration and organization—parish, diocese, and archdiocese, under Rome—is hurting us in a time when the whole world is quickly becoming a global village. On top of all this, when talented leaders do emerge, we don't advance and empower them; we make their paths almost impossible.

Why are we so unwilling to raise these leaders up when they do emerge? Why do we keep them down? Why do we regionalize them? Why do we persecute them? Are we afraid they will become too popular, that we won't be able to control them? Whatever the reason, we should try to pinpoint it, because in the absence of this desperately needed leadership, the Church will have to content herself with mere survival. We must address the issue of leadership. If the Catholic Church is to thrive in the twenty-first century, it will be because of bold and inspiring leadership.

The fact that we cannot put forth a single spokesperson who can be nationally recognized to speak about different Catholic issues in a bold, brilliant, articulate, and inspiring fashion should send up a red flag. Something is amiss.

It may be true that most of us cannot do anything about this particular situation, but let's pray that God will raise up a great voice for our time. Where is our Francis or Ignatius? And when God does raise up this great voice, let us pray that the hierarchy and the laity together recognize this person and the role he or she has been called to.

• Paralyzed by Fear •

There is a great fear that has seized the leadership of the Catholic Church. I am referring not only to bishops and priests but also to lay leadership. Fear has paralyzed all our leaders.

The rapid change in the world over the past seventy-five years caught the Church almost completely unprepared. Six hundred years passed between the invention of the plow and the invention of the automobile. Only sixty years passed between the invention of the automobile and the space age. It is during this period of rapid change that the whole model of the Church was challenged by a culture that completely reoriented the hearts and minds of humanity.

Before this period of rapid change, many men were humbled by their lack of education and accepted the authority, teachings, and leadership of the Church based upon faith. But by the mid-1960s, men, women, and children of modern Western nations had begun questioning absolutely everything. This questioning is a wonderful opportunity to engage people in deeper ways, but the Church was caught unprepared for this massive cultural shift. This lightning-fast cultural shift put the Church on the back foot. This defensive posture was the beginning of the fear that has seized the Church. The Church was simply unwilling or unable to adapt to these changes fast enough. We were unable to retool and refocus our educational institutions fast enough to respond to the new demands of the modern intellect. We were unable to reeducate our clergy and religious in such a way that they could respond to the changing criteria of the modern mind. As a result, we find ourselves continuously on the back foot, perpetually in the defensive position, struggling just to survive.

Stifled by this fear, over the past fifty years too many of our leaders have hidden behind inaction, using discretion, prudence, and discernment as their excuses. There is a difference between fear and discretion, between fear and prudence, between fear and discernment. Fear is not a virtue.

The most common phrase that appears in the New Testament is "Do not be afraid." The most common phrase that appears in the Old Testament is "Be not afraid." Between the Old and New Testaments, this phrase appears more than one thousand times. Do you think God is trying to get a message across to us?

• Courage •

The most dominant emotion in our modern society is fear. We are afraid—afraid of losing the things we have worked hard to buy, afraid of rejection and failure, afraid of certain parts of town, afraid of certain types of people, afraid of criticism, of suffering and heartache, of change, afraid to tell people how we really feel. We are afraid of so many things. We are even afraid to be ourselves. Some of these fears we are consciously aware of, while others exist subconsciously. But all these fears play a large role in directing the actions and activities of our lives. Fear has a tendency to imprison us. Fear stops more people from doing something incredible with their lives than lack of ability, contacts, resources, or any other single variable. Fear paralyzes the human spirit.

Courage is not the absence of fear, but the acquired ability to move beyond fear. Each day we must pass through the jungles of doubt and cross the valley of fear. For it is only then that we can live in the high places, on the peaks of courage.

Take a moment to wander through the pages of history—your family's history, your nation's history, human history—and extract from those pages the men and women you most admire. Who would they be without courage? Nothing worthwhile in history is achieved without courage. Courage is the father of every great moment and movement in history.

I have felt the chilling winds of fear and self-doubt rush against my skin. I have discovered that courage is learning to recognize and master that single moment. That moment is a prelude, a prelude to courage or a prelude to fear. So much can be accomplished in one moment of courage. And so much can be lost to one moment of fear.

No one is born with courage. It is an acquired virtue. You learn to ride a bicycle by riding a bicycle. You learn to dance by dancing. You learn to play football by playing football. Courage is acquired by practicing courage. And like most qualities of character, when practiced our courage becomes stronger and more readily accessible with every passing day. Virtues are like muscles—when you exercise them they become stronger.

Everything in life requires courage. Whether it is playing or coaching football, crossing the room to ask a girl out on a date or rekindling a love that has grown cold, starting a new business, battling a potentially fatal disease, getting married, struggling to overcome an addiction, or coming humbly before your God in prayer, life requires courage.

Courage is essential to the human experience. It animates us, brings us to life, and makes everything else possible. And yet, courage is the rarest quality in a human person.

The measure of your life will be the measure of your courage.

• Bold Leadership •

What we need is bold leadership. Goethe, the famous German author, once wrote, "Be bold and mighty forces will come to your aid." It is this boldness that the Church needs. And I promise you that whenever and wherever a leader emerges with this boldness, the people will clamor to support such leadership. They will respond like people dying of thirst who have just been offered a cool drink of water. It will be as true for a local pastor in his parish as it was for John Paul II on an international scale. The people are desperate for authentic leadership. They are lost and lonely, like sheep without a shepherd. People don't follow titles and authority. They follow courage.

There is boldness in Catholicism when it is truly lived. People are hungry for the truth, but we are afraid to give it to them. The truth will set them free, but we don't have the courage to proclaim it (cf. John 8:32).

In the last chapter, I shared, "The ironic thing is that most young people are looking for someone who has the courage to look them in the eye and tell them the truth. Young people want above all to be their own person, but not just any version. They yearn deeply to be the-best-version-of-themselves. Sometimes they are aware of that yearning and sometimes they are not. To discover and realize their highest potential they need and want guidance." This is true not only of young people, but of *all* people.

Where will this courage we so desperately need come from? Perhaps the answer lies in the lives of our spiritual ancestors, the saints. They were not timid, whimpering, and noncommittal. They were brave and bold. Why? They knew their essential purpose. They moved always in the direction of the great spiritual North Star. They formed habits that helped them become the-best-version-of-themselves. They knew that happiness was impossible if separated from the ways of God. And they took seriously the opportunity to share the truth and wisdom of Catholicism with others. Where did they get all this from? Prayer. In its many forms, prayer nourished their lives.

Cervantes's counsel was this: "He who loses wealth loses much; he who loses a friend loses more; but he who loses courage loses all." Shakespeare wrote, "Virtue is bold, and goodness never fearful."

To be a Catholic leader is to hold a position of spiritual leadership; therefore, the primary concern of a Catholic leader must be dedication to the spiritual life. I've never met a prayerful coward. Virtue is bold, goodness is not fearful, and prayerful leaders are courageous leaders. And courage, like every other virtue, is contagious.

• Servant Leadership •

Some people think of Jesus as just a good guy, others as a prophet, some as a sage, and yet others as God and Savior. At one level or another, Jesus is universally admired. Yet, few people consider him as a relevant leadership model for their lives.

Jesus gave birth to a method of leadership that had never been seen before. Throughout history, all the great kings, queens, and emperors have measured their strength, power, and greatness by their wealth and the number of servants they ruled. But Jesus, the greatest leader of all time, did not come to be served. Jesus came to serve:

> He rose from supper and took off his outer garments. Then he took a towel and tied it around his waist. Then he poured water into a basin and began to wash the disciples' feet and dry them with the towel around his waist. . . . When he had washed their feet and put his garments back on and reclined at table again, he said to them,

"Do you realize what I have done for you? You call me 'teacher' and 'master' and rightly so, for indeed I am. If I, therefore, have washed your feet, you ought to wash one another's feet. I have given you a model to follow, so that as I have done for you, you should also do. (John 13:4–15)

Even some of his disciples were expecting him to use his power to rule in some earthly capacity, but again Jesus' methods of leadership were very different from anything that had ever been experienced before. For thousands of years, kings, queens, and emperors had been sending their people off to die for them. Jesus was the only leader who chose to die for his people.

Jesus' whole method of leadership focused on turning the hierarchy upside down. The model of leadership that Christ himself left us was one of service and sacrifice.

If you use your power to make people do things they don't want to do, you are not a leader; you are just another dictator or tyrant. But if you can inspire people to do things that are difficult but good for them and their community, then you are a leader.

The most effective leaders are authentic leaders. In Chapter One, we discussed how in our own time there is an abundance of leaders standing at the crossroads pointing us down a path they have never traveled themselves. But what we need is authentic leaders, men and women willing to lead humanity along the right path with the example of their own lives. Authentic leaders lead by example.

The laws of authentic leadership seem to have been universally proven throughout human history, whether in business, in battle, in the sporting arena, or in church. I think we find a reasonable summary in the following anonymous quotation:

I submit to you that leaders will never be more or less than their soldiers' evaluation of them. This is the true efficiency report. From most of your troops you can expect courage to match your courage, guts to match your guts, endurance to match your endurance, motivation to match your motivation, esprit to match your esprit, a desire for achievement to match your achievement. You can expect a love of God, a love of country, and a love of duty to match your own. They won't mind the heat if you sweat with them, and they won't mind the cold if you shiver with them.

You see, you don't accept the troops; they were there first. They accept you. And when they do, you'll know. They won't beat drums, wave flags, or carry you off the drill field on their shoulders, but you'll know. You see, your orders will appoint you to command. No orders, no letters, no insignia of rank can appoint you as a leader. Leadership is an intangible thing. Leadership is developed within yourselves; and you'll get stronger as you go.

At different times, we are called upon as leaders. Some as mothers and fathers, others as CEOs and presidents, and yet others as priests and bishops. Whatever form of leadership we are called to, let us exercise it with one thing in mind: People don't fail because they want to fail. People fail because they don't know how to succeed.

Chapter Twenty-one

RETURN TO VIRTUE

Eight hundred years ago, a young Italian man searching for meaning in his life went into a dilapidated old church and heard the voice of God speak to him: "Rebuild my Church. As you can see, it is in ruins." If you and I listen carefully, I believe we will hear the same voice saying the same thing in our hearts today.

Francis's first response was to repair and rebuild a number of churches in and around Assisi, but the voice kept calling to him: "Francis, rebuild my Church. As you can see, it is in ruins."

Over the past twenty-five years, we have spent a lot of time, energy, and money building and restoring the physical facilities of our churches. But the voice of God continues to call to us. Once again, God is saying, "Rebuild my Church," and the rebuilding that needs to be done now is of a spiritual nature.

The only way for our lives to genuinely improve is by acquiring virtue. Similarly, it is impossible for a society to genuinely improve unless its members grow in virtue. The renewal that the Church so desperately needs is a renewal of virtue. And it is our relationship with Christ that gives us the strength, the grace, and the wisdom to grow in virtue. What is virtue? It is "a habitual and firm disposition to do good." (The Catechism of the Catholic Church [CCC] #1833)

The great fallacy of the lukewarm moral life is to believe that our sole responsibility is to eliminate vice from our lives. In the absence of a sincere and focused effort to grow in virtue and an openness to God's will for our lives, vice will creep into our lives in the form of a hundred different self-centered and self-destructive habits.

No man or woman is born virtuous. Good habits are not infused. Virtue must be sought out and can be acquired only by continual practice. You learn to ride a bicycle by riding a bicycle. You learn to play baseball by playing baseball. You learn to be patient by practicing patience. You become virtuous by practicing virtue.

For thousands of years, politicians, philosophers, and priests have all argued about the best way to organize society. Many organizing concepts, including duty, obligation, law, force, obedience, tyranny, and greed, have been employed throughout history by various societies and organizations. In America at present we employ the organizing principle of law, which supports our Constitution, the Bill of Rights, and capitalism. But what is the ultimate organizing principle? It is virtue, because two virtuous people will always have a better relationship than two people without virtue. Two patient people will always have a better relationship than two impatient people. Two kind and generous people will always have a better relationship than two selfish people. Two humble people will always have a better relationship than two proud people. Not sometimes, but every single time. And the world is just an extension of your relationship with me. If we are both striving to live virtuous lives our relationship will prosper. But when we give up our striving for virtue, our relationship will disintegrate. In the same way, two humble nations will have a better relationship than two prideful nations. Virtue leads to better people, better living, better relationships, and a better world. If humanity is to flourish in the twenty-first century it will be because we realize once and for all that the key organizing concept of a truly great civilization is virtue.

The connection between virtue and the flourishing of an individual is unquestionable. To live a life of virtue is to move beyond the chaos and restlessness that agonize the human heart, and embrace a life of coherence. Similarly, the relationship between the virtue of the members of a community and the flourishing of their society is proven time and time again throughout history.

I have never met a thief or a liar who was truly happy or genuinely flourishing. If we hope to ever have our desire for happiness satisfied it is essential that we turn our attention toward the acquisition of virtue.

On my eighteenth birthday, my mother and father gave me a card with Rudyard Kipling's poem "If" printed on the front. For years, I kept the card in the top drawer of my bedside table. Often, while I was lying awake at night pondering a situation in my life, I would read over these words. The poem contains a wonderful list of human virtues. Kipling's list is by no means exhaustive, but it is filled with profoundly practical suggestions, and it certainly provides an inspiring starting point.

> If you can keep your head when all about you
> Are losing theirs and blaming it on you,
> If you can trust yourself when all men doubt you,
> But make allowance for their doubting too;
> If you can wait and not be tired by waiting,
> Or being lied about, don't deal in lies,
> Or being hated, don't give way to hating,
> And yet don't look too good, nor talk too wise:
>
> If you can dream—and not make dreams your master;
> If you can think—and not make thoughts your aim;
> If you can meet with Triumph and Disaster
> And treat those two impostors just the same;
> If you can bear to hear the truth you've spoken
> Twisted by knaves to make a trap for fools,
> Or watch the things you gave your life to, broken,
> And stoop and build 'em up with worn-out tools:
>
> If you can make one heap of all your winnings
> And risk it on one turn of pitch-and-toss,
> And lose, and start again at your beginnings

And never breathe a word about your loss;
If you can force your heart and nerve and sinew
To serve your turn long after they are gone,
And so hold on when there is nothing in you
Except the Will which says to them: "Hold on!"

If you can talk with crowds and keep your virtue,
Or walk with Kings—nor lose the common touch,
If neither foes nor loving friends can hurt you,
If all men count with you, but none too much;
If you can fill the unforgiving minute
With sixty seconds' worth of distance run,
Yours is the Earth and everything that's in it,
And—which is more—you'll be a Man, my son!

The Church has always proclaimed that the seven foundational virtues are the cornerstone of the moral life. This foundation is made up of the supernatural virtues (Faith, Hope, and Love) and the four cardinal virtues (Prudence, Justice, Temperance, and Fortitude). The supernatural virtues free us from self-centeredness and protect us from the ultimate vice—pride—and dispose us to live in relationship with God. The cardinal virtues, which are sometimes referred to as "the human virtues," allow us to acquire the self-mastery necessary to make us free and capable of love. They do this by ordering our passions and guiding our conduct in accordance with reason and faith (CCC #1834).

The only way for our lives to genuinely improve is by acquiring virtue. To grow in virtue is to improve as a person. Virtues are the tools God uses to build the-best-version-of-ourselves.

• The World Needs the Church •

As I have already said, it seems the only acceptable prejudice in this hypersensitive, politically correct modern climate is anti-Catholicism. This prejudice is growing as it is subtly—and not so subtly—nurtured by the arts and the media, and furthered by the way prevailing philosophies undermine Catholicism.

Tolerance is proclaimed as the ultimate secular virtue. And yet, those who espouse tolerance are completely intolerant of all things Catholic and Christian, as well as any common code of moral conduct.

In the midst of this blatantly obvious anti-Catholic environment that our culture has created, it is easy to overlook some fundamental and practical realities. The world needs the Church today more than ever before. And this trend shows no signs of slowing. In a modern schema in which people are becoming more self-absorbed and completely fixated on the fulfillment of their own selfish desires, the Church is only going to be needed more and more.

The Catholic Church feeds, clothes, houses, and educates more people than any other organization in the world. And when the modern media and the secular culture have finished tearing down the Church as best they can, let me ask you, who will take our place? Who will feed the hungry? Who will clothe the naked? Who will visit the lonely and imprisoned? Who will house the homeless? Who will comfort the sick and dying? Who will educate the masses?

The world needs the Church. Even your hardened and cynical politicians with nothing in mind but personal gain recognize this reality with alarming clarity. If for no other reason than from an economic standpoint, they know they wouldn't be able to pick up the broken pieces that would be left if the Church disappeared from their community.

The Church may be massively unappreciated and woefully persecuted, but we must press on all the same. After all, that is always the way it has been. Jesus didn't promise an easy way. He promised that we would be ridiculed, persecuted, and unappreciated as he himself was, but that we would nonetheless experience joy and fullness of life.

We should try not to forget that when Jesus was on the cross, he didn't turn to the man next to him and say, "You did the crime, now pay the price."

No, he offered him a better life. That is the responsibility that now falls on our shoulders as followers of Jesus.

One part of our ongoing mission as the Church is to offer people a better life. The key word in all of this is *offer*. The Church doesn't force people to do things. The Church is a lover who comes to propose to the beloved (you and me). The Church proposes certain courses of action for certain situations, just as a physician offers you a prescription. But your physician does not force you to get your scrip filled. Nor does she force you to take the medicine. We are free to choose. The Church proposes to you and me a certain way of life. Each of us, like the beloved who is proposed to, can accept or reject the proposal. But whatever our decision, we will live with it forever.

• Something Wonderful Is About to Happen •

For a long time I have wanted to write this book, and yet, at the same time I wish I had another fifty years to prepare. In this book I have not tried to answer all the questions that surround Catholicism, nor have I tried to cover all the controversial issues. This book is not, strictly speaking, a theological work, and it is not a book that promises to deliver monumental virtue with seductive ease. These are merely reflections on my experiences as a Catholic and on Catholicism at this time. I have simply tried to share what I have witnessed, learned, discovered, and experienced about Catholicism so far in my short life. In doing so, I have attempted to demonstrate that Catholicism is an incredible learning system, a lifestyle, and a spiritual odyssey that God the Father invites us to through the Catholic Church. It is because we respond to that invitation that an adventure of epic proportions begins, one that will leave no corner of our lives as it was before.

The problem with books is that they are never really finished; they are only ever abandoned. You could keep writing and rewriting the same book for your whole life and never be fully satisfied with it. As I read back over these pages I realize there is so much more that I would like to share with you. They seem so inadequate when compared to the love and affection that I have for Catholicism. I hope the words on these pages are a celebration of faith, a celebration of all it is and all it can be. I hope that as we read them and apply them to our lives, our lives in turn will become a celebration of Catholicism. More than anything I hope these words have filled you with hope and renewed your enthusiasm for your spiritual life.

On the desk in my office I have a Post-it note that reads simply, "Something wonderful is about to happen!" It has been there for a long time now. I have thought of having these words printed in calligraphy and putting them in a nice frame, but there is something powerful about this simple Post-it note.

I believe something wonderful is about to happen. I believe it for my life, I believe it for your life, and I believe it for the life of the Church. I pray that you and I will make ourselves radically available to God so that he can use us to make it happen. You see, God doesn't necessarily use the most talented people, he doesn't necessarily use the people in positions of power and authority, and he doesn't necessarily use those who are the best educated. Very often education, power, authority, and talent can become the prideful impediments that keep us from doing God's work. What type of person does God always use in powerful ways? Whom has God always used throughout history to do his work in the world? The people who make themselves available to him.

God uses those who make themselves available. How available are you willing to make yourself to God?

It is true that the Church finds herself in the midst of a difficult time in her life. The dilemmas we face as a Church are a cause of sadness for all who love the Church. In mythology, for thousands of years it has been believed that the darkest hour is right before the dawn, and that in the hour of greatest darkness the great heroes of the new times are being born. The darkness that the Church is passing through at the moment will not last. There is a light at the end of it all.

Sometimes people ask me what stops me from becoming depressed or falling into despair. Two things, I tell them. First, I know the renewal that the Church so desperately needs is not my sole responsibility, and second, hope. Where does the hope come from? What feeds that hope? It comes from my God and from my neighbor. My hope comes from God, who loves me, and from my neighbor, who loves me.

In a world filled with so much cynicism, the supernatural virtues—Faith, Hope, and Love—are often laughed at and dismissed as foolish and naive. Some people say that hope only sets you up for disappointment, and because of that hope is a bad thing.

Hope is a good thing, maybe the best of things. Hope is one of those things that you can't buy, but that will be freely given to you if you ask. Hope is the one thing people cannot live without. Hope is a thing of beauty.

I hope . . .

I hope I can live up to the gifts and talents God has given me. I hope I can have the courage to be a true friend, a good father, and a loving husband. I hope I never stop striving to become the-best-version-of-myself. I hope I will continue to take time to listen to the voice of God each day. I hope I will have the courage to follow where his voice leads me. I hope we can build a world where our children can grow free and strong. And I hope we grow wise enough to realize that we have no better ally than Catholicism in achieving these hopes.

I hope . . . and that is a wonderful thing. Join me in that hope and together we will awaken all men and women to discover the incredible dream God has for their lives and for the world.

ABOUT THE AUTHOR

Matthew Kelly has dedicated his life to helping people and organizations become the-best-version-of-themselves. Born in Sydney, Australia, he began speaking and writing in his late teens while he was attending business school. Since that time, more than four million people have attended his seminars and presentations in more than fifty countries.

Today he is an internationally acclaimed speaker, bestselling author, and business consultant. His books have been published in twenty-five languages, have appeared on the *New York Times*, *Wall Street Journal*, and *USA Today* bestseller lists, and have sold in excess of three million copies.

Kelly is also a partner at Floyd Consulting, a Chicago based management-consulting firm. His clients include: Pepsi, Procter and Gamble, Chick-fil-A, General Electric, FedEx, HSBC, the Department of Defense, McDonalds, US Bank, 3M, Ernst & Young, the U.S Navy, the U.S. Air Force, and dozens of other Fortune 500 companies.

The Matthew Kelly Foundation was established in 1995 to help young people discover their mission in life. Over the past fifteen years Kelly has visited several hundred high schools, inspiring students to use their lives to make a contribution. The foundation's most recent initiative is a grade-school program entitled, *Why am I Here?*

Matthew is also one of the most passionate Catholic speakers and authors of our time. Raised Catholic, Kelly discovered what he calls 'the genius of Catholicism" in his teens and has spent the past two decades inspiring millions of men, woman, and children to explore the faith in a fresh way. He foundered The Dynamic Catholic Institute to research why Catholics engage or disengage and determine what it will take to establish vibrant Catholic communities in the 21st Century.

Matthew Kelly's core message resonates with people of all ages and from all walks of life. Whether he is speaking in a business forum, at a high school, or in a church, he invites his audience to become the-best-version-of-themselves.

NOTES

NOTES

NOTES

NOTES

NOTES

NOTES

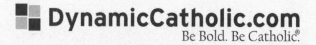

THE
DYNAMIC CATHOLIC
INSTITUTE

[MISSION]

To re-energize the Catholic Church
in America by developing world-class
resources that inspire people to
rediscover the genius of Catholicism.

[VISION]

To be the innovative leader in the
New Evangelization helping Catholics
and their parishes become
the-best-version-of-themselves.

DynamicCatholic.com
Be Bold. Be Catholic.®

The Dynamic Catholic Institute
2200 Arbor Tech Drive
Hebron, KY 41048
Phone: 859-980-7900
info@DynamicCatholic.com